THE CHURCH IN THE
WORLD

THE CHURCH IN THE WORLD 〜 〜

COLLECTED ESSAYS BY WILLIAM RALPH INGE

C.V.O., D.D., F.B.A.: DEAN OF ST. PAUL'S

Essay Index Reprint Series

BOOKS FOR LIBRARIES PRESS
FREEPORT, NEW YORK

First Published 1927
Reprinted 1969

LIBRARY OF CONGRESS CATALOG CARD NUMBER:
68-57324

PRINTED IN THE UNITED STATES OF AMERICA

PREFACE

THIS book differs from my two volumes of ' Outspoken Essays ' in containing no discussions on politics or sociology. I had intended to include in it at least part of my Lyman Beecher Lectures at Yale University, on the Social Teaching of the Church. It has been usual to publish the Lectures given on this foundation, and I should have been glad of the opportunity to thank my American hosts for the generous hospitality and friendliness which made my visit so agreeable to myself. But I made the mistake of treating the subject historically, a plan which demanded a larger book than a course of eight Lectures, and much more research than I could find time for in a single year of a busy life. I have therefore decided to leave these Lectures unpublished. If Troeltsch's massive ' Soziallehre ' is ever translated, the want, for English readers, of an authoritative and impartial book on this important subject will be fully supplied.

The first essay appeared in the *Edinburgh Review* for January, 1925. It is based on four recent books named in the text, which deal with the character and genius of the Church of England, and the conflict of ideals within it.

The second, reprinted by courtesy of the *Quarterly Review*, appeared in July, 1923. It is a critical review of Professor Heiler's much-discussed work, ' Der Katholizismus,' which is on the whole an apology for that kind of Modernism which does not appeal to me. The peculiarity of Heiler's position is that he does not, like Loisy, Tyrrell, and other members of the same school, write as a Roman Catholic, but as a Lutheran who has once been a Catholic. His attitude towards the historical Jesus, and his idea of the Church, are nevertheless very much like those of the Catholic Modernists whose position I have discussed in my other writings.

The third essay, on the Quakers, is almost entirely new, though it contains parts of a short article contributed to the *Contemporary Review*. After the two essays on Anglicanism and Roman Catholicism, I wished to add a third on what Troeltsch calls the Sect-type of Christianity. I am convinced that the Quaker type of belief and practice will be of great and increasing importance in what remains of the twentieth century. Its influence already extends far beyond the narrow limits of the Society of Friends. For it is in this Society, it seems to me, that the spirit of Protestantism has found itself more completely than in the larger Reformed Churches. It is more invulnerable than any of them on the side of intellectual difficulties, though it shrinks at once under any cooling of the spiritual life itself. Its philanthropy is disinterested ; it has hitherto never tried to make a deal with a political party ; and it steadily refuses to appeal to those sub-Christian religious tastes and instincts which are so strong in the population at large. I could hardly join the Society of Friends myself, not only because I value the Sacrament of Holy

Communion as administered in the Church of England,
believing it to be a special means of grace, but because
I cannot agree with the Quakers that ' force is no
remedy,' and that capital punishment is wrong. A
gardener has a right to weed his garden ; and our
national garden unfortunately contains a good many
weeds which I should like to see torn up by the roots.
But I do not hesitate to say that in my judgment the
Quakers are the truest Christians in the modern world.

I am very grateful for permission to include in this
collection the essay which I wrote for that admirable
book, ' The Legacy of Greece.'   Until the age of forty-
four, it was my business to teach the classics, so I am
here on familiar ground. A friendly critic remarked
after reading my essay, ' It is too closely packed.'   It
is so, and I believe it is a fault into which I often fall ;
but in this case I had a great deal to say in a small
space.   There is in some quarters a strange disinclina-
tion to admit that Christianity is much more European
than Asiatic. To an unprejudiced mind it is quite
obvious that it is so, and that it could not be otherwise.
Our Lord Himself is above national limitations, but
the Jewish leaders soon made up their minds that
His teaching was unacceptable to them. St. Paul
was not a Jerusalem Rabbi, but a Hellenised Jew of
the Dispersion ; we all know with what intense hatred
he was regarded by his countrymen in Palestine.
I have no prejudice whatever against the Jews ; but
as a matter of fact, Christianity, as it has existed since
St. Paul began to preach, is not a Semitic religion. It
grew in the soil of the old classical culture ; its philosophy, its ethics, and the constitution of its most
imposing branch, the Church of Rome, are alike

unintelligible unless we realise its historical continuity
with the civilisation of Greece and Rome. There is
at present an anti-Hellenic reaction—I am thinking
especially of such French Modernists as Le Roy and
Laberthonnière. This is, I believe, a very dangerous
path for a Christian apologist to follow.

The fifth essay is also reprinted from a com-
paratively new book—'Science, Religion, and Reality'
(Sheldon Press, 1925)—and I again record my thanks
for a generous permission. It is a survey of the whole
field as mapped out by the other essayists ; but I have
attempted to supply certain omissions, and have
stated my own position. I have tried to consider
candidly the outstanding questions at issue between
Science and Theology. It is frivolous or dishonest to
deny that any such exist. The assertion is made by
some who are not interested in intellectual problems,
but wish to turn their attention to matters which they
consider more practical. But we have no right to
cry peace when there is no peace. The Church must
come to terms with the scientific view of the world,
and I see no reason why there should be any permanent
antagonism between them.

The Fison Lecture (1926) was given at Guy's Hospital.
The Lectureship was founded in memory of an honoured
teacher attached to that institution. It is a defence
of theism, as the theory of creation which involves
fewer difficulties than any other. Some pages of it
are a criticism of the Hegelian doctrine of God, which
in spite of the religious language which Hegelians,
quite sincerely, love to use, can hardly be reconciled
with theistic belief as Christians understand it. I have
taken religious Hegelianism at its very best, in the

writings of Professor Pringle Pattison; I earnestly
hope that I have not seemed to fail in respect and
admiration for one of our greatest teachers, to whom
I am personally much indebted.

I have added, next in order, a Presidential Address
given at a summer meeting of the Churchmen's
Union. This Society is beginning to be aware of
amicable differences—a body of Liberal Churchmen is
sure to be an awkward squad. Some of its members,
like myself, are Protestants and, in a sense, rationalists;
others are attracted by pragmatism and Continental
Modernism. I mention this only because my Address
must not be taken as a profession of belief to which all
members of the Churchmen's Union would be willing
to subscribe.

The concluding paper is reprinted with permission
from ' Cambridge Essays on Education ' (Cambridge,
1918). Short as it is, it pleased its author, and won
praise from the editor, my dear friend the late Arthur
Christopher Benson.

W. R. INGE.

St. Paul's,
   April, 1927.

CONTENTS

THE CHURCH IN THE WORLD

THE CONDITION OF THE CHURCH OF ENGLAND

' IT hath been the wisdom of the Church of England,' says the Preface to the Prayer Book, ' ever since the first compiling of her Publick Liturgy, to keep the mean between the two extremes.' In more precise and picturesque language, a divine of the same period defines the extremes as ' the meretricious gaudiness of the Church of Rome, and the squalid sluttery of fanatick conventicles.' But the Englishman, like a sailor on shore, preserves his equilibrium by rolling heavily from side to side, still keeping somewhere near the middle of the road. His institutions, both secular and religious, reflect this national habit. An ecclesiastical historian, the late Mr. Warre Cornish, has said that the average duration of a lurch, or ' movement,' in the Church of England, is about two generations. If this is so, a reaction from the tendency which has been dominant since the Oxford Movement is somewhat overdue.

The conflict of ideals in the National Church can be understood only through its history. As Mark

B

Pattison said : ' Both the Church and the world of
to-day are what they are as the result of the whole
of their antecedents. The history of a party may
be written on the theory of periodical occultation ;
but he who wishes to trace the descent of religious
thought and the practical working of the religious
ideals must follow these through all the phases they
have actually assumed.' All parties alike are prone
to forget that their rivals have a historical claim to
be in the Church, and that the attempts made by one
faction after another to expel their opponents have
come to nothing.   When the Anglo-Catholics proclaim,
through their favourite newspaper, that they intend
to drive out the Modernists, and to encourage the
Evangelcals to join the Protestant dissenters, they
only prove how completely they have lost touch with
the realities of the situation.

The conflict has always centred in the question :
' What is the seat of authority in religion ? ' To this
question, four answers may be given. The seat of
authority may be the Church, the Bible, human reason,
or mystical revelation. Since all Christians agree that
some authority attaches to each of these four, the
important question is, which of them comes first ?
Hooker, omitting individual inspiration, or what is
now called religious experience, as a separate source,
declares : ' What Scripture doth plainly deliver, to
that the first place both of credit and obedience is
due ; the next whereunto is whatsoever any man can
necessarily conclude by force of reason ; after these,
the voice of the Church succeedeth.' Laud pronounces
that all four are necessary—' no one of these doth it
alone ' ; and he distinguishes the testimony of the

Holy Ghost within us from the work of the natural reason, to which he assigns the negative office of ' disproving that which misguided men conceive against' the truth.

The Church and the Bible are two external and historical authorities ; where either of them is supreme, reason and illumination have only a subordinate function. The two external authorities became inevitably the watchwords of the fierce conflicts between Catholicism and Protestantism. The authority of both Church and Bible was emphasised in the face of a hostile environment, just as in the early Church the creeds were formed to exclude each error as it arose. In all warfare, the independence of the individual is sacrificed. It is only when a fresh breath of inspiration is blowing that the rights of personality are recognised, the demands of the institution are relaxed, and Christianity reverts to what it was at first—an individual and universal religion. In such favourable circumstances reason and illumination—philosophy and mysticism—become again the guides of thought and practice. The Platonic tradition, which has always been an integral part of Christianity, by the side of—though not independent of—the Catholic and Protestant elements, emerges again and produces its characteristic fruits.

The Reformation, which was no sudden revolt, but the culmination of a long agitation for national independence in religious matters, was precipitated by the moral corruption of the Papal hierarchy, and by the intolerable political claims of the Roman See. It unfortunately brought to an end a promising development of religious Humanism, which nowhere

took so attractive a form as in England, under the
guidance of More, Colet, Erasmus and their friends,
the fine flower of the late-blooming northern Renaissance. What happened could not have been
averted ; rougher hands than those of scholars were
needed to burst the shackles which bound Europe to
the expiring Middle Ages. But it was a real misfortune that the conditions of warfare, as stated in
the preceding paragraph, hardened and narrowed both
sections of divided Christendom, just at a time when
secular knowledge was advancing from triumph to
triumph, with clear eye and confident step. Both
the Reformation and the Counter-Reformation' were
reactionary ; though they brought the Middle Ages
to an end, they were themselves medieval in spirit
and method. The Humanists, who had the forward
view, declined in influence ; two religions of authority
fought against each other. The result was that
Christianity failed to make the necessary adjustments
to growing secular knowledge. Freedom of thought
and of speech, as always during war, was branded as
treason or rebellion, and a cleft opened between sacred
and profane science, which has not yet been closed.

The changes in modern thought to which the
Church has been slow to adapt itself have been well
summarised by Lecky. (1) The decline in the sense
of the miraculous, involved by the new conception of
natural law. (2) The growth of new ideas of God,
man and the universe, and a consequent new moral
movement resulting in the decay of belief in witch-
craft, in rejection of religious persecution, and
of ghastly notions concerning future punishment.
(3) The decline of belief in the guilt of error, and the

rejection of an asceticism which had paralysed the progress of mankind. (4) The operation of the rational spirit, which gradually secularised every department of political life, and formed habits of thought which affected all judgments. (5) The rise of the industrial and democratic spirit in Europe.

These developments were not contemplated at the time of the Reformation. It contained implicitly the promise of an emancipation of the human spirit, which at first was neither fully realised nor welcomed. The sectaries, whether political or mystical, were the step-children of the Reformation, who only came into their own in the days of Cromwell, and then only for a short time. But there were other questions which did not come to the front at first.

For instance, the question of Orders was not much agitated in the sixteenth century. Bancroft, a very able Primate, blamed the Puritans not because they were uncatholic, but because they ' walked disorderly.' He opposed the re-ordination of Presbyterian ministers. ' The ordination given by presbyters,' he said, ' must be esteemed valid ; otherwise it might be doubtful if there was any lawful vocation in most of the Reformed Churches.' The political controversy at this time centred in the Papacy, the religious controversy in the Mass. The question about Parker was not whether he was a Catholic priest, but whether he was legally archbishop. It was only the Council of Trent which closed such open questions as the free use of the Bible, Communion in both kinds, the vernacular liturgy, and even the marriage of the clergy. The Reformers, on their side, were mainly concerned to reject the Roman interpretation of three passages of the New Testament: (1) *Tu es Petrus*; (2) *Hoc est corpus meum*; (3) *Ave Maria plena gratia*.

The Reformation in England was effected with singularly little disturbance. Bernard Gilpin, who was ordained under Henry VIII, was unmolested by Edward VI, Mary and Elizabeth. Only 200 parish priests were deprived in 1559; 2000 in 1662, and 400 in 1689. 'These be not matters for burning,' thought the average Englishman. But Tunstall of Durham declared without fear of contradiction that 'if the King [Henry VIII] should go about to renew the abolished authority of the Bishop of Rome, he should find much more difficulty to bring it about in his parliament, and to induce his people to agree thereunto, than anything that he ever proposed in his parliament since his first reign.'

In the seventeenth century the three historic parties which have ever since divided the Church of England made their appearance, and the conflict now centred on questions of Church government. Many of the Marian exiles had imbibed a strong admiration for Calvin's discipline at Geneva, and after the accession of James I the Puritans headed a parliamentary movement, not primarily ecclesiastical. They professed, however, to find episcopacy unscriptural. In opposition to their movement, a vigorous 'Church and King' party arose, under the leadership of Laud, and the theory of the apostolical succession was invoked in defence of episcopacy. The Caroline Laudians emphasised the importance of the Sacraments, the idea of the Church, and the value of patristic literature. But the Laudians were never Latinisers; their form of Catholicism was distinctively English, and avowedly

Protestant. Laud himself claimed this name both for the King and himself. It was also learned ; foreign scholars were not only welcomed in England, but promoted to ecclesiastical preferments, like Voss and his son.

Meanwhile, the party of comprehension and liberal thought was represented by Lord Falkland, Hales of Eton, Chillingworth and Stillingfleet, who prepared the way for the Cambridge Platonists, a small group of scholars and teachers who in troubled times upheld the supreme authority of the rational, moral and spiritual consciousness. Such sayings as : ' Sir, I oppose not rational to spiritual, for spiritual is most rational ' ; ' The state of religion lies in a good mind and a good life ; all else is about religion ; and men must not put the instrumental part of religion for the state of religion,' indicate the spirit of their teaching, which, on the intellectual side, was an appeal to the Church to ' return to her old loving nurse, the Platonick philosophy.' It was not their fault that their successors in the next century became rationalists instead of Platonic mystics. As Mr. Richardson says in his excellent little book : [1] ' Natural science, with its doctrines of a creative process still proceeding, and a creative force existing within the universe, was required to create the point of view which would make the spiritual theology of the Cambridge Platonists credible and acceptable to the many. The great achievements of the human spirit in the Cambridge Platonists were destined soon to be submerged and forgotten in the recrudescence of religious and political conflict towards the end of the seventeenth century.'

[1] *Conflict of Ideals in the Church*, John Murray, 1923.

The fissiparous tendency of Protestantism had already shown itself in the secession of the Baptists, who may be said to have given almost exclusive attention to the moral consciousness, and of the Quakers, who represented pure mysticism. The Unitarians, who represented rationalistic theology, broke off later. These secessions, of which the latest, that of the Methodists, was the most unnecessary and disastrous, have repeatedly weakened the National Church, upsetting the balance of opinion within it, and finally endangering its representative character.

The eighteenth century, from the religious point of view, is a period of rather cold and prosaic common sense, followed by an emotional reaction under Wesley and the Evangelicals. The most interesting figure is not Bishop Butler, whose famous refutation of Deism is a double-edged weapon, which might easily be turned against theistic beliefs generally, but William Law, nonjuror, moralist and mystic, who bridges over the gap between the Cambridge school and the Romantics of the early nineteenth century.

The Romantic movement sprang from literature and philosophy rather than from the Churches. It was the beginning of that lay influence upon religious opinion which has been a marked feature of the last hundred years. The nineteenth century learned more religion from its poets than from its preachers, and more theology from its philosophers than from its divines. It was, in England, the age of amateurs of genius, and our countrymen have always preferred to listen to unprofessional advice ; but the influence of the lay prophet is one of the results of

Protestantism, and we may hope to see it still further extended.

Romanticism, as Canon Storr says,[1] has the following notes. It recognised the depth and largeness of human nature, and restored their rights to the emotions and affections. It revived the spirit of wonder and the sense of mystery in man and nature. It laid stress on the importance of the imagination. It revealed the treasures of the past in their value for the present, and especially discovered an interest in the Middle Ages, which had been despised as merely barbarous. It created a sense of sympathy between man and nature, a half pantheistic or immanental reverence for the spirit which is ' deeply interfused ' in all that lives.

It is easy to see that the Romantic movement, as soon as it touched religion, was certain to stimulate a Catholic revival. Ritualism and medievalism were the natural offspring of Romanticism. Its influence on psychology, through the sympathetic study of ' religious experience,' was perhaps even more important, though less in evidence, and slower to take effect. The scientific observation of human nature, its beliefs and joys and sufferings, in its inner spiritual life, was quite alien to the mind of the eighteenth century, and became possible only under the influence of the Romantic movement. Connected with this attention to the inner life is the revival of interest in mysticism, which during the last thirty years has been studied far more thoroughly than ever before. It is now generally recognised that the centre of

[1] *The Development of Theology in the Nineteenth Century*, vol. i, Longmans, 1913.

gravity in religion has changed from authority to experience, and that in consequence the testimonies of the saints have acquired a new evidential import- ance. The old arguments from miracle and prophecy are now seldom adduced, since it is felt that not only are the proofs lacking in cogency, but that it is impossible to build a spiritual faith on such a basis, even if the evidence were conclusive.

The success of the Tractarians was further facili- tated by the break-up of the old Evangelical party. The Evangelicals had never been very strong intellectually, and they had embarked all their fortunes on a dogma which has no essential connexion with Protestantism, and which could not survive any attempt to criticise the Bible ' like any other book '—the doctrine of the verbal inspiration and consequent inerrancy of Holy Scripture. Another heavy blow was struck at the theology of this school by the discoveries of Darwin, which were almost as destructive to the scheme of redemption as taught by the old Evangelicals—resting on the drama of a ruined perfection and a lost Paradise —as the Copernican astronomy is to belief in a geographical heaven and hell. The party was also handicapped by its tendency to Millenarianism—a doctrine which in an acutely secularised form has passed to the Socialists, with their dreams of a good time which is coming soon, though nobody is able to say how ; but which in its original shape of a belief in the approaching end of the world, is quite dead, except among persons of very low intellectual cultiva- tion. Again, the party had appealed very much to fear, and had not shrunk from horrible pictures of the torments of hell. This appeal also lost its force in the nineteenth century. In a word, the whole spirit of the age, the advance of science and of criticism, the Romantic movement and the new emphasis on the ideas of the Church and of corporate unity, combined to shatter the old Evangelical party. Its surviving supporters are either old people, or those who have isolated themselves from all the currents of modern thought.

The collapse of their rivals gave the Anglo-Catholics an easy victory. Very many sons and daughters of prominent Evangelicals joined the High Church camp ; some ended by seceding to Rome. I hope to show before the end of this article that a new Evangelical school is arising, which has sacrificed nothing of what is really essential to Protestantism, while it has gained enormously in strength by shedding a mass of extraneous and untenable theories and beliefs. The eclipse of the party, which has had so much to do with the success of Anglo-Catholic propaganda, is now, I believe, nearly at an end.

Canon Storr says, truly no doubt, that the influence of Tractarianism has been felt less in the sphere of thought than in that of practical Church life. Its theological, as opposed to its ecclesiastical, significance has, he thinks, been greatly over-estimated. An able article, which appeared in one of the leading quarterlies in 1924, went further, and spoke of the Anglo-Catholics as intellectually a feeble folk. This statement, which is somewhat uncourteous, does not accord with the facts. If we except the professors of divinity and other professional scholars, who are seldom attracted by Anglo-Catholicism, and consider only those clergymen who are engaged in administrative or pastoral work,

we shall have to admit that this party has at present
more than its share of the brains of the clerical profession.   It would be easy to draw up a list of a dozen
names of living Anglo-Catholics which could not be
mentioned except with respect—men of the highest
academical distinction and unquestionable ability.
But the movement has from the first been intensely
insular.   The very idea of a separated Catholic Church,
which divides all other Christians into those who
unchurch it and those whom it unchurches, is unintelligible to Continental Christians, whether Catholic
or Protestant ; and the apologetic theology of the
school, so much esteemed at home, is very little read
abroad.

The generation after the Napoleonic War, when the
Oxford Movement began, was perhaps the period when
England was most isolated from the main current of
European ideas.   It was a time of great men, but our
learning and scholarship lagged far behind those of
Germany.   This insularity is emphasised both by
Canon Storr and by Mr. Fawkes.[1] ' The distinctive
note of the unreformed Oxford in which the movement
arose,' says the latter, ' was provincialism ; the University stood outside the current of European mind.
Newman's genius, though great, was spasmodic and
incidental ; the theology to which it lent a glamour
was below the level even of the average theology of the
age.'   Newman was fond of denouncing ' Reason ' as
officious, captious, forward, usurping, or rebellious.
His pulpit commentary on the massacres of the
Canaanites is memorable.   ' Doubtless as they slew
those [the little children of the people of the land] who

[1] *The Genius of the English Church*, John Murray, 1917.

suffered for the sins of their fathers, their thoughts turned first to the fall of Adam, and next to the unseen state where all inequalities are righted.' ' Kill them all—God will know his own,' as was said at the massacre of St. Bartholomew. But what must have been the intellectual and moral state of the University, when this teaching was regarded as the utterance of an almost inspired prophet and saint ?

There was, even then, a Liberal or ' Noetic ' movement at Oxford, but Newman and his friends declared war against it, though they were even more alarmed by the political Liberalism which threatened to abolish some of the most flagrant abuses in the Church of England. The proposal to suppress certain Irish bishoprics in 1868 was the occasion of Keble's sermon on ' National Apostasy,' which is regarded as the beginning of Tractarianism. The alliance between Romanticism, which stands for individual freedom, and Tractarianism, which stood for sacrosanct authority, was precarious. Nor were the Oxford leaders enamoured of the Middle Ages, like most of the Romantics. They looked back to the ' undivided Church,' and to the Anglican divines (not the Cambridge School) of the seventeenth century. Their whole ideal was reactionary, while the Romantics, in spite of their idealisation of Gothic architecture and feudal chivalry, looked forward. Both were ignorant and uncritical, but their very ignorance helped them to construct golden ages in the past for the imitation of the present. A successful revival is always an attempt to restore something that never existed. The Tractarians were driven to formulate a theory of the Church, or rather of the ministry, which should justify the exclusive claim of Anglicanism to be the Church of Christ in these islands, while rebutting the arguments of Rome. The doctrine of Apostolical Succession, which is not held in this form by any other Church in Christendom, gave them the weapon which they wanted, vindicating against Rome their title to be Catholic priests, while denying the validity of all other Protestant Orders. The essence of Tractarianism lies in this peculiar doctrine.

The growth of ritualism came later, and was not encouraged by the Oxford leaders, who were very conservative in these matters. When Tractarianism went out into the streets and lanes of the city, the necessity of appeals to the eye became obvious, and the inner logic of Catholicism gradually broke down all the barriers which the Tractarians had honestly meant to keep between High Anglicanism and Popery. The Roman doctrine of Transubstantiation could not be preached in an English church, but it could be implied, and imparted more effectually, by symbolism borrowed from the Latin rite. The extreme Romanising faction, dragging the main body of High Churchmen reluctantly after it, has now established a purely Latin sect within the Church of England. This sect is especially strong in the districts served by the London Brighton and South Coast Railway; but it exists sporadically in most other parts of England.

The Anglo-Catholic party has thus wandered far since the days of Keble and Pusey. Perhaps a not less remarkable change than that which has been just mentioned is the complete political *volte-face* which it has made since the Oxford divines tried to put new life into the old ' Church and King ' school of High Churchmen. In those days it was the Broad Churchmen, under Maurice and Kingsley, who interested themselves in social reforms. The change came with the advent of the ' Lux Mundi ' school, and at present a compound of sacerdotalism and socialism is characteristic of Anglo-Catholics. Several causes have contributed to this new development. Many ritualists have been honourably distinguished by their devoted work among the poor, and it is natural that they should tend to look at social questions from the point of view of the people among whom they work. They find that in these quarters the Church is suspected of being an ally of ' capitalism,' and that their influence is lessened in consequence. Having for the most part no knowledge of political economy, and a considerable command of rhetoric, they indulge in vague declamations against the existing social order, which only serve to spread discontent and darken counsel, but which are none the less sincere. There have been two or three notorious instances of ambitious and bitter fanatics who have deliberately fanned the flame of class hatred ; but this cannot be laid to the charge of the majority.

There are, however, other reasons which have detached the party from its former political Conservatism. The change in the social position of the clergy since the palmy days of Anthony Trollope has been enormous. Their social status, like that of the national school master and mistress, is not well defined; they have to bear snubs which they resent, and the prospects of their children, if they have any, are black indeed. In fact, the clergy are becoming an educated proletariat —always a dangerous class. This, of course, does not apply to the well-born and well-endowed leaders ; but in their case it is sometimes possible to trace an aristocratic disdain and dislike of the bourgeoisie, whose virtues and shortcomings are alike displeasing to both the upper and the lower classes. The bourgeois is despised by the aristocrat and by the working man for his thrift and industry; and besides these vices he is apt to be a dissenter, or at least a strong Protestant. So it has come about that the new type of ecclesiastic has no sympathy with Toryism or Liberalism, but woos the favour of the Labour party.

This is hardly a legitimate development of the Catholic movement. Catholicism has always been an anti-revolutionary force. The Gospel views economic disputes with lofty detachment. The only answer Christ deigned to give to the appeal, ' Speak to my brother that he divide the inheritance with me,' was ' Take heed and beware of all covetousness, for a man's life consisteth not in the abundance of the things that he possesseth.' The avaricious man is stigmatised as ' Thou fool,' not as ' Thou thief.' The Church looked to charity, not to legislation, to redress social wrongs; legislation might be necessary, but it was not the Church's business. Private property was said to be in accordance with the Law of Nature, not, perhaps, the original Law of Nature, but the Law of Nature as adapted to man's fallen state. ' Christian men's goods are not common.' In this respect the Catholic tradition has been firm and consistent; the Law of Nature is still appealed to by Catholic casuists as a sacred and final authority. Collectivist movements within Christianity have proceeded almost entirely from the Anabaptists and other sectaries.

The most recent activity of Christian social reformers has been the widely advertised and cleverly engineered ' Conference on Christian Politics, Economics, and Citizenship,' called, from its initials, ' Copec.' A large number of workers was enlisted, and the educative value of their labours to themselves was doubtless considerable. Parts of their lengthy Report show ability as well as painstaking research ; but the whole was rendered slightly ridiculous by the pontifical language in which their conclusions were given to the world. If words mean anything, they claimed to have been divinely inspired. We may hope that such assistance is always given to those who humbly seek it ; but in the rather sloppy Socialism which pervades this document there is nothing which seems to transcend the limits of unaided human intelligence.

Liberalism in the Church has never been organised as a party. The Liberal as such is a free-lance ; he does not wish to have to conform himself to any programme or policy. But the advance of Liberal opinions during the last fifty years has been far more noteworthy than the loudly trumpeted triumphs of the Catholic revival ; and, unlike these last, it has gained ground which can hardly be lost. It is difficult for us to believe that in 1829 Dean Milman's ' History of the Jews ' had to be withdrawn by the publisher in consequence of the commotion which it made in ecclesiastical circles. ' Essays and Reviews,' in 1860, raised a storm which swept the bishops off their feet, and soon after, Colenso was excommunicated by Bishop Gray of Capetown for views on the Old Testament which are now taken for granted. But Canute soon had to move his chair backward. ' Lux Mundi ' evoked a few protests, and embittered the last days of Canon Liddon ; but the

c

protagonist of this group, who has changed none of his opinions since that early venture, is now justly regarded as the main pillar of theological Conservatism. Much bolder books of essays, such as ' Contentio Veritatis ' and ' Foundations,' were widely read without getting their authors into trouble. Attempts at heresy-hunts have collapsed ignominiously, and a Liberal bishop to-day would have nothing worse to fear than the attacks of the ignoble obscurantist Press and an organised boycott by some theological colleges. The two other recognised parties have been quite unable to prevent the infiltration of Liberal ideas into their own circles. The more thoughtful of the Anglo-Catholics show a leaning to the Continental type of Modernism, represented by Loisy (in his earlier phase), and by Le Roy, Tyrrell, and Baron von Hügel ; the younger Evangelicals read the critical and philo-sophical works of German Protestants, and are in process of reconstructing their party on new lines. Thought within the Church of England is now much freer than ever before ; the battle for liberty has been practically won, though the extreme factions would gladly silence or expel the Liberals if they could.

Liberalism in the Church has in truth a tradition and a history which make attempts to expel it absurd. It is, especially in England, closely connected with the Platonic or Renaissance tradition, which in its turn may be traced back to the Greek Fathers and the Fourth Gospel. Anglican Liberalism is for the most part orthodox about the Person of Christ, but it believes that Christianity is primarily a way of living, based on Christ's teaching. The Liberal, feeling himself independent of ' proofs ' from miracles, wishes to terminate the long feud between the Church on one side, and Humanism and Science on the other. He is convinced that a frank abandonment of certain dogmas which are intelligible only by the geocentric hypothesis, would strengthen the influence of Christianity by removing the stumbling-blocks which keep many candid and intelligent persons out of the Church. If the Liberals expect quick results, they are too sanguine, for the love of truth is not very common, and superstition grows rankly in the soil through which the war-god lately drove his plough. But no form of Christianity which flouts science is in the true line of progress ; it may have a disastrous success for a time ; but the conscience as well as the reason of civilised man demands a reconciliation between secular knowledge and faith. An obscurantist religion can only assist at the euthanasia of decadent nations.

The isolation of the Church of England causes distress to all Anglicans, but the remedies suggested are very diverse. The theory of the Apostolical Succession obliges its supporters to recognise as true Churches only the Anglican, Roman, Eastern Orthodox, and perhaps the Swedish Lutheran. No reunion with the English Free Churches is even desired by this party, except on condition of their ministers submitting to episcopal ordination. After the war, there was a general wish for fraternisation among Protestants ; but the Anglo-Catholic party blocked the way. The contribution of this party to reunion was to open a ridiculous flirtation with a Belgian Cardinal, although the Vatican had recently pronounced with full authority that Anglican Orders are

other country could Catholics and Protestants dwell
together as members of the same Church. But the
genius for illogicality of the English people is unique,
and in the present case I shall try to show that it is
not unreasonable. The danger of disruption certainly
exists. It has been averted hitherto partly by the
long experience and great sagacity of the present
Primate. A less judicious successor might overturn
the coach. There is also a possibility that the Anglo-
Catholics, some of whom are utterly reckless and
actually desirous to make things intolerable for the
other historical parties, may introduce changes which
neither Evangelicals nor Liberals could conscientiously
accept. But, personally, I do not expect it. There
are traditions which would curb the rashness of any
occupant of Lambeth ; and the fanatics, even in the
dominant party, are really a small minority. The
practical difficulties of a great secession would be
enormous, and it must be remembered that the mass
of the laity are intensely conservative. They have no
wish for a new Prayer Book, or new teaching of any
kind. The Church, for them, if they belong to it, is
the Church of England, not a sect. They will bow
their heads under each violent wind of doctrine as it
comes ; in their hearts they know that fashions change,
and that the old Church has already weathered many
storms. Perhaps the most probable secession will be
from the extreme wing of the Latin party. To judge
by their utterances, they are living in a fool's paradise,
persuaded that the Church is rapidly becoming
Catholic, in their sense. When they awake from this
dream, the very thin trickle of Roman converts which
flows year by year may become a more copious stream.

But, on the other hand, those may be right who think that the Catholic reaction has already passed its climax. It is not likely that an attempt will be made to found a new independent Church ; for experience seems to prove that secessions of this kind are usually a mistake. The Nonjurors and the Old Catholics were not saved from failure by the high character and ability of their leaders. Even the Free Churches of England, numerous and powerful as they are, seem to be on the down grade; they were most prosperous while their chief supporters (the shop keeping class) wielded political power. Signs are not wanting that the Anglican Church may have another opportunity of leading and representing the religion of the English people.

The question, ' What does the Church of England stand for ? ' must, of course, be answered. It can be answered only by considering what it has stood for since the Reformation and before it. It has been—in intention, and sometimes in fact—the Church of the English people. This is the principle upon which Hooker most insists. ' There is not any man of the Church of England but the same man is also a member of the commonwealth ; nor any man a member of the commonwealth, which is not also [a member] of the Church of England.' The Royal Supremacy had very little to do with the seventeenth-century figment of the divine right of kings ; it meant that there was to be no dual control in any section of the commonwealth. The king—or, as we should now say, the law—was to be supreme in all causes, ecclesiastical as well as civil. There was to be no appeal to any tradition or authority outside the realm. In 1792 Burke

(quoted by Mr. Fawkes) asserts the old doctrine again.
' An alliance between Church and State in a Christian
commonwealth is an idle and a fanciful opinion. An
alliance is between two things that are in their nature
distinct and independent, such as between two
sovereign States. But in a Christian commonwealth
the Church and the State are one and the same thing,
being different integral parts of the same whole.'

Mr. Fawkes also quotes a magnificent passage
from ' John Inglesant,' the more remarkable as written
by a Nonconformist. I regret to have to abbreviate
it. ' The English Church, as established by the law
of England, offers the supernatural to all who care to
come. It is like the Divine Being Himself, whose
sun shines on the evil and on the good. . . . Shall we
throw this aside ? It has been won for us by the
death and torture of men like ourselves in bodily
frame, infinitely superior to some of us in self-denial
and endurance. If we cannot endure as they did, at
least let us not needlessly throw away what they have
won. It is not a question of religious freedom only,
it is a question of learning and culture in every form.
. . . As a Church, it is unique ; if suffered to drop
out of existence, nothing like it can ever take its
place.'

Is it quite too late to revive this ideal of a National
Church ? Those who think so may be cured of their
despondency by reading the Primary Charge of the
Bishop of Gloucester, Dr. Headlam,[1] the most noteworthy episcopal pronouncement that we have had
for many years. Dr. Headlam has learning, statesmanship and courage. He knows the history of the

[1] *The Church of England*, John Murray, 1924.

Church of England, and his knowledge gives him a confidence in its future which is none too common to-day.

He proves that ' our Church claims, and rightly claims, for it is dependent on the whole position it has adopted, to have authority to arrange and put forth for itself a national use.' ' The fundamental principle is that the authority of the Pope is an usurped authority.' ' We recognise the competence of our Church to ordain its services for itself, and we intend loyally to adhere to its principles and obey its directions, even when we disagree with them.'

It would be impossible even to summarise Dr. Headlam's argument. He insists that the Church of England is absolutely independent, that it has a character of its own, which corresponds with the national character of our people, that it has had a glorious history, that it meets the needs of the present age as no other Church can do, being comprehensive and adaptable without any uncertainty about the fundamental principles of the Christian religion, and that it should have a great future, if it remains true to its character as the most Catholic of Reformed and Protestant Churches. It is the old principle of the ' via media,' ably and fearlessly applied to present-day conditions.

The attempt which is now being made to drag Anglicanism away from its history and traditions will fail. The ship will right itself by degrees. And the chief influence in restoring the balance will be, I think, the new school of Liberal Evangelicals, who are now freeing themselves from the cramping influences of their party tradition, and are facing the future with

clear eyes and unflinching faith. For the strength of
Protestantism lies not in theories of inspiration and
special providences ; it lies in personal devotion to
Christ, and in the duty of individual judgment, under
the guidance of the Spirit of Truth.   Institutionalism
may be decaying, and there are at present few signs
of a revival of it ; but personal religion may even
gain by the decline of authority and ecclesiastical
discipline ; and it is in personal religion that the
Christian recovers the faith of the original Gospel,
and an unassailable basis for confronting the problems
of the future.

THE CRISIS OF ROMAN CATHOLICISM

PROFESSOR FRIEDRICH HEILER, of Marburg, is, in the opinion of some men well qualified to judge, the most outstanding among the younger theologians of Germany. He is well known as the author of a standard work on Prayer (' Das Gebet '), which has passed through several editions ; and he has now republished, in a much enlarged form, a comprehensive study of Roman Catholicism, which is probably the most important book on the subject. The Professor has lately left the Church of Rome to become a Lutheran ; but he retains a warm affection and admiration for the Catholic system, and explains in a masterly way the many-sided attractiveness of that majestic institution, which appeals to nearly all the religious instincts of human nature. Heiler was driven out of the Roman communion by the disciplinary measures taken by the Vatican against the Modernists. It does not appear that he was personally censured ; but he is an ardent disciple of George Tyrrell and Archbishop Söderblom of Upsala, and still more, perhaps, of Baron Friedrich von Hügel, who must certainly be ranked as a Modernist, though this profound and loyal lay theologian is too great an asset to his Church to be molested. Heiler writes with burning indignation of the fate of Tyrrell and his friends, but he makes no attempt to defend

Loisy, the great Biblical critic, and even denies that he
has had much influence on the Modernist movement.
The unflinching condemnation of Modernism by the
Pope made it impossible for Heiler to remain a Catholic
without denying his convictions and deserting his
friends.

The main facts about the Modernist controversy
are well known. The group of men whom Pope Pius X
called Modernists are, or were, some of them
philosophers and some New Testament critics. In the
latter capacity they tend to accept the extreme
destructive position, holding with Loisy that the
historical Jesus was merely an enthusiastic prophet
who went about preaching that ' the Kingdom of
God '—a supernatural cataclysm which would bring
the world-order to an end—was close at hand. All
the supernatural elements in the Gospel narrative are
either openly rejected or tacitly set aside. Albert
Schweitzer's one-sided insistence on the so-called
eschatological (apocalyptic) character of Christ's teaching has had a strong influence upon the Modernists.
The historical Jesus, according to these critics, founded
no Church and instituted no Sacraments ; the real
founder of Catholicism was St. Paul, who inaugurated
the cult of the Lord Christ (Kyrios Christos), and
thereby gave the new religion a form which was
intelligible to the Hellenistic population of the Roman
Empire. The Church grew, like any other organism,
by responding to its environment ; it adapted itself to
human needs, and gave scope for the unchanging
popular religion of the Mediterranean peoples to find
expression within its comprehensive system. Since
religion is fundamentally ' irrational '—Heiler repeats

this statement many times—it can easily survive the
loss of its factual basis. The fatal error of Catholic
theology has been the attempt to find a rationalistic
foundation for faith.

That this treatment of the historical Founder of
Christianity is ' deeply repulsive to the large majority
of believers ' is admitted by Baron von Hügel ; but
the more drastic Modernists maintain that it is, or
soon will be, forced upon us by honest criticism ; and
their anti-intellectualist philosophy helps them to face
the crisis with equanimity. Christianity, as Tyrrell
said, is at the cross-roads. The arguments from
miracle and prophecy are gone. The ' historical '
articles in the Creeds are, for the Modernists, myth,
not fact. The claims of the Roman Church are
buttressed by fraud. And lastly, the official philosophy, that of St. Thomas Aquinas, is quite out of
date, being based on preconceptions which modern
philosophy has rejected. Either, then, Catholicism
must be abandoned, or it must justify itself by a new
apologetic. Tyrrell, in a letter which he did not mean
to be published, used the strong phrase, ' Catholicism
must die to live.'

The Vatican made no terms with its dangerous
defenders. Modernism was pronounced to be ' a
compendium of all the heresies,' and its theses were
anathematised in detail. A very searching anti-
Modernist oath was, and still is, exacted, which was
intended to make it impossible for any Modernist to
hold office in the Catholic Church, except by deliberate
perjury. Loisy protested that it is impossible to kill
ideas by a *coup de bâton*, but he seems to have become
convinced that his position was really incompatible

with membership of a Christian Church, and he
accepted a lay professorship. Other members of the
school considered themselves deeply injured by being
branded as heretics, and protested their loyalty and
devotion to Catholicism. Heiler's position, as will be
seen, is peculiar. He thinks that the Church in
becoming Roman has ceased to be Catholic. Since
the Reformation it has, he says, been growing steadily
narrower, till it has lost the right to speak in the
name of ' universal ' Christianity.

The question whether the Church has, since its
very beginning, substituted a mythical figure for the
martyred prophet of Galilee must be argued as a
problem of historical criticism. Liberal theology in
this country sees no reason to accept the position of
Loisy and Schweitzer. The present writer has elsewhere stated some of the difficulties which the advocates
of the theory fail to meet ; the matter cannot be
discussed here. To the Protestant, the severance of
the Church from its roots in the Person of the Redeemer
would be a blow from which his faith could not recover ;
official Catholicism is equally emphatic to the same
effect. But it will be well to let Heiler speak for
himself, since we must not attribute the same opinions
to all members of the school.

Heiler gives us a sketch of the entire history of
Catholicism from the first century to the present day.
His survey covers the same ground as Auguste
Sabatier's ' Les Religions d'Autorité et la Religion de
l'Esprit,' but he never mentions the work of the French
scholar, which is in truth a bitter anti-Roman polemic.
A comparison between the two books is nevertheless
very interesting and instructive.

The author, though he follows Schweitzer in holding that the essential part of Christ's message was the near approach of the ' Kingdom of God,' does not disparage the rest of the Gospel message as mere ' Interimsethik.' He finds in the Gospel a revival, ' pure and strong, of the most precious heritage of Israel, the religion of the prophets.' He also points out that the Judaism of Palestine at the beginning of our era was already affected by ' Greek wisdom, esoteric asceticism and mysticism, and Platonic ideas.' Since, however, the teaching of Christ, as he admits, shows no traces of these accretions, it is doubtful whether he has the right to speak of ' a background of syncretistic religion ' in the Gospel. The Judaism of Palestine differed widely from the Judaism of the Dispersion. It is much more important that Heiler fully recognises the universal and revolutionary character of Christ's teaching. ' He lays the axe to the root of Judaism,' and ' not less tears to pieces all exclusive Christian church-manship.' ' Jesus overcame the traditional religion, though without a formal breach.'

Heiler thus emphasises what might be called the Protestant character of the Gospel ; he does not leave much standing of the Catholic claim that Christ instituted the Catholic Church. 'Salvation [in the Gospel] lies alone in faith, hope, and love; faith in God's mercy, hope in the eternal kingdom, and self-sacrificing love. These are not bound up with institutional religion ; they make their own way to the kingdom of heaven.' Jesus resembled Savonarola, but ' unlike Savonarola, He stood above all Churchman-ship, independent of institutions.' ' He is inwardly indifferent to every Church-ideal.' ' Inwardness and

brotherly love break down all the barriers of legal
and ritual Church-religion.' ' The Gospel is super-
ecclesiastical and unecclesiastical ; His judgment on
the Jewish Church is valid also against the Christian
Church of the later centuries.' ' The use of the word
Ecclesia in St. Matthew is unhistorical ; Jesus can
never have said this ' (Matt. xvi, 18). ' The words
about binding and loosing have been transferred from
another context.' ' Jesus gave no primacy or privileged
position to any of His apostles.' ' The commission of
primacy to Peter is plainly an interpolation.' ' The
Gospel of Christ and the Roman World-Church are
united by no inner band ; a gulf yawns between
them.' ' The Catholicising of Christianity begins
immediately after the death of Jesus. The Pentecost
is the birthday of the Catholic World-Church ; not
the man Jesus, but the Kyrios Christos and His
Spirit founded the universal Church.'

These are precisely the arguments which lead the
Protestant to reject the Catholic position as historically
untenable ; but to the Catholic Modernist they cause
no uneasiness. ' If you want to establish the identity
of an individual,' says Loisy, ' it is not necessary to
squeeze him into his cradle.'

' The system of Catholic dogma has its root in the
Pauline myth of the Son of God.' (By a ' myth '
Heiler says that he means ' a fact-like historical
picture ' or ' symbolical narrative '—phrases which he
borrows from Baron von Hügel.) St. Paul is also the
father of Catholic mysticism ; through him ' the
Orphic-Platonic piety,' with which the Hellenistic
world was ' saturated,' was permanently amalgamated
with Christianity. St. Paul ' lived in the higher world

of the Spirit, the world of mystical inwardness.' ' The whole Christ-drama of salvation passes into this mystical inner life '; the whole process of Christ, His death, resurrection, and ascension, must be re-enacted in the personal experience of the Christian. Therewith came a certain indifference to the merely historical aspect of the revelation : ' though we have known Christ after the flesh, henceforth we know Him so no more ' (2 Cor. v, 16).

In the later books of the New Testament, the Pastoral Epistles and the Gospel of Matthew, we find another spirit. ' The Pastoral Epistles are the first document of narrow and stiff Roman Churchmanship.' The editor of our First Gospel has also done much to turn the announcement of the Kingdom of God into the proclamation of a legal ecclesiastical system. It has been the favourite Gospel of the Roman hierarchy, which finds in it its most impressive texts. ' The Apocalypse is the first document of the Catholic popular (" vulgar ") religion.' ' Old Oriental cosmology, Jewish eschatology, Chaldæan astrology, Assyrian number-symbolism, Hellenistic magic and Sibylline prophecy, Persian dualism and Christian belief in redemption, are here thrown together in a chaotic syncretism.' Most of these elements lived on in the popular religion of the Middle Ages.

The Fourth Evangelist is neither a missionary nor an ecclesiastic ; he is a mystical theologian, the Origen of primitive Christianity. The Johannine Christ is a figure of unmoved, passionless majesty ; the picture makes a strong appeal to Buddhist students. The nameless disciple, who leaned on Jesus' breast, is the mystic, who penetrates furthest into the secrets of

D

the divine. The piety of this Gospel is ' Gnostic Mysticism,' if we may use the word Gnostic, as Clement did, as a title of honour. Nevertheless, the Evangelist is a loyal Catholic : ' the mother of Jesus ' is an allegory of the Church, and ' Peter ' of Church authority. (Heiler, I think, is quite mistaken in attributing a half-magical sacramental doctrine to this Evangelist, who, on the contrary, carefully dissociates his sacramental teaching from the rites, and describes only one institu-tion of a sacrament, namely, the feet-washing, which never established itself in the Church as a recognised ' mysterium.') ' The dogma of the Incarnation is the great creation of this writer.' For the rest, his Gospel of love is the genuine Gospel of Christ ; and the Reformers naturally prized ' St. John ' above all the other Evangelists. The ' native air ' of this treatise is of course not Palestine, but ' the Alexandrian religious world.'

Heiler next traces the development of Catholicism during its ' campaign on two fronts,' against Marcion and the Gnostics. Gnosticism was a ' hot-house growth,' which the early Church could not incorporate without danger ; Marcionism was an attempted return to the primitive Gospel. The Church steered a middle course between them, borrowing something from both, but continually strengthening the hands of authority and checking the ' liberty of prophesying.' In this kind of statesmanship Rome took the lead.

The Alexandrian philosophy of religion is not much to Heiler's taste. He begins to talk about ' intellectual-ism,' that bugbear of modern thought, which it is the custom to attribute to the Greeks. The Platonic school, to which Catholic theology is so much indebted,

is certainly not 'intellectualist' in the disparaging
sense. The organ of divine knowledge (νοῦς) is not
the logic-chopping faculty, but the whole personality
unified by a discipline which is at least as much moral
as intellectual, for the quest of truth, goodness, and
beauty. The root-principle of Platonism, as of all
Christian mysticism, is that spiritual things are spiritually discerned, so that the soul must commit itself
whole-heartedly to the upward path before it can form
true conceptions of supersensual reality. Certainly
the statement that religion is 'irrational' would seem
to Platonists and mystics of all ages nothing less than
treason against our highest endowment. The 'seven
gifts of the Holy Spirit' are gifts of intellectual enlightenment, and have always been recognised as such by
the General Councils, which opened with a special
invocation of the Holy Ghost. Heiler's notion that
Catholic philosophy lost sight of faith and love in verbal
disputations is quite untrue. The Catholic theologians
never, in theory at least, forgot the truth which is
emphasised by Plotinus, that the mind (or spirit) *in
love* can alone reach the full attainment of divine
knowledge. Heiler regards Origen as the founder of
Scholasticism ; but he reserves his strongest censures
for St. Thomas Aquinas, whose theology is still authoritative in the Church of Rome. The whole of the
' proofs of God's existence,' and the rest of the demonstration which claims to establish by the light of reason
the fundamental principles of religion, Heiler regards as
a disastrous blunder, an attempt to rationalise the
irrational. He reminds us of what of course is true,
that the mental state of the philosophic theologian is
quite different from that of the saint at prayer.

Spiritual experience is not gathered by dialectic ; no one ever supposed that it was ; but it is difficult to understand how an earnest and candid mind can be content to leave religious convictions entirely unco-ordinated with human knowledge, a mere mass of emotions nowhere in contact with external fact. When we remember how Heiler and his school have dealt with the Jesus of history, we can only read with amazement such a sentence as this : ' The living Christ-piety, the belief in the incarnate Son of God, the following of the poor and meek Jesus, the love of the heavenly Saviour and bridegroom of the soul, the prayers to the eternal Christ as the King of Kings—all this has nothing to do with the *Christuspopanz*, for which the traditional apologetic strives.   As the God of speculative dogmatics is other than the God of devout piety, so the Christ of apologetics and dogmatics is other than the Christ of real piety.'   It is plain that ' the object of real piety ' is for this school a Being who never existed.   It is enough to say that the early Church was quite familiar with cults of non-historical dying and rising Saviour Gods, and suffered persecution because it refused to have anything to do with them or to recognise any truth in them.

Scholastic theology was, as we all know, the child of an utterly unscientific and half-barbarous age.   It attempts to prove some things that cannot be proven, and other things that we now know to be untrue. Some Thomists are justly accused of that abuse of logic which consists in moving counters about as if they were known entities with a fixed connotation. But to condemn their whole method and object is ' misology ' of the worst description.   Even the

famous ' proofs of God's existence ' were not killed
by Kant ; they may all be stated in forms which are
still valuable and even cogent.

After the concordat with the State in the reign of
Constantine, the Church was rapidly paganised. ' The
whole ancient piety, with its magical Beings, its cult of
gods and heroes, its fear of demons and its belief in
miracles, clothed itself with a thin Christian dress and
so found entrance into the consecrated precincts of the
Church.' The expiring heathen temple-liturgies took
a new life within the Church, and brought its rites
nearer to the old worship of the temples. The priest
became a privileged official and mystagogue. Before
long, the ancestral religion of the barbarian invaders
began to exert its influence. ' German heathenism,
Aristotelian logic and metaphysics, and the mysticism
of Dionysius the Areopagite, are the new factors which
the medieval Church took into its bosom.' In Gregory
the Great this ' vulgar Catholicism ' becomes authoritative. ' The Catholicism of the present day is more
the creation of the Christian Middle Ages than of
Christian antiquity.'

This is perhaps the best place to consider Heiler's
conception of the essence of Catholicism. It is, he
says, essentially a comprehensive religion, a *complexio
oppositorum*. Of the Eastern Church he says : ' The
combination of these heterogeneous elements makes it
Catholic, and has enabled it to endure during all the
centuries.' Again : ' Catholicism has proclaimed the
whole gay congeries of religions, which it embraces, as
genuinely Christian.' It not only incorporated the
whole religious philosophy of the Neoplatonists, but all
the popular beliefs of the half-heathen masses. This

unlimited hospitality is for Heiler the note of true
Catholicism. The power of assimilation has been
gradually lost, and so Rome is no longer truly Catholic.

To the present writer, this seems to be a miscon-
ception of the part which Catholicism has played in
history. The name Catholic indicates universal extension in a geographical sense rather than intellectual
comprehensiveness. So far from desiring to include
heterogeneous and irreconcilable elements, the Church
defined its position mainly by the exclusion of errors,
and endeavoured from the first to leave no contra-
dictions unsolved. The 'narrowness' which to our
author seems a modern error was in reality present
from the first. For example, there never was a time at
which the statement that the historical Christ was
purely human (ψιλὸς ἄνθρωπος) was not anathematised. Judaisers, Pagans, Gnostics, Arians, and even
Nestorians were condemned. No compromise was
made with the popular ' Religionsgemenge,' which was
then called *theocrasia.* If we put aside for the moment
the political evolution of Catholicism, on which more
must be said presently, and regard it as a religion
consisting of a body of beliefs, we find that the Church
belongs quite definitely to a particular type of religion
and even to a particular type of thought, and does not
try to make room for all religion, nor for all philosophy. It is, for example, a system of personal theism,
a supernational religion, an other-worldly religion, a
religion of brotherly love. It does not deny that there
is much which is noble and valuable in Buddhism
which denies the first of these, in Judaism which denies
the second, in Positivism which denies the third, and in
the creed of self-culture which dispenses with the fourth.

But it does not try to include these religions ; they are not Christian.

In the same way, Catholicism is not hospitable to every philosophy. It is, as Troeltsch says, the last creative achievement of classical antiquity, the heir of Greek thought. The whole structure of Catholic dogma, apologetic, and philosophy is built upon the foundation of Greek speculation and Greek mental discipline. It is impossible to tear them asunder, because there never was a primitive Church unaffected by Hellenistic ideas. They are apparent in the earliest books of the New Testament. They determined the dogmas and creeds of Christendom. They imposed upon the Church an eschatology which is incompatible with the Jewish beliefs of the first Christians. They introduced into the Church that combination of speculative thought, ascetic discipline, and mystical intuition which belongs essentially to the Platonic tradition. Now this Catholic philosophy, which is a continuation of the thousand years of unfettered debate which the Greek race enjoyed before the closing of the schools of Athens, has a quite definite character of its own. It is rationalistic, and also mystical, like the philosophy of the Neoplatonists. A Platonist need not be a Christian, still less a Catholic ; but the main presuppositions on which Christian philosophy has always been based are also his.

Aristotelianism is a more questionable ally of the Christian faith. It is significant that the scholastic semi-Aristotelianism, which was before long accepted by the Church, was at first received with suspicion. Heiler quotes with satisfaction the letter which Pope Gregory IX wrote to the Professors of the University

of Paris in 1223, condemning the Modernists of the
thirteenth century as severely as the Encyclical ' Pas-
cendi dominici gregis ' condemned Loisy and his school.
' Some of you, distended like a bladder with the spirit
of vanity, busy themselves in altering the limits laid
down by the fathers with profane innovations . . .
inclining to the teaching of natural philosophers.
Misled by various and strange doctrines, they put the
head where the tail ought to be, and force the queen to
serve the maid-servant.   And while they endeavour to
buttress the faith by natural reason more than they
ought, do they not render it, in a manner, useless and
empty ? '   The Pope exhorts them not to bedizen
the spouse of Christ with rouge and extraneous orna-
ments, but to ' teach theological purity without the
ferment of worldly science, not contaminating the
word of God with the figments of philosophers.'   The
Church distrusted rationalism untempered by mysticism.   Like its precursor, Neoplatonism, it neglected
the scientific studies to which Aristotle devoted much
of his life, and feared that science would end by under-
mining the supernatural.   It was a crisis in Christian
thought, and we see that authority, after an unsparing
condemnation, admitted the new learning as a bulwark
of orthodoxy.   But Aristotle the natural philosopher
was never really accepted.   The Schoolmen were less
of Aristotelians than they supposed.   Some of the
doctrines and treatises which they believed to be
Aristotle's really belonged to the later Platonists.
The Schoolmen, too, had no desire to make philosophy
anything more than an *ancilla fidei ;* they were anything rather than dangerous rebels.   They did nothing
to prepare the Church for the great decision which it

had to make in regard to the discoveries of Copernicus and Galileo. With hardly a qualm, authority then came down on the side of obscurantism, and ever since, the faithful have been condemned to live in a pre-Copernican universe, from which they can only escape by formal heresy or obvious inconsistency. This, however, is not because the Schoolmen and their successors were rationalists, but because, like the medievals in general, they were timid traditionalists. They did not know that a great Renaissance was dawning.

Heiler shows a bitter hostility to the philosophy of the Middle Ages, and the grounds of his dislike throw much light on the character of Modernist thought. We have to remember that logic had a much larger place in medieval education than it has in our own day. With us, natural science is more and more the basis of all constructive theories of history and philosophy; but in the Middle Ages, when there was no natural science worthy of the name, right reasoning —*recta ratio*—was the *praeambula fidei*. The scholastic apologists felt, surely rightly, that a supernatural revelation must have at least a foundation within the domain of human reason, and it was by logic that they attempted to demonstrate the essentials of the theistic position. Heiler objects that these proofs, even were they more valid than they are, do not lead us to 'the God of living piety.' 'The God of living piety is excluded from all possibility of rational proof, because He is essentially irrational.' Rational proof may demonstrate the existence of the Absolute, but 'the introduction of proofs of the existence of the Absolute into theology is a dangerous error, which has bitterly revenged itself in later times.' 'The proofs of God's

existence have never brought any one to believe in
God, but have torn belief in God out of the hearts of
many.' In the same way ' the philosophical arguments
for the immortality of the soul are a very poor substitute for the belief in the Kingdom of God. Rational
philosophy stands here also in a totally different
sphere from irrational faith.'

We naturally ask—while apologising for the absurd
form which the question must necessarily take—what
reasons there are for believing the irrational ? We can
imagine two answers, but it is difficult to find any clear
explanation in Heiler. It might be said : Since knowledge of things as they are is entirely beyond our
capacity, it is our wisdom to believe, or to behave as if
we believed, whatever helps us to live as we wish to
live. If any belief ceases to help us, we may give it up
and try something else. The proof of the pudding is in
the eating. Whatever helps souls may be called true.
This is pragmatism ; it goes back to Protagoras, with
his maxim, ' Man is the measure of all things.' Some
of the Modernists have coquetted with this philosophy,
which is popular in America. In that country ' bluff '
is so successful that men are not without hope that
they may bluff nature and its Author. But it is difficult to imagine any view of life more incompatible
with Christianity.

The other possible answer is that we know God by
mystical intuition, which makes reason superfluous.
Heiler actually appeals to Plotinus in support of this
reply : God is ' beyond thought ' ($\epsilon\pi\epsilon\kappa\epsilon\iota\nu\alpha$ $\nu o\hat{v}$ $\kappa\alpha\grave{\iota}$
$\nu o\acute{\eta}\sigma\epsilon\omega s$). There could hardly be a more fundamental
misunderstanding of mystical philosophy. The Absolute,
whom Heiler dislikes so much, is said by the mystics to

be ' beyond Being and beyond thought ' ; he is the ultimate unity, the One, who is presupposed in all distinctions, even in the distinction between thinker and
thought.　It is not necessary to quote the language in
which writers like Plotinus, Dionysius, Erigena, and
Eckhart have tried to express the absolute transcendence of the Godhead as He is in Himself.　It is also
true that the life of the beatified spirit, which can be
experienced in a measure by the mystic on earth, is lived
in a higher atmosphere than that of discursive reason.
' The soul that has become spirit,' as some of these
writers express it, is in more immediate correspondence
with eternal and spiritual reality than can be attained
by mere dialectic.　This is enough to disprove the
charge of ' intellectualism,' but it by no means implies
that the mystical quest is ' irrational.'　If the mystic
were not convinced that the heaven of his desire exists
objectively and independently of himself, he would at
once cease to be a mystic ; and if he did not believe that
the quest to which he is committed involves the con-
secration of the intellectual faculties no less than of the
will and affections, he could not believe, as he does, that
only the unified personality can come into touch with
the Godhead.　The dictum of Plotinus that to aspire to
rise above intelligence is to fall outside it shows how
determined he is to take no short cuts to the beatific
vision.　The best Catholic theologians reject explicitly
the argument of ' ontologism,' the claim that immediate and irrefragable certainty of the being of God is
granted to us.　The proof of God's existence is for them
in the nature of a valid inference.　The life of faith is
justified to the intellect by this conclusion of the reason ;
but it remains a venture, without which it would not be

faith.   The venture is progressively justified by spiritual experience, which at last reaches intuitive certainty. The spiritual ascent gives as it were new data on which a true philosophy can be founded.   Our earlier pro-visional syntheses may have to be discarded in the light of higher and fuller knowledge ; but never, even in the highest stage, does faith become irrational.

There seems to be a curious dualism in the mind of the Modernist. In dealing with history, he is an extreme rationalist. He rejects the notion that there was any-thing unique or supernatural in the career of Jesus of Nazareth ; he would, one imagines, not dissent from the harsh statement of Loisy that the historian does not banish God from history ; he never meets Him there. And yet he values the creeds, the sacraments, and the liturgy of the Catholic Church, which are based on the belief that in the historical Christ ' dwelleth all the full-ness of the Godhead bodily.'   The Catholic worship is for him, we must suppose, symbolic : it represents spiritual truths which can move our affections and imaginations only when they are translated into these images.   Now we must all admit that we see through a glass darkly, and know only in part.   But is it not a matter of experience that as soon as we see that an alleged miracle is only a parable, it loses its value for us as a miracle, and becomes only an aid to the imagination, or more often even a hindrance ?   To the ' vulgar Christian ' (the phrase is less offensive in German), Catholicism guarantees facts, past, present, and future. To the man in the street the alternative is fact or fraud ; and in view of the powers claimed by the priesthood, which depend on the factual truth of their doctrines, it is difficult to deny that this is the alternative.   Heiler seems to say in effect, ' All that the rationalists say is true, but it does not matter.' But we live in a scientific age, which will not readily agree that the question is irrelevant whether an event which is presented to us as immensely important ever went through the form of taking place.

Heiler traces the development of post-Tridentine Catholicism with growing disapprobation. After the Reformation the Church became narrower, and no longer produced men of genius like Augustine, or even like Thomas Aquinas. Its most outstanding figures are Ignatius of Loyola and Alfonso of Liguori, in whom ' vulgar Catholicism' overwhelms the mystical and evangelical elements of Christianity. The Prussianism of Ignatius is briefly but sufficiently sketched. In Alfonso of Liguori Catholicism seems to him to have descended to a still lower plane. This modern Catholic saint is the author of the statement, ' It is difficult to be saved through Christ, but easy through Mary.' His extravagant Papalism is the main reason why his works, which Döllinger stigmatised as ' a magazine of errors and lies,' have been made authoritative, and exalted to the level of the earlier doctors of the Church.

There is much in this book which I must leave without comment, though it is full of interest—a sympathetic elucidation of the liturgy, discipline, and institutions of the great Church which the author quitted with so much sorrow. In some ways, these chapters are the most illuminating in the whole volume. But my space is needed for a judgment on the book as a whole. I have dealt with the Modernist attitude towards history and dogma, and have not disguised my conviction that Rome would have committed suicide by admitting and

sanctioning a disintegrating philosophy of religion, the
tendency of which would have been to change Catholicism into a religion of a different type, depriving it both
of the advantage which gave it the victory over Isis and
Mithra—its basis in history, and of its philosophy, in
which it affiliated itself to the great Hellenic tradition.
Nevertheless, Tyrrell was right in saying that the
Church of Rome stands at the cross-roads.   It is encum-
bered by an immense mass of falsified history and anti-
quated science, which it cannot repudiate, and which it
can no longer impose upon its adherents, except where
its priests still control and stifle education.   The plea
that truths of fact and truths of faith are different
things, which do not conflict because they are on
different planes, certainly suggests a way out.   It is a
way which would lead the Roman Church to disaster ;
but perhaps no other solution of the problem is in sight.

It remains to consider whether the history of
Christianity in general, and of Western Catholicism
in particular, does not suggest rather different conclusions from those which lie at the root of Heiler's
position.   And first of all, the unwelcome fact must be
faced, that to find a form of religion which shall be
acceptable to all the great races of mankind, divided
as they are by immemorial differences of mental
structure and ancestral customs, is a problem which,
if not insoluble, has never yet been solved.   The
Gospel of Christ Himself, we may gladly admit, speaks
in his own tongue to the Greek and the Roman, the
Teuton and the Celt, the white man and the black.
But this cannot be said of any institutional Church.
Just as Buddhism, in gaining China and Burma, lost
India, the home of its origin, so the Christian Church,

in gaining for Christ the whole domain of Graeco-
Roman culture, lost its power of appealing to the
Semitic nations. It became the religion of the Roman
Empire. Christians may hope for a time when Asia
and Africa may own allegiance to the Founder of their
faith ; but the historian will not cherish the expecta-
tion that the people of these continents will ever
become adherents of any European Church. To speak
plainly, an universal Church is as much a chimaera
as an universal empire. The double dream of an
universal Roman Church and an universal Roman
Empire floated before the minds of men in the Middle
Ages ; but now that man knows his home from end
to end, the Roman Empire seems a small thing, and
the Latin Church a smaller. One who has been
brought up under the magic of the Roman name,
like Heiler, may ask, Why should Rome not be the
capital of the world-religion ? Others will more
reasonably ask, Why should it ?

For Latin Catholicism is an institution much
narrower even than European Christianity. It is the
religion of the Latin-speaking Mediterraneans, and
of the barbarian invaders whom they were able to
assimilate. What Heiler calls vulgar Catholicism is
the ancestral religion of south-western Europe. The
medieval Church borrowed what it could understand of
Greek philosophy ; it neglected and lost Greek science ;
it thoroughly understood and eagerly developed the
theory and practice of Roman Imperialism. ' Tu
regere imperio populos, Romane, memento.' As long
as Northern Europe was under the tutelage of the
more advanced nations of the south, it remained
Catholic ; but there were many precursors of the

Reformation in England and Germany, and the great cleavage of the sixteenth century so nearly followed racial lines that it bears the character of a Nordic secession. There is no likelihood whatever that the Northern Europeans will ever return to the Italian allegiance. It is curious that Heiler does not seem to have considered the racial limits of Romanism, though history has marked them out very clearly. He is obsessed by the ideal of one fold and one shepherd.

' The tragedy of Catholicism,' then, is not to be found in its failure to maintain the character of a *complexio oppositorum*, a combination of opposite tendencies, for this was never a part of the Catholic ideal. Nor is there any tragedy in its failure to establish a world-empire, for no such empire can ever exist. We shall find the tragedy rather in the political evolution of the Western Church, which Sabatier has described with much insight. Rome is to-day the only surviving autocracy, the one remaining example of a type of government which has had a notable past, and may have a future, but which for the present has been discredited and abandoned in all secular States. This unique position makes the Latin Church a very interesting object of study for the political philosopher, but the means by which this centralised despotism was acquired, consolidated, and perpetuated, furnish grounds for an unanswerable indictment against those who claim any peculiar sanctity for the Catholic Church as an institution. It is the Church as a political organisation which has made so many enemies ; and unhappily the will to power has infected every branch of the institution, determining doctrine no less than policy.

The Roman Empire, as is well known, became more centralised and more despotic until it fell to pieces. Both the Court and the system of government approached more nearly to the Asiatic type, chiefly because only a very strong central government could cope with the evils of praetorianism, which was wrecking civilisation by repeated pronunciamientos. The same tendency showed itself in the Church, though the problems of ecclesiastical government were different. As Sabatier says: ' After having been in apostolic times a pure democracy, the Church became a great federation governed by its bishops ; this was an aristocratic régime. Then the primacy of Rome turned it into a monarchy, at first tempered by the Councils, afterwards more and more centralised, omnipotent, and finally absolute.' The same political necessity, he says, determined the whole evolution, which culminated in the dogma of infallibility. But we are tempted to ask whether this steady movement towards a complete autocracy was inevitable from the first, or whether, quite early in Church history, there was a parting of the ways, when the alternative course might have been taken. I shall not attempt to decide this very difficult question, but a few considerations may be offered.

It is certain that the Gospel of Christ levels all institutional barriers, whether sacred or secular, by ignoring them. Faith and love are the only and sufficient passports to membership of the ' little flock.' But even within the circle of the Twelve instances are recorded of the characteristic Jewish intolerance, and the early Church narrated with satisfaction how St. John fled from a public bath when the heretic

E

Cerinthus entered it. Jewish fanaticism combined
with Roman imperialism to create the idea of a Church
world-wide *de iure*, which regarded all dissentients as
rebels and traitors, to be justly subjected to persecution
here and eternal torments hereafter. This intolerance
was not Greek in origin, though it is significant that
Plato, who sketched with marvellous foresight the
forms which his philosophic Republic must assume,
sanctioned coercive measures against atheists and
others, and even provided for a ' Nocturnal Council,'
terribly like the Inquisition. Plutarch tells us that
Cleanthes the Stoic ' thought that the Greeks ought
to prosecute Aristarchus for impiety, for moving the
centre of the universe ; because Aristarchus tried to
account for the phenomena by the hypothesis that the
firmament is stationary, and that the earth revolves
round the sun in an oblique circle, at the same time
rotating on its own axis.' But this precursor of
Galileo was a Greek, and escaped the fate of the
Renaissance astronomer.

We have to account for the instinctive fear of the
Church which the imperial government soon began to
manifest. The pagans despised the Christians as a
' tenebrosa et lucifugax natio,' but at the same time
they considered them an association of a peculiarly
dangerous kind. They were not so foolish as to suppose them to be social revolutionaries, though this
has been suggested ; but they saw in the Church an
imperium in imperio, independent of the empire and
ostentatiously indifferent to it. They feared that the
triumph of the Church would mean the disappearance
of the old civilisation, and that ' a shapeless darkness
would destroy all the beauty of the world.' The

effect of the persecutions was to foster a spirit which would have been easily exorcised by a different treatment. At Alexandria the adherents of many religions met in friendly intercourse and attended the same university lectures; a Christian philosophy soon sprang up which did not wish to deny its debt to the old culture. But in the Church as a whole authority was becoming more rigorous and more centralised; the Church was preparing for its final struggle for recognition and supremacy. The historian may think that what happened was inevitable. The effect certainly was that Roman imperialism received a new lease of life under the form which Celsus and Julian would have considered the least desirable.

The Concordat under Constantine pointed to the form of government called Caesaro-papism, in which the secular and sacred hierarchies support each other. This was in fact the Byzantine system; but the Eastern patriarchates, for various reasons, remained 'autocephalous'; there has never been an Eastern Pope. The jealousy of the Tsars even deprived the Russian patriarch of his power, which was put into commission under the Holy Synod. But the crumbling and collapse of the Western Empire left the Roman Church supreme, or only confronted by the embarrassed phantom of the Holy Roman Empire. It is interesting to observe how little the progress of the Papacy was retarded by the 'Pornocracy' and other scandals of the Middle Ages. The feudal idea played into the hands of the Pope. In a state of society where every one was some one else's 'man,' there must be one supreme head on earth of the Church.

The Renaissance seemed to promise a stable alliance

between Christianity and Humanism, which after bringing to perfection a glorious Catholic art, might at last have ended the conflict between orthodoxy and natural science. But Northern Europe, now becoming conscious of its right to political and spiritual independence, revolted against the Roman obedience, and the savage wars of religion followed. They ended in a permanent cleavage on racial lines, and Rome became distinctively the Church of the Latins. In the struggle with Protestantism some abuses were remedied ; but Heiler is right when he says that the whole character of the Roman Church was changed for the worse. Not only Protestantism, but modern civilisation gradually became the enemy, till in 1864 a Papal Bull pronounced that, ' If any one says that the Roman Pontiff can and ought to reconcile himself with progress, liberalism, and modern civilisation, let him be anathema ' ; and thirteen years later the same infallible authority condemned the theory of evolution as ' contradicted by history, by the tradition of all peoples, by exact science, by observed facts, and by reason itself ; it is in truth not worth refutation.' It goes without saying that no Protestant Church would wish or dare to use such language, which seems to mark the Roman Church as a home of lost causes, a survivor of modes of thought which the civilised world has outgrown. But history has shown that the Papal hierarchy has never been deficient in astuteness and political wisdom. It is not, and seldom has been, interested in theological questions as such ; its motives are purely political. And it stands committed, on political grounds, to this truceless war against all the ideas of the modern world. These declarations, let us remember, belong to the generation which put the coping-stone on the Papal autocracy.

The policy, apparently, is to regard all independent thinkers as already lost, and to bring the rest under a tighter discipline. The discipline, as is well known, is not strictly enforced upon the laity, who are practically invited to take what suits them in the Catholic system, and only to abstain from contradicting the rest. The officers, the priests, are to be bound to implicit obedience, even if they are ordered to swear that black is white. ' La chiesa non è un credo, la chiesa è una disciplina ' ; from the private soldiers loyalty only is exacted. It is true that the Canons say : ' Nec sufficit ut obedientia sit externa, sed etiam interna esse debet, neque contenta obsequioso silentio ' ; but this is an ideal, and practically means only that doubts must be crushed out like the suggestions of sensuality. This, and not any particular doctrines, is the real essence of Catholicism. As Mark Pattison said : ' Those rites and those doctrines which have made noise in the Roman controversy are those which are least of the essence of Romanism. The Virgin and the Saints, Reliques, Images, Purgatory and Masses—these bywords with the vulgar and unthinking are powerless decorations or natural developments. The one essential principle of the Catholic system is the control of the individual conscience by an authority or law placed without it, and exercised over it by men assuming to act in the name of heaven.'

Autocracy and the claim of universal empire go together. It is necessary for the Roman Church to discredit completely all other forms of Christianity, denying any efficacy to their rites, and threatening all their members with eternal damnation, without respect to their moral characters. The only loophole by which a Protestant can hope for the mercy of God is by the plea of ' invincible ignorance.'

From the institutional and professional point of view, the Roman system has very obvious advantages, so long as the laity can be kept on the level of culture which is favourable to belief in magical or super-natural powers. In backward communities, where the strength of Catholicism lies, the priests still exercise considerable influence, which is not sensibly impaired by declarations of war against modern science. The one essential thing is that the hierarchy should not lose its control of primary education.

The rigid discipline of the Church is also a source of great political strength. Protestantism has no wish to influence the political action of citizens ; there is no Protestant vote. Nor do the Protestant Churches, as a rule, attempt to intimidate the Press, to work for their own ends through the jury system, or to control town councils. All these things the Roman Church does as a matter of course. It makes bitter enemies ; but it can extort bargains from governments, suppress adverse comments in newspapers, injure opponents and help friends. It is significant that no one has yet exposed the wide-reaching influence which the Vatican used on the side of the Central Powers during the war.

Even more significant is the disposition to turn towards Rome whenever a nation feels itself to be in danger of internal disruption. In France between 1871 and 1914 there was a revulsion against the ' ideas of 1789,' under which the country seemed to be disintegrating, and a disposition to look for national redemption to what was sometimes called the

hierarchical idea. This movement was especially represented by men of letters, several of whom rallied to
Catholicism, more, it would seem, from patriotism than
from real religious conviction. They believed that
the Church was the only force which could consolidate
the nation and check fissiparous tendencies. So Heiler
quotes 'one of the most distinguished Liberal theologians in Germany' as saying, 'The Catholic Church
is the only salvation for our poor fatherland.' The
real strength of the Roman Church lies in its wonderful
organisation. It is quite possible that if international
revolutionary conspiracies become really menacing,
European civilisation may find no other protector
than 'the Black International,' round which all supporters of law and order may, in terror of a general
upheaval, gather themselves. If this ever happens,
the Church will once more have the support of the
educated portion of society, and may even ally itself
again with Humanism and Science, and so recover from
the blunders of the last four centuries.

This, however, is not likely to happen except in
the Latin countries. In England it is hardly con-
ceivable. Our people are not prone to revolution, and
are conspicuous for a sturdy independence which is
the very antithesis of the Catholic spirit. Even before
the Reformation the English were not contented subjects of a foreign Church, and to suppose that they
will ever submit themselves to an Italian priest is the
dream of a few bigoted ecclesiastics.

At the same time, no one supposes that Protestantism as we have known it in the eighteenth and nineteenth centuries—the religion of bibliolatry and
whitewash—has a great future, and it may well be
that in the externals of worship there will be less

difference between Northern and Southern Europe a
hundred years hence than there is to-day. But each
country must develop on its own lines, in religious no
less than in secular institutions. The system of independent national churches, which to Heiler appears
a scandal, is probably more hopeful than the idea of
a single central authority or a world-wide ecclesiastical
polity. Christ spoke of ' one flock,' not of ' one fold ' ;
the Vulgate *unum ovile* lends itself to a theory of the
Church which cannot claim divine authority. Mutual
recognition between the Churches is possible and
desirable ; political amalgamation is neither possible
nor desirable.

For some of us, the most valuable part of Latin
Christianity, next to the gentle piety which it often
shelters, is just that theological or philosophical tradition against which the Modernists are in sharp revolt.
It is not necessarily connected with the obsolete science
and popular mythology which it has incorporated
and which it endeavours to defend. The whole idea
of the supernatural as a ' higher order ' dovetailed
into the natural order is extraneous to the philosophy
on which Catholic theology rests. But much more
alien to this philosophy is the anti-intellectualism of
the last thirty years. This new metaphysic is trying
to support itself by appealing to the new psychology,
as we see in another remarkable German book of last
year, Otto's ' Das Heilige.' But it is, in my opinion,
irreconcilable with the Christian view of the world,
which trusts human reason, and never supposes that
we can make for ourselves the objects of our worship
or the goal of our efforts. The God of Christianity is
at once the *valor valorum* and the *ens realissimum*.

THE QUAKERS

THE full history of the Society of Friends, which
Professor Rufus Jones has now completed, and several
other recent books about the life and opinions of
modern Quakers, have given to the world for the first
time an adequate picture of one of the most interesting developments of the Christian religion. Several
causes have united to attract the attention of thoughtful men and women to this numerically insignificant
society, which has never tried to court popularity.
The first of these is the transference of the centre of
gravity in religion from authority to experience. Our
generation likes to think for itself, and is little inclined
to respect a tradition on the sole ground of its antiquity.
Science and historical criticism have shaken the foundations of the old apologetic ; and the modern science
of religious psychology has awakened a new interest
in the lives and writings of the mystics. It is natural
that many have turned their attention to the one
religious body which in its earliest period, and now
again when it has recovered consciousness of its original
inspiration, has based faith upon the witness of the
inner light. The crumbling of traditional theology
has left the foundations of Quakerism untouched.
This type of belief has nothing to fear from the new
knowledge, since it rests on the apprehension of

spiritual values, not on the proof of supernatural phenomena.   Next, the splendid record of the Friends in social work of all kinds, and particularly their eager response to such special calls as have arisen from the distressed condition of a world exhausted and distracted by war, have evoked unstinted admiration from all who have witnessed them, without distinction of race or creed.   And thirdly, the growing conviction that the Great War was a ghastly and unnecessary blunder, which need not have happened and ought not to have happened, has far more than compensated for the temporary unpopularity of a sect which swelled the ranks of the conscientious objectors.   It has been said, bluntly but not irreverently, that the only person who emerged with intellectual credit from that tragic business is Jesus Christ, because if the belligerents had listened to His precepts they would not now be weltering in bankruptcy and misery.   The Quakers, in their uncompromising condemnation of war, have testified consistently to their belief that the wrath of man worketh not the righteousness of God, and may claim that if they had been able to make their views prevail, Europe would have been spared four years of scientific butchery and most unscientific expenditure. It is not surprising, then, that some notable conversions to Quakerism among persons of high intellectual culture have lately occurred, and that even in the Anglican Church attempts have been made to introduce the most characteristic Quaker service, the silent prayer meeting.

It has been sometimes said that a sect of ' individualistic mystics,' like the Quakers, finds a congenial soil only among Anglo-Saxons, who are supposed to have something of Robinson Crusoe in their composition. But individualism is hardly the right word to use of a body which has a very strong group-consciousness, and which has shown unusual capacity in co-operative organisation for social work. There are individualistic mystics, but they do not, as a rule, leave their own denominations to become Quakers. Outside the Society of Friends there is a large number of persons whose religion is of the Quaker type, but who are content to remain in the Church or sect in which they were born and bred. They may be more or less indifferent to ecclesiastical rites and doctrines, but they do not usually care to quarrel with them. They often value the shelter of a great institution, and in many cases would be sorry to cut themselves off from the beauty and dignity of Catholic or Anglican worship. The Quakers themselves are not zealous to make converts. Caroline Stephen, whose wide culture and great literary gifts made her an important acquisition to the Society, which she joined late in life, wrote : ' So long as our principles continue to gain ground, we need not, I think, be anxious about outward and definite membership, and we may even rejoice in the lessening of our isolation. Our fundamental principle of obedience to the Light of Christ in the heart is certainly not to be regarded as the distinguishing mark of a sect. The very growth of that obedience must, I believe, lead to the effacing of outlines and boundaries made by human hands. Our framework, beautiful and elastic as it is, certainly belongs to the outward and perishable. To subordinate, and if need be to sacrifice, whatever is outward and perishable to the innermost, the central and supreme, is the very ground-work of our ideal.' [1] This attitude distinguishes the Quakers from almost all other religious bodies, and especially, it need hardly be said, from Catholicism.

The Quaker type of Christianity did not appear for the first time in the seventeenth century. It would be possible to trace a succession, though hardly an unbroken chain, from Tertullian and the Montanists to George Fox. Robert Barclay in his famous ' Apology ' (1678) is able to point to ' ancient Fathers ' and ' primitive Christians ' as maintainers of the unlawfulness of war ; and the medieval sects which Dr. Rufus Jones describes as precursors of Quakerism tended to exalt the priesthood of the laity, to disparage sacraments and ritual, to refuse military service and judicial oaths, and sometimes to object to capital punishment. Such, with minor differences, were the Paulicians, the Cathari, the Waldenses, some of the Spiritual Franciscans, some of the Lollards, and some of the early Baptists. The Pilgrim Fathers under John Robinson set up in America a spiritual democracy not unlike that of the Quakers. The little group of Grindletonians, founded by Roger Brerely, a Lancashire clergyman who died in 1637, had a great influence upon the Seekers in the north of England, many of whom welcomed the teaching of Fox.

The nation at this time was seething with new life ; it was a time of spiritual as well as of political ferment. Milton in his ' Areopagitica ' (1644) describes the condition of England in his day. ' I see a noble and puissant nation rousing herself like a strong man after sleep and shaking her invincible locks. Methinks I see her, as an eagle mewing her mighty youth, and

---

[1] *Quaker Strongholds*, Preface to ed. of 1907.

kindling her undazzled eyes at the full midday beam,
purging and unscaling her long-abused sight at the
fountain itself of heavenly radiance, while the whole
noise of timorous and flocking birds, with those also
that love the twilight, flutter about amazed at what
she means, and in their envious gabble prognosticate
a year of sects and schisms.' The sects and schisms
were not to be avoided. As Marsden said : ' Absurd
excesses of opinion now appeared, as exotics in a hot-
bed. The distractions of the times suspended the
restraints of Church discipline ; opinions monstrous
and prodigious started up every day, and were broached
with impunity in public and in private, and multi-
tudes were led astray. The number of new sects,
religious and political, with which England swarmed
appears almost incredible.' [1] Most of them were what
we call movements rather than sects. The ' Seekers '
were to be found in all the sects, and in the Church
itself. They were quietists, who had no wish to make
schisms. The movement was essentially mystical, a
longing for what some of them called ' upper-room
Christianity.' Its adherents were mostly simple folk,
unlearned in theology, but very much in earnest about
moral reformation. They were partially discredited
by an offshoot of the movement, those who were called
Ranters, and preached a vague antinomian pantheism.
Fox denounced this perversion of his teaching with
justifiable indignation. Ranterism was a revival of
the ' Brethren of the Free Spirit ' who brought scandal
upon medieval mysticism in the thirteenth and four-
teenth centuries. Cromwell in 1651 denounced these
' opinions destructive of the power of godliness.'

[1] Quoted by Rufus Jones, *Studies in Mystical Religion.*

Fox, then, was no isolated phenomenon ; he was the child of his age, though Penn was substantially right in saying that ' as a man, he was an original, being no man's copy.' Unlike most of his contemporaries, he was a religious genius, who saw intuitively, as the great Reformers had not seen, what principles were implicit in the Reformation, what its affinities are with primitive Christianity, and where we are to look for an unshakeable foundation on which the faith of a Protestant may rest. This foundation, he saw clearly, is not to be found in institutionalism, nor in the Scriptures, but in the interior life and spirit of man.

George Fox was the son of a Puritan weaver. He was born at Fenny Drayton in Leicestershire in July 1624. He was apprenticed to a shoemaker and grazier, and like many shepherds found ample time for meditation on high things while tending his sheep alone. At the age of nineteen came what in some sects would be called his conversion ; but there is no evidence that he was ever a careless liver, nor did he at any time show that deep consciousness of sin which many saints have experienced. It was the deep unreality of conventional Christianity that afflicted him, and he found no help from the accredited teachers, whether of the Established Church or the sects. The revealing message came to him as ' a voice which said, There is one, even Christ Jesus, that can speak to thy condition ; and when I heard it, my heart did leap for joy.' In 1648 ' the Lord opened to me by His invisible power that every man was enlightened by the Divine Light of Christ, and I saw it shine through all.' This was the keynote of all his subsequent preaching, which was offensive to the Calvinists because it denied that any are predestined to reprobation, and to other Protestants because it appealed directly to the inner light and not to the Scriptures. It was dissatisfaction with Calvinism that caused him his first searchings of heart, when at the age of nineteen he left his home, in obedience to an inward call to ' forsake all and keep out of all and be as a stranger to all.'

So he became a wandering preacher, at a time when there were but few popular interests to compete with religion. There were no novels, no newspapers, no theatres, no football or racing. A great missionary, of the type of St. Paul, had a grand opportunity. The parallel between Fox and St. Paul has often been drawn. Not only had the English prophet to endure similar persecutions and imprisonments ; not only were the priests and ' professors ' whom Fox encountered very like the Jews and Judaisers who plagued St. Paul ; but the mystical experiences of the two men were strikingly similar. On one occasion he was actually struck blind, like St. Paul after his vision on the road to Damascus. In both cases the blindness was probably due to auto-suggestion ; this condition, though rare, is not unknown among persons subject to trances. On another occasion he records that, at the age of twenty-three, ' a priest in high account ' wished to have him bled, and that ' they could not get one drop of blood from me, my body being as it were dried up with sorrows, grief and troubles.' This, I believe, is hardly possible ; but many mystics have recorded equally strange phenomena in good faith. A little later, he tells us, he lay in a cataleptic trance for about fourteen days—a much severer visitation

than is recorded of St. Paul. Whether the great
apostle went through such experiences during his
retirement in Arabia, we cannot tell ; but it is not
improbable. Fox, during his period of searching for
the light, ' fasted much and walked about in solitary
places many days, and often took my Bible and went
and sat in hollow trees and lonesome places till night
came on, and frequently in the night walked mourn-
fully about by myself.' ' I had some intermissions
and was brought into such heavenly joy that I thought
I had been in Abraham's bosom.' These alternations
between ' the dark night of the soul ' and unspeakable
rapture are very typical of the mystical temperament.
Illumination is generally described by him as sight,
not hearing. ' I saw, through the opening of the
invisible Spirit, the blood of Christ.' ' I saw that
there was an ocean of darkness and death, but an
infinite ocean of life and love that flowed over the
ocean of darkness.' ' From the top of this hill the
Lord let me see in what places He had a great people
to be gathered.' ' He let me see a great people in
white raiment by a river side coming to the Lord.
And the place that I saw them in was about Wensley-
dale and Sedbergh.' [1] He was once caught up through
the Spirit ' into the paradise of God,' so that the whole
creation gave a new *smell*—another familiar symptom
of mystical visions. These violent experiences belong
to Fox's youth ; in mature life he became ' a bulky
person,' with strong health and a commanding presence.
Force seemed to radiate from him ; the Cambridge
undergraduates, who had tried to ' rag ' him by pulling

---

[1] Quoted by Rufus Jones in *George Fox: Some Modern
Appreciations.*

him off his horse, saw him ' ride through them in the
Lord's power, and they cried, He shines ! he glistens ! '
In this majestic presence he had the advantage of
St. Paul, but his literary compositions, impressive as
they are, can hardly be described as ' weighty and
powerful.' There were a few returns of extreme
instability in later life. At Stratford he again
temporarily lost his sight, and also his hearing, while
he lay for some time at death's door, and ' was under
great sufferings, beyond what I have words to declare.
For I was brought into the deep, and saw all the
religions of the world and the people that lived in
them and the priests that held them up.' This deep
conviction of the discordance between profession and
practice in the world around him had been the beginning of his inward life, and it tended to overpower
him again when he was physically exhausted. But
he died in jubilant confidence that ' the Seed of God
reigns over all, and over death itself.'

He suffered in all eight imprisonments, covering
about six years of his life, and most of them were
spent in ' nasty stinking ' cells. The longest was at
Lancaster and Scarborough, for two years and eight
months. He was punished for interrupting a preacher
in church, for blasphemy, for refusing a commission
in Cromwell's army, and (practically) for mere refusal
to conform. These persecutions throw some light on
the persecutions of the early Christians. Magistrates
and populace were incensed at a refusal of customary
marks of courtesy and respect for the laws, which in
their eyes was purely contumacious ; and neither Fox
nor the Christian martyrs made it easy for their judges
to be indulgent. Fox was a pacifist ; but his tongue

was not always peaceable. It was hardly prudent, when a Welsh magistrate asked him whether he believed in election and reprobation, to answer, ' Yes, and thou art in the reprobation.' How did he know ? The angry magistrate at first said he would send Fox to prison till he proved it ; but in the end ' the Lord's power so came over him that he confessed to the truth.'

Over four thousand Quakers were thrown into prison at the Restoration ; but after his liberation from Scarborough gaol Fox was able to resume his missionary journeys, and in 1669 married Margaret Fell, widow of Judge Fell of Swarthmoor Hall, near Ulverston. In 1671 he crossed the Atlantic, visiting Barbados, Jamaica, and the British colonies on the mainland ; on his return he was imprisoned again. He went to Holland in 1677, and again in 1684 ; there were already groups of Friends for him to visit there. Towards the end of his life he preached chiefly in London, defying the authorities, who, it will be seen, were only half-hearted in their attempts to suppress him—another parallel to the treatment of the Christians by the Pagan Empire. The Toleration Act was passed in 1689, and he died very soon after.

William Penn has given us a portrait of his friend, which I transcribe with a few omissions. ' He was of an innocent life . . . so meek, contented, modest, easy, steady, tender, it was a pleasure to be in his company. He exercised no authority but over evil, and that everywhere and in all, but with love, compassion and long-suffering. A most merciful man, as ready to forgive as unapt to take or to give an offence. . . . Having been with him for weeks and months together on divers occasions, and those of the nearest and most exercising nature, and that by night and by day, by sea and by land, in this and in foreign countries ; and I can say I never saw him out of his place, or not a match for every service and occasion. For in all things he acquitted himself like a man, yea a strong man, a new and heavenly-minded man, a divine and naturalist, and all of God Almighty's making. . . . Civil, beyond all forms of breeding, in his behaviour. . . . The most awful, living, reverent frame I ever felt or beheld, I must say, was his in prayer.'

Auguste Comte chose George Fox for a place in the Positivist Calendar, as one of the great religious geniuses of the world. The more we study his life and writings, the more plain it becomes that he deserves to be ranked among the greatest.

Fox was not a philosopher or speculative theologian, like Jacob Böhme. His interest was concentrated on moral issues, and in this respect he was more Puritan than mystic. But he differed from the Puritans on three heads. He rejected the doctrine of total depravity and predestination. The ' Divine Seed ' is given to every man. He believed in the possibility of human perfection, and insisted that righteousness is imparted, not merely imputed. And he taught that it is only through the indwelling Spirit that we can understand the Scriptures. The Spirit that inspired the Scriptures is still at work. The seat of authority, which Catholics found in the Church, and Puritans in the Book, he most distinctly placed in the enlightened human soul. His great assumption was that the inner light is sufficiently real, constant, and available to be a guide for the whole of a man's life.

At the passing of the Toleration Act it was estimated that the Quakers were as numerous as all the other Nonconformist sects put together. The Quakers began by expecting a rapid conquest for the religion of the Spirit over the religions of authority. Before the death of George Fox his Society had extended its operations to the Continent of Europe and to the New World. In America the aggressive period continued into the eighteenth century, though the intolerant Puritanism of the New England colonies stained the soil of America with the blood of Quaker martyrs. But in England a great change came over the Society, a change which overtakes all mystical movements, and which usually enables the priest to capture, under pretext of preserving, the harvest which the prophet has sown. This is the great tragedy of religious history ; a revelation which for a time glowed with white heat, cools down, and either petrifies or evaporates. Institutionalism bides its time, and re-covers all that it had lost, fortified, it may be, by the inspiration of the prophets whom it killed or per-secuted, and whose sepulchres it now builds. The Quakers of the eighteenth century were still ready to suffer for their convictions, but they lived increasingly in a little world of their own, rather influenced by the movements of their time than influencing them.

Mysticism is always in danger of relapsing into Quietism. It is only when a collective inspiration is fresh and glowing that the mystic dreams of converting the world. The compromises which are essential to corporate action on a large scale are hateful to him, and the mere contact with the rough-and-tumble life of human societies threatens to sully the purity of his

contemplation. Even the writer of the First Epistle
of St. John declares that ' the whole world lieth in
the wicked one,' and points to the sanctification of a
remnant rather than to an appeal to the ' Seed ' which,
as Fox taught, is imparted to all men alike. Quietism
springs from despair of unaided human nature, combined with unbounded confidence in the power of
supernatural grace. It is fundamentally dualistic.
Whatever comes from below is of the evil one, and it
is safest for the human will to remain entirely passive,
waiting for the recognisable motions of the Spirit
within the soul.

The tendency towards Quietism was not peculiar
to the Quakers. It was equally prominent in the
Catholicism of the Counter-Reformation, and wherever
it was preached by an attractive personality, such as
Molinos or Madame Guyon, it spread like wild-fire,
and alarmed the hierarchy. In fact it is never far
from mystics of the Neoplatonic type, for whom the
highest devotion is the prayer of quiet, when no words
are uttered, and the self seems for a time to have been
utterly submerged or transcended. The silent worship
of the Quaker meeting was, and was intended to be,
of this type. On a wider stage the Quietist movement
had two stages—the fierce, heroic asceticism of men like
St. John of the Cross, and the gentler, more sentimental,
less exacting teaching and practice of Fénelon and
St. François de Sales. This type of piety is safe only
when it is severely ascetic. Even Molinos was accused
of condoning and practising acts of immorality with
which only the body, and not the spirit, was concerned ;
such was the excuse offered. Molinos was probably
calumniated ; but the Cynics taught the same, and

even Plotinus suggests something of the kind as a
pis aller when the flesh becomes too importunate. The
hierarchy doubtless suppressed Molinism mainly because it taught the people that they could dispense
with priests and sacraments ; but the advice to abstain
from all outward activity in the service of God is really
deadly. For what purpose, it may be asked, was the
world created, and immortal spirits sent to sojourn
in it, if we have no duties except to make our escape
from contaminating surroundings ? The Incarnation,
rightly understood, corrects this error.

Before describing the fortunes of the Society of
Friends in the eighteenth century, something should
be said of the chief immediate disciples of Fox, and
of their writings.

Isaac Penington was the son of a wealthy City man,
High Sheriff and Lord Mayor of London, and member
for the City in the Long Parliament. Alderman
Penington was one of the High Court who tried
Charles I. Isaac, however, was not the man to embrace
a public career with paternal backing. Like Fox, he
was deeply religious from childhood, and like Fox he
was revolted by the Calvinist doctrine of reprobation.
He passed through ' the dark night of the soul,' and
came out on the other side. ' When my nature was
almost spent, and the pit of despair was even closing
its mouth upon me, deliverance came and light sprang
within me, and the Lord my God owned me, and sealed
His love unto me ; which made not only the Scriptures,
but the very outward creatures glorious in my eye,
so that everything was sweet and pleasant and light-
some round about me.' He joined an Independent
Congregation ; but soon after completely lost his faith,

and was solitary and miserable. At the age of thirty-eight he married a kindred spirit, the widowed Lady Springett, the mother, by her first marriage, of William Penn's wife. In 1658 he met George Fox, and cried out almost in the words of Plotinus when he first heard Ammonius Saccas, ' This is he whom I have waited for and sought after from my childhood.' From that time he never wavered. He soon fell upon evil days. His father the Alderman was done to death in the Tower as a regicide, and Isaac suffered six imprisonments, amounting to nearly five years. Two of them were by the illegal order of Lord Bridgewater, whom he had offended by omitting the customary tokens of respect. A letter to his persecutor will illustrate both his Christian temper and the simple grace of his style. ' That which thou hast done to me hath not made me thy enemy ; but in the midst of it I desire thy true welfare ; and that thou mayest so carry thyself in thy place, as neither to provoke God against thee in this world nor in the world to come. I do not desire that thou shouldst suffer either from man or from God, on my account, but that thou mightest be guided to and persevere in that which will bring sweet rest, peace and safety to all who are sheltered by it, in the stormy hour in which the Lord will make man to feel his sin and misery.' [1] Both Penington and his wife were tormented and robbed in various ways till 1672, when the Declaration of Indulgence enabled him to pass the last seven years of his life in peace. His voluminous works are very little read ; but one sentence at least contains in outline a deep philosophy of religion. ' All truth is a shadow except the last.

[1] Quoted by J. W. Graham, *The Faith of a Quaker*.

But every truth is substance in its own place, though it be but a shadow in another place. And the shadow is a true shadow, as the substance is a true substance.'

William Penn (1644–1718) belongs to the history of his time. His character has been variously judged, and need not be discussed here, though few will now be found to endorse the unfavourable picture of him in Macaulay's History. His chief work, ' No Cross No Crown,' is one of our religious classics, and is still fairly well known outside Quaker circles. It is partly a defence of Quaker practice, and partly an exhortation to holiness of life. No one can read it without searchings of heart, but its extreme severity, in which it far surpasses even William Law's ' Serious Call,' seems to make the yoke of Christ unnecessarily heavy. He begins by saying that ' the unmortified Christian and the heathen are of the same religion,' and that ' Christ's enemies are now chiefly those of his own profession.' ' Religion has fallen from experience to tradition, and worship from power to form, from life to letter.' In the Church of his day he can find ' only a by-rote *mumpsimus,* a dull and insipid formality, made up of corporeal bowings and cringings, garments and furnitures, perfumes, voices, and music, fitter for the reception of some earthly prince than the heavenly worship of the one true and immortal God, who is an eternal, invisible Spirit.' There is no attempt to understand the meaning of ritual and cultus, in these early Quakers ; what to many is the natural language of worship is to them mere corruption and vanity. The seventeenth-century atmosphere was not favourable to the perception of half-lights and *nuances* ; these zealots saw only black and white.

No more beautiful words on death and bereavement have been written than the following from Penn's ' Solitude ' : ' They that love beyond the world cannot be separated by it.   Death cannot kill what never dies, nor can spirits ever be divided that love and live in the same Divine Principle, the root and record of their friendship.   If absence be not death, neither is theirs ; death is but crossing the world, as friends do the seas ; they live in one another still.   For they must needs be present that love and live in that which is omni-present.   In this Divine Glass they see face to face, and their converse is free as well as pure.   This is the Comfort of Friends that though they may be said to die, yet their friendship and society are, in the best sense, ever present, because immortal.'

Penn lies buried at Jordans, that simplest and most moving of all *campo-santos*.   There, in a meadow sur-rounded by trees, and flanked by a little chapel, under the plainest of tombstones, all exactly alike, lie many of the early prophets and confessors of Quakerism. The stones do not mark the exact resting-places of the dead.   The Friends were afraid, we may hope without reason, that the Pennsylvanians might attempt to carry off the bones of their eponymous hero to Philadelphia !   But in that field repose the remains of Penn, Penington, and several members of their families.

The famous ' Apology ' of Robert Barclay, a Scottish gentleman, was written in Latin and printed at Amsterdam in 1676.   An English version appeared two years later, and 8000 copies, bound in leather, were at once subscribed for—a very large sale in those days.   The book became for a whole century a sort of second Bible for the Society. The author was punished, like the other apostles of Quakerism, with cruel imprisonments, and died at the age of forty-two. It has perhaps been a misfortune for the Society that their chief apologist was trained in the Calvinistic schools of Scotland, and never came in contact with the contemporary mystical school of the Cambridge Platonists. Barclay exalts the Scriptures into an external and infallible authority, thus departing from the teaching of Fox. He returns, most unhappily, to the doctrine of the total corruption of man's nature, and takes throughout that harshly dualistic view which was one of the causes of Quietism. In short, the book, with all its merits, had much to do with drawing Quakerism away from its unassailable basis, and assimilating it to the current Evangelicalism.

Some of the ablest modern Quakers, such as Mr. Edward Grubb, heartily regret the turn which Barclay helped to give to their theology. ' They were wholly unable to think of a Reason in man that was not merely human but also divine, a natural faculty that was also spiritual. If man was totally corrupted by the Fall, the light in his soul could not be any part of his nature, it must be a supernatural agency, as separate from himself as a candle is from the lantern that contains it. On Barclay's theory, which became the accepted view of the Society of Friends, the mind of man was incapable of instruction in the things of God ; only a supernatural faculty would bring him knowledge of God and order his life therein.' [1] Thus the inner light became itself external, and the foundation was laid for a new religion of authority, singularly

[1] E. Grubb, *Quaker Thought and History*.

destitute of safeguards against self-deception and even absurdity. But there has been a fundamental sanity among the Quakers which has kept them from the vagaries of other mystical sects. One curious difference is that while other congregations of mystics have broken out into ' speaking with tongues ' and ecstatic prophesyings, the Quakers in the eighteenth century tended more and more to meet in unbroken silence for hours together. Thus the desire for simplicity may overleap itself, and produce the most unnatural and artificial mode of worship that can be imagined. Short silences, for not more than half an hour, are exceedingly helpful, as many who are not Quakers can testify ; but there are probably few who could sit through two hours, silent and motionless, without wandering thoughts and extreme boredom.

The most serious charge that the Quakers had to meet, and that from the beginning of their history, was that of denying the historical Christ. Christ, for them, was the quickening Spirit in their own souls ; there seemed to be no necessary connexion between this experience and the Gospel narratives. Some eminent contemporaries of Fox were not slow to throw this accusation in their teeth. Richard Baxter in his ' Quaker's Catechism ' (1657) charged the Quakers with denying that there is any such person as Jesus Christ who suffered at Jerusalem, and John Bunyan in the same year asserts that the Quakers, whom he couples with the Ranters and Familists, ' either deny Christ to be a real man without [= outside] them, blasphemously fancying him to be only God manifested in their flesh, or else make his human nature, with the fullness of the Godhead in it, to be but a type of God

manifested in the saints.' Bunyan himself crudely
asserts that Christ went away from His disciples into
heaven, ' in his body of flesh and bones,' and that our
only hope of felicity is in the belief ' that the Son of
Mary is now absent from his children in his person and
humanity, making intercession for them in the presence
of his Father.' [1] Thus the question whether the
Pauline identification of Jesus with Christ is justifiable
was squarely raised in the seventeenth century ; but
the antagonists on both sides were poorly equipped for
a philosophical controversy. For Fox the identification
was certain and obvious, revealed to him by the light
within ; it had been much the same with St. Paul.
Penington, however, wrote ' An Examination of the
causes or grounds ' which had induced the Bostonians
to expel the Quakers from Massachusetts on pain of
death, and to hang four of them on Boston Common.
On the Person of Christ he writes that ' there is no
being saved by a belief of Christ's death for them, and
of his resurrection, ascension, intercession, &c., without
being brought into a true fellowship with him in his
death, and without feeling his immortal seed of life
raised and living in them. And so they disown the
faith in Christ's death which is only received and
entertained from the relation of the letter of the
Scriptures, and stands not in the Divine power and
sensible experience of the Begotten of God in the heart.'
This is common mystical doctrine ; we find it in
Angelus Silesius, in William Law, and many other
writers. But he goes on to say that ' they [his Society]
distinguish, according to the Scriptures, between that

[1] E. Grubb, *The Historic and the Inward Christ: A Study in
Quaker Thought.*

which is called Christ and the bodily garment which he wore. The one was flesh, the other spirit. The flesh profiteth nothing (saith he), the spirit quickeneth; and he that eateth me shall live by me, even as I live by the Father. This is the manna itself, the true treasure; the other but the visible or earthen vessel which held it.' Elsewhere he says, 'We can never call the bodily garment Christ, but that which appeared and dwelt in the body.' This implicates Penington in the Docetic heresy. Penn says more brusquely: 'that the outward person which suffered was properly the Son of God, we utterly deny.' In the next generation attempts were made to explain away these statements.

So far as the Quakers fell into Docetism, the fault lay in their dualistic way of conceiving the divine and human as mutually exclusive categories. They did not understand the Christology of St. Paul and St. John, which makes it possible to combine belief in a historical Incarnation with belief in the indwelling of Christ in the soul. The Puritans could not have taught them better; but Whichcote, Smith, and Cudworth could. It is a pity that prejudice kept these groups so much apart. Nevertheless it must be admitted that mysticism at all times has refused to attach primary importance to the merely historical. The mystic believes that Christ rose, because he knows that He has risen; and his knowledge is almost independent of what are usually called Christian evidences.

Our sketch of Quaker history has now brought us to the first half of the eighteenth century, the period of the Deistic controversy, when, if we may believe contemporary records, a dry rationalism and prosaic common sense marked a general decay of real religious conviction. The opponents of Deism, who brought in God at the end of a syllogism, were not much more edifying. The Deist, Anthony Collins, said that nobody doubted the existence of God till the Boyle Lecturers undertook to prove it.[1] William Law, one of the most virile controversialists of the century, saw that ' the debate was equally vain on both sides, doing no more real good to one than the other,' seeing that ' a set of scholastic logical opinions about history, facts, doctrines and institutions of the Church' could neither save a soul nor consign it to perdition. This is very much what Fox had said about what he called ' notions.' Law had as much in common with the Quakers as the Cambridge Platonists had, but he was a stalwart Churchman, and showed no sympathy with the sectaries. Once again we see that nothing divides kindred spirits so much as institutional loyalties, whether ecclesiastical or secular. The Friends, in their almost complete isolation, were the chief sufferers by being cut off from men who were treading the same path, with a far better intellectual equipment than they, at this time, could command.

The Quakers, whose numbers probably culminated in the reign of Queen Anne, suffered severely from the anti-mystical tendency of the next generation. The fresh springs of their religion were cut off, and there are complaints of frequent backslidings within the Society. The revival of English religion came, as everybody knows, in the Evangelical movement, both within the Established Church, and in the amazingly active

[1] Rufus Jones, *Later Periods of Quakerism.*

mission preaching of Wesley and Whitefield. Although
the movement began as an awakening of faith, coloured
by much more emotionalism than the Deists and their
opponents found to their taste, it was soon associated
with a definite system of theological opinions, which
became known as Evangelical. Among these the chief
were the belief in total depravity, against which we
have seen the early Quakers protesting; the theory
of verbal inspiration, with an almost superstitious
reverence for copies of the English Bible; a somewhat
arbitrary selection of popular amusements as inconsistent with the profession of a strict Christian; a
tendency to observe Sunday as if it were a continuation
of the Jewish Sabbath; and a strong emphasis on the
Atonement, rather than the Incarnation, as the central
doctrine of Christianity. The Crucifixion of Christ
was almost taken out of its historical framework and
was regarded as the one supremely important event
in the history of the world. Combined with this
theology was a new zeal for the redress of certain
social iniquities, such as the slave trade.

As the Society of Friends had been influenced by
Quietism, and adversely affected by the paralysing
rationalism of the reigns of the first two Georges, so
they were strongly attracted by the Evangelicalism of
the later part of the eighteenth century. There were
indeed signs of a revival of mysticism in the Society,
and of a slight Liberalising tendency, but these movements were weak compared with the attraction of
Evangelicalism as then understood. For a time
mysticism was not only discouraged, but actively
denounced. But before dealing with this period, it
will be a pleasure to give a brief account of one of

the most attractive Quaker saints, John Woolman (1720–1772). It would be difficult to find a more beautiful character in any of the Christian Churches.

His father was a farmer in New Jersey, and John was one of thirteen children. In those days the Anglo-American stock, a very fine one, multiplied like rabbits. His parents were devout Quakers, and very severe upon childish delinquencies, which John himself was disposed to magnify. He accuses himself of loving ' wanton company,' but as he stopped short of ' profane language and scandalous conduct,' his companions do not seem to have misled him very seriously.

From early years he was convinced that the voice of God within him was guiding all his actions and desires. He found the ' pure silent worship ' of the meetings most refreshing to his soul ; ' in silent worship the soul feeds on the divine.' In 1742 he was appointed minister of the Mount Holly meeting, where he opened a school. But before long the question of slavery, which at that time troubled the consciences of few, began to agitate his mind. ' It appears to me,' he wrote in 1752, ' that the slave trade was founded, and hath greatly been carried on, in a wrong spirit ; that the effects of it are detrimental to the real prosperity of our country, and will become more so, except we cease from the common motives for keeping them, and treat them in future agreeably to truth and pure justice. Forced subjection of innocent persons of full age is inconsistent with right reason. Seed sown with the tears of an oppressed people makes bread less sweet to the taste of an honest man.' His attention to this question was diverted for a time by the horrors of Indian warfare near Philadelphia, where he went

to reside. The Quakers, who had their chief seat in
that town, would not join in war for the destruction
of the Indians, and were very unpopular in consequence, especially as they objected even to pay war-
taxes.

In 1761 we find him again travelling on behalf of
the slaves ; and he published an earnest appeal called
' Considerations on the keeping of Negroes.' His
' Journal ' at this time contains comments on other
worldly matters, which show in what sense the typical
Quaker feels sympathy with Labour movements. He
blames himself for having ' accustomed himself to
some things which have occasioned more labour than
I believe Divine wisdom intended for us. I believe
that the Lord hath provided that so much labour shall
be necessary for man's support in this world as would,
being rightly divided, be a suitable employment of
their time ; and that we cannot go into superfluities,
or grasp after wealth in a way contrary to His wisdom,
without having connexion with some degree of
oppression, and with the spirit which leads to self-
exaltation and strife, and which frequently brings
calamities on countries by parties contending about
their claims.' He enjoins ' a life where no unnecessary
care, nor expenses, may encumber our minds nor lessen
our ability to do good ; where no desires after riches
or greatness may lead into hard dealing,' contrasting
this mode of living with those which ' tend to oppression,' when ' people do that to others which they
know would not be acceptable to themselves, either
in exercising an absolute power over them or otherwise
laying on them inequitable burdens. Hence a fear
lest that measure should be meted to them which they

G

have measured to others incites a care to support
that by craft and cunning devices which stands not
on the firm foundation of righteousness. Thus the
harmony of society is broken, and from hence com-
motions and wars do frequently arise in the world.'
Once more he says, ' The money which the wealthy
receive from the poor, who do more than a proper
share of business in raising it, is frequently paid to
other poor people for doing business which is foreign
to the true use of things.'

These quotations explain the ethical basis of the
Quaker frugality, which, together with the steady
industry enjoined upon them, has made some Quaker
families richer than the austerer members of their
Society would have approved. Money must be made
honestly, without fraud or oppression ; it must not
be spent frivolously, destroying idly the results of
human labour and bribing men to waste their lives in
producing superfluities ; and we must not be content
while any class of the community is unable to live in
simple comfort. The maxim ' Waste not ' would, in
the opinion of Friends, solve most of our economic
difficulties. This is quite different from the Com-
munism which was ascribed to the Lollards, who must
be reckoned among the precursors of Quakerism, and
which was certainly preached by the Anabaptists.
There has always been a tendency to Socialism among
such bodies ; and quite lately the Quakers, who had
been suspected of an undue tenderness for accumulated
capital, have shown a disposition to support the
Labour Party in politics. But their most characteristic economic doctrine is that unnecessary expenditure
is a public injury.

There are some fine descriptions in Woolman's 'Journal' of his intrepid visits to the camps of Indians on the war-path. He walked straight up to fierce savages armed with tomahawks, and was never hurt. These expeditions were treated calmly enough by the evangelist and by his flock. The minutes of the Mount Holly meeting record : 'First of 8th month, 1763. Our friend John Woolman, being returned from his visit to some religiously disposed Indians of Susquehannah, informed the last meeting that he was treated kindly, and had satisfaction in his visit.'

Towards the end of his life Woolman visited England, characteristically travelling in the steerage, because he observed 'superfluities' in the shape of 'sundry sorts of carved work and imagery' in the cabin. His impressions of England are disappointingly meagre. His attention was concentrated almost entirely on the English Friends ; though he records his indignation at finding many of the English working-class living 'mainly on bread and water, and there are many poor children not even taught to read.' He was displeased by the dirtiness under foot and 'the scent arising from that filth which more or less infects the air of all thickly settled towns.' These sights and smells, and the custom of concealing dirt in old garments by dyeing them, 'produced a longing in my mind that people might come into cleanness of spirit, cleanness of person, and cleanness about their houses and garments. Real cleanliness becometh a holy people ; but hiding that which is not clean by colouring our garments seems contrary to the sweetness of sincerity.' This dislike of all concealment, even in the externals of life, is characteristic of Quakers ;

and we cannot help contrasting the healthiness and refinement of Quaker asceticism with the cult of dirt and vermin which Christian devotees inherited from the Cynics.

There is indeed a robust common sense in most of Woolman's opinions. On 'Labour' he writes: 'Having from my childhood been used to bodily labour for a living, I may express my experience therein. Right exercise affords an innocent pleasure in the time of it, and prepares us to enjoy the sweetness of rest, but from the extremes each way arise inconveniences. Moderate exercise opens the pores, gives the blood a lively circulation, and the better enables us to judge rightly respecting that portion of labour which is the true medium. . . . Idle men are often a burden to themselves, neglect the duty they owe to their families, and become burdensome to others also. But I have observed that too much labour not only makes the understanding dull, but so intrudes upon the harmony of the body that after ceasing from our toil we have another to pass through before we can be so composed as to enjoy the sweetness of rest.' [1]

The insanitary condition of our English towns was the cause of his death; for he contracted smallpox at York, and died there, carefully tended by English Friends.

The tendency to substitute the current Evangelicalism for belief in the inner light was fostered by two men who were very influential in the Society. The two books of Henry Tuke (1801 and 1805) on the faith and principles of 'the people called Quakers,' show how completely the centre of gravity had altered since

---

[1] W. Teignmouth Shore, *John Woolman.*

the days of Fox and Penington. All the doctrines characteristic of the Evangelical school are emphasised ; literal inspiration of the Scriptures, man's depravity and Christ's propitiatory sacrifice are the parts of the Christian scheme on which he likes to dwell. The other, born later, was Joseph John Gurney of Earlham, the leader of English Quakerism in the nineteenth century. Gurney came early under the influence of the leading Evangelicals, such as Charles Simeon and William Wilberforce ; and though he thought it his duty to ' testify ' as a Friend by entering a bishop's drawing-room with his hat on, he was never a Quaker after the type of the founders of the Society. So far as his influence extended, there was little to distinguish the Quaker theology from that of the Evangelical school generally. When we remember that George Fox had revolted as much against ' notions ' and theological doctrines as against priests and sacraments, it is plain that at this time Quakerism had lost its bearings and its reason for a separate existence. But so it had to remain, until a new outpouring of the Spirit should come.

The Quakers in America were and are far more numerous than in England. The ' Great Separation ' under Elias Hicks is therefore an important event in the history of the Society. It occurred in 1827 and 1828. Hicks led a revolt against the tendency to disparage the inner light, and to turn vital Christianity into a system of doctrines. He wished to go back to the mystical Quakerism of the seventeenth century. Hicks is said to have been a powerful preacher, but his theology is poor and crude. Technically, his doctrine of the Person of Christ seems to be a mixture of Adoptionism and Docetism. He succeeded in dividing the American Quakers into two bodies ; and this schism, which greatly weakened the Society, lasted on till the present year, when (as I am informed by a leading American Friend) it is in process of being healed. In England there was no disruption, but a general weakness and loss in membership. The religious census of 1851 revealed so small a membership that the Society was alarmed, and from that time proposals for reform were seriously considered. It was felt that the external peculiarities of dress and manners had become far more peculiar than Fox intended them to be. There was nothing unusual in the costume when it was first chosen ; but the customs had become a burden grievous to be borne for the young, who in fact refused to obey them. Even more important was the rule of ' disowning ' members who married outside the Society. It was not without reason that one Quaker exclaimed : ' We have done a great deal to reform the criminal law of the nation ; why cannot we reform our own ? ' The change was made, after long deliberation, in 1859. In the same year J. S. Rowntree published an ' Enquiry into the Causes of Decline,' and gave his opinion that ' the peculiar form of public worship adopted by Friends has had not a little to do with their declining numbers.' In this view he was confirmed by Elizabeth Fry, who said with much common sense : ' For babes in Christ I have great fears, inasmuch as true, solemn, silent worship is a very high administration of spiritual worship. I frequently fear for such that more external aid is wanted.' From this time on there has been a great relaxation of the old rigidity.

Quakerism, as we have seen, began with a fiery zeal for moral reform. The first Quakers were itinerant missionaries like John Wesley. But in the eighteenth century they withdrew into themselves, and even pledged themselves to take no part in politics (1712). The reawakening of social enthusiasm is strongly marked in John Woolman, the denouncer of slavery, and it would be impossible to name a date when no members of the Society were interested in social questions. In America the Friends were among the first to protest against slavery ; the Pennsylvania Society for Promoting the Abolition of Slavery (1775) was the first abolitionist association. ' The practice of holding slaves,' says Dr. Rufus Jones, ' had practically ceased among Friends by the year 1780.' In London the Society censured the slave trade as ' not a commendable nor allowed practice,' as early as 1727, and in 1758 members were warned to be careful ' to avoid being in any way concerned in reaping the unrighteous profits arising from the iniquitous practice of dealing in slaves.' The language of the yearly messages becomes more and more vigorous. In 1774 there is a call for the suppression of ' that flagrant injustice to our fellow-creatures, for whom our Saviour shed His precious blood, as well as for others ' ; and two years earlier that the trade ' may be utterly abolished as a reproach to the Christian profession.' [1] Petitions to Parliament against the traffic in slaves followed, and the Quakers gained powerful allies in Wilberforce, Clarkson, and Thomas Fowell Buxton. Victory was won in 1807, and in 1838 all slavery within the British Empire was abolished by Act of Parliament. The

[1] Rufus Jones, *Later Periods of Quakerism*.

resounding language of the Act seems to echo the triumph of a great moral victory.

It would take too much space to recount all the philanthropic and humanitarian movements to which the Quakers, now emancipated from the notion that all initiative in such matters is an attempt to force the hand of the Almighty, devoted themselves in the nineteenth century. Two Quakers, William Allen and Stephen Grellet—the latter a Frenchman—acquired a considerable influence over the Tsar Alexander I, who received them in his capital and knelt in prayer with them. Allen gave the Emperor an account of his famous experiment at the New Lanark mills ; for the travels of these men always had a practical object. To improve the condition of the labourer, to stop the cruelties practised in prisons, and to mitigate the barbarity of the criminal law, were now—with the final abolition of slavery—their chief practical aims. The labours of Elizabeth Fry among the prisoners at Newgate are celebrated. The name of Tuke is equally famous as the founder of a rational mode of dealing with the insane.

Nor has there been any slackening in the devotion of Friends to philanthropic movements, though the worst scandals have now been removed, partly through their agency. The Great War, which placed patriotic Quakers in a terrible dilemma, gave them a unique opportunity of relieving suffering in the countries where the effects of the war had been most ruinous. In Germany and Austria they quickly disarmed suspicion, and won the love and gratitude of countless hungry children and their parents. It was observed also that all Quaker funds were well administered ; there was very little waste or leakage. Some Quakers have been afraid that the Society may become a merely philanthropic agency—the accusation has been brought against it by Roman Catholic writers, who are naturally anxious to discredit a body whose existence and record are a crushing disproof of their exclusive claims. But from what I have observed, there is no real danger of the religious basis being weakened.

The Victorian age produced two Quakers of perhaps greater distinction than had ever before adorned the Society—John Bright in England and John Greenleaf Whittier in America. Bright was one of the greatest Parliamentary orators that this country has known, and he has the almost unique distinction of having made speeches which were both effective when delivered and also models of literary eloquence. His diction owed much to the Authorised Version of the Bible, and we need not doubt his assurance that he had never used an argument which he did not believe to be sound, or stated anything as a fact which he did not believe to be true. His speeches during the Crimean War, which hardly anybody now defends, but which was undoubtedly popular at the time, are still remembered, read, and quoted. With equal courage he championed the cause of the Federals in the American Civil War, and prophesied their victory. American schoolboys still learn this splendid piece of rhetoric by heart. Time has justified his wisdom on some, but not on all points. He was one of the best and noblest representatives of the middle class to which he belonged, in the days of its ascendancy.

Whittier, whose poetry, though not of the highest class, deserves to be more read than it is by our generation, was prevented by ill-health from taking part in political life, as he would have liked to do. He belonged to a very devout Quaker family, and in his private life, as well as in his writings, he showed the Quaker characteristics at their best. It was said of him as a youth that ' when a wrong was to be righted or an evil to be remedied, he was readier to act than any young man I ever knew, and was very wise in his action—shrewd, sensible, practical.' He obeyed what he felt to be the call of duty in putting aside a literary career to devote himself to the abolition of slavery. He says of himself :

> And one there was, a dreamer born,
> Who, with a mission to fulfil,
> Had left the Muses' haunts to turn
> The crank of an opinion-mill,
> Making his rustic reed of song
> A weapon in the war with wrong,
> Yoking his fancy to the breaking-plough
> That beam-deep turned the soil for truth to spring and grow.

He showed in this cause not only the enthusiasm of an idealist, but the sagacity of a practical leader.

One specimen alike of his poetry and of his faith may be quoted :

> Wherever through the ages rise
> The altars of self-sacrifice,
> Where love its arms hath opened wide,
> Or man for man has calmly died,
> I see the same white wings outspread
> That hovered o'er the Master's head.
> I trace His presence in the blind
> Pathetic gropings of my kind—
> In prayers from sin and sorrow wrung,
> In cradle-hymns of life they sung,
> Each in its measure but a part
> Of the unmeasured Over-Heart.

He lived to old age, and saw the triumph of the Emancipation movement.

More recently, the Society has had some notable names in England, of whom perhaps the most conspicuous are Thomas Hodgkin, the historian; Caroline Stephen, whose mystical books have had a large sale and a well-deserved reputation ; Silvanus Thompson, the scientist; and among the living, Sir George Newman, Dr. Rendel Harris, Mr. H. G. Wood, and Mr. Grubb.

The new Quakerism is far more intellectual than the old. The issue was faced in a Conference at Manchester in 1895, at which J. W. Rowntree, Thomas Hodgkin, and Silvanus Thompson all urged a forward policy in the direction of accepting modern science and criticism. Hodgkin boldly declared that ' what was spoken unscientifically in the childhood of the world by the unscientific Hebrew sage is no essential part of Christ's message to the world to-day.' Thompson asked : ' What is a Friend but one who, illuminated by the quickening Spirit, has learned to cast off the incrustations which ignorance and intellectual pride or intellectual folly have during the centuries built up around the simple code of Christ's teaching ? ' [1] Thus an attitude of confidence towards the new knowledge has been quite definitely taken up by the Society. The Friends can well afford to discard external aids to faith, some of which now offer only very treacherous support. This change in policy issued in a permanent institution for religious and social study at Woodbrooke, near Birmingham. There are also summer schools, one of which, held at Jordans, I was privileged

[1] Rufus Jones, *Later Periods of Quakerism.*

to attend recently. It is clear that this Liberal Quakerism has broken entirely with the belief in verbal inspiration, which has been recognised as the result of alien influence. Henceforth Quakers must fall back upon the mystical faith of their founder. But their leaders will naturally, being highly educated men, seek to give mysticism an intellectual or philosophical expression, endeavouring to find a place for spiritual illumination in their view of God, the world, and the self. This will bring them definitely into line with the long and honourable succession of Christian Platonists, their affinity to whom they have been rather slow to discover. We may expect that this will be the next development in the Society. They ought to do valuable work on the philosophy and psychology of mysticism, all the more because they have kept wonderfully free from the *Schwärmerei* of many mystics, and from the queer pseudo-science of ' mystical phenomena '—levitation, incandescence, stigmatisation, and the like—which fills some of the Catholic literature on the subject. Their active participation in social work will also tend to keep their speculation in touch with concrete realities.

The peculiar customs of the Quakers have already been mentioned. Most religious bodies have found it expedient to make a few more or less irrational rules, which act as a pledge of loyalty. Such are the fish-days of the Catholics, miscalled fasting, and the prohibition of card-playing, theatre-going, and Sunday recreations among some Protestants. The early Quakers made a principle of certain rather absurd scruples, and suffered much persecution on that account. The same herd-instinct which causes a flock

of animals to turn upon one of their number who shows
any peculiarity leads the majority of mankind to take
it as a personal injury if any of their neighbours break
away from accredited custom. It was a very simple
matter for any magistrate to convict a Quaker of
disloyalty by merely requiring him to take the oath of
allegiance, knowing that he would refuse to take any
oath. We are reminded of the sacrificial test imposed
upon Christians by Roman magistrates. The trivial
peculiarities on which the Quakers laid such store were
highly irritating to their neighbours, and as time went
on they put too great a strain on the loyalty of the
Quakers themselves. They have now been almost
entirely dropped, and there is little, in dress and
outward deportment, to distinguish a Quaker from
other people. No inquisitorial questions are any
longer asked ; it is left to the conscience of the individual to interpret the rule of ' plainness ' on which
the Society still lays stress. Of late years there has
been a tendency to urge total abstention from alcohol
upon members of the Society ; but no binding rule
has been laid down.

For many people the distinguishing feature of
Quakerism is its total condemnation of war. But, as
Mr. Graham shows, pacifism was not the heart of the
Quaker preaching. Barclay puts it last among his mis-
cellaneous ' testimonies,' and deals with it very briefly.
What is more surprising, George Fox himself upbraids
Cromwell for his peaceful policy ! The passage, found
in a parchment-bound book in Devonshire House, is
quoted by Mr. Braithwaite in his book on ' The Beginnings of Quakerism,' and will be read by the profane
with amusement and astonishment. ' O Oliver, hadst

thou been faithful and thundered down the deceit, the Hollander had been thy subject and tributary, Germany had given up to do thy will, the Spaniard had quivered like a dry leaf wanting the virtue of God, the King of France should have bowed his neck under thee, the Pope should have withered as in winter, the Turk in all his fatness should have smoked, thou shouldst not have stood trifling about small things, but minded the work of the Lord as He began with thee at first.' A truly comprehensive scheme of European conquest, from the North Sea to the Dardanelles! It sounds like an echo of the famous Ode by Andrew Marvell, Oliver's court poet :

> A Caesar he ere long to Gaul,
> To Italy an Hannibal,
>   And to all states not free
>   Shall climacteric be.

But Fox had a clear leading that it was wrong to fight for Charles II. 'All that pretend to fight for Christ are deceived ; for his Kingdom is not of this world, therefore his servants do not fight. Fighters are not of Christ's kingdom, but are without Christ's kingdom ; His kingdom stands in peace and righteousness, but fighters are in the lust ; and all that would destroy men's lives are not of Christ's mind, who came to save men's lives. . . . All that pretend fighting for Sion are in darkness, for Sion needs no such helpers.' Fox lost no time in sending a Declaration against war to the restored monarch.

From that time the testimony of the Friends has never wavered, and their refusal to bear arms has exposed them to many indignities and sufferings, both in England and America. In the Napoleonic War

Pitt exempted the Quakers as a body from conscription, and they were not acutely tried till 1916, when the safety of the country required that every able-bodied man should take his part in national defence. In America the Friends refused to bear arms against the Indians ; and in most cases the savages were careful to leave Quaker families unmolested. In the American Civil War the question of conscience was very difficult, because the Quakers were among the stalwarts of the Abolitionist party. Many of them bore arms against the South, for which some were forgiven, others ' disowned '—driven from the Society. In the South the Quakers were severely dealt with. Some were driven forcibly into the firing-line, where they refused to shoot.

In the Great War, according to Mr. J. W. Graham, the Quakers refused a denominational exemption, which would have saved them from the punishments inflicted on other ' conscientious objectors.' Ultimately 32 per cent. of those liable to military service joined the forces. The remaining two-thirds either served their country as ambulance-men, mine-sweepers, or in other work recognised as ' of national importance,' or they went to prison. The prisoners are said to have amounted to 279.

It is very difficult to judge this case of conscience fairly. War is perhaps the greatest of all human evils and follies. In old days it was possible to glorify it as a school of chivalry, courage, and self-sacrifice. Courage and self-sacrifice have never been more signally displayed than in the Great War of 1914–1918 ; but those who took part in it agree that it was a hideous business, in which nearly all the humane alleviations of brutal violence, introduced and practised in the days when professional armies fought for a dynasty or for a point of honour, were disregarded. Now that wars are between nations, no longer between governments or armies, they have become far more horrible and far more insane. The distinction between combatants and non-combatants hardly exists any longer, and with the disappearance of this distinction war becomes pure savagery. The Great War shook civilisation to its base ; it is generally agreed that another conflict on the same scale would shatter it, and probably introduce another Dark Age. Nor is there any safeguard against the nations being misled and deceived by their governments into sanctioning another great war ; it is fatally easy to represent that though peace is almost always to be chosen if possible, on this one occasion the egregious wickedness of the other side makes chastisement a moral duty. So all the belligerents were told in the Great War. The manufacture and dissemination of propaganda-literature, for the purpose of rousing the passions of the people by garbled statements, became an important war-industry.

Since all other methods of combating this monstrous evil have hitherto failed, the Quakers plead for their own remedy—refusal to take part in any war, whatever excuses may be made for it. They argue that this is the method prescribed by Christ, both in precept and example. He refused to let His disciples defend Him, telling them that those who take the sword shall perish by the sword ; He bade us turn the other cheek to the smiter, and, as an all-embracing principle, to overcome evil with good. Everything else, say they, has been tried in vain. Why not give Christian ethics a trial ?

There are, of course, many degrees in accepting the

principle of non-resistance. The Quakers, whether
they are rigidly consistent or not, are much saner than
the Russian Tolstoy, who wished to make an end of all
coercion, even in children's schools. The Quakers are
quite ready to accept the protection of the police, and
even to serve as special constables when civil trouble
is feared. They do not, for the most part, even declare
categorically that no war can ever be right. Few
Quakers would condemn the Government of India in
1857 for taking steps to protect the English non-
combatants, women and children, from the fury of the
mutineers. Some Quakers, as has been said, were
willing to fight for their country in the Great War,
because they were honestly convinced that the enemy
had morally no case. There were, as we might expect,
great differences of opinion within the Society as to the
right course of action. But since the Armistice, the
feeling against war has hardened among Friends ; they
realise that during the conflict the people were not
allowed to know the whole truth, and they think that
the only safety against being deceived lies in an uncompromising refusal to bear arms on any pretext.

The chief question perhaps is whether we ought
always to follow what is ideally best, or whether we
may allow ourselves to take into account conditions
which would not exist if the world were all that it
should be, but which do exist in the world in which we
live. Practical statesmen, as Lord Morley was fond
of pointing out, have usually to be content with a
second-best course. But, he adds, ' we misunderstand
the conditions which should rightly lead us in practice
to acquiesce in a second-best course of action, and go
on to suppose that there are the same grounds why we

H

should in our own minds acquiesce in second-best opinions.' The successful statesman, however, is usually a man with first-rate abilities and second-rate opinions. The philosopher in politics is a failure. Lord Morley is doubtless right in justifying the acceptance by the politician of the *pis aller* at every turn. The alternative is to cease to be a politician. He raises the same question which was often argued in the Middle Ages, whether there is not a *relative* Law of Nature, determined by our fallen state, which, while we live here, we are as much bound to obey as if it were part of the absolute Law of Nature, which is suited only to an ideal society. In such an imperfect world as ours, we have to consider the consequences of applying the principles of the Sermon on the Mount to national and international affairs.

If this be admitted, the lawfulness or unlawfulness of taking part in deeds of violence must be judged on the merits of each particular case. Jesus Christ Himself, it may be urged, did not follow literally His own precept. When He was struck, He did not turn the other cheek, but addressed a dignified remonstrance to the smiter. When the Great War had actually broken out, the question for every Briton was whether the Kingdom of God, or the welfare of mankind, would be advanced most by his country's victory or by her defeat. If he was conscientiously convinced that the success of the Allies was desirable in the highest interests of Europe and the rest of the world, it does not seem to me that he was justified in refusing to take any active part in bringing that result about. Our duties are always relative to the position in which we find ourselves. Even if the war was the result of human sin, crime, and folly, we must accept the conditions which those errors have introduced, and join in what seem to be the most practical means to cure them. Even if we belong to a small minority, the obligation remains so to act that our conduct might be a standard for all.

The mere condemnation of force shows, as a rule, some mental confusion. There are more ways of coercing a man than by pointing a gun at his head. A pacifist society may be unjust and oppressive ; a government resting openly on force, like that of the Fascists in Italy, may be the only alternative to a blood-stained tyranny such as exists in Russia. A General Strike is as much an act of civil war as a Gunpowder Plot, and it would be absurd to argue that society may not use weapons to protect itself against those who are planning its destruction. To assert that Christianity forbids violence is to make Christian ethics too external. Christ always went behind overt acts to the motives which inspire them.

Nevertheless, the Quaker protest against war has been and is very valuable. The Quaker refuses to be satisfied with what William James says on the subject. ' The plain truth is, people want war. They want it anyhow. It is the final bouquet of life's fireworks. The born soldier wants it hot and actual. The non-combatants want it in the background, and always as an open possibility to feed imagination on, and keep excitement going. . . . Let the general possibility of war be left open, in heaven's name, for the imagination to dally with. Let the soldiers dream of killing as the old maids dream of marrying. But organise in every possible way the practical machinery

for making each successive chance of war abortive.'
William James would hardly have written with such
levity after 1914. If the peoples wanted war, no
machinery could prevent them from having it ; but
they do not want, and did not want it—not one of
them—in 1914. The Quakers are right in thinking
that human nature is sound on this subject, and that
they can appeal to a very strong opinion on their
side. The weakest point in the peace campaign is
that it is supported by many who do not desire peace,
but only class-wars instead of national wars. These
men are poisoning the movement, and bringing
suspicion upon it, and I think that there are some
Quakers among them. As for the soldiers, they do
not ' want war hot and actual.' Those who passed
through the ordeal a few years ago are more apt to
echo the opinion of the American General Sherman.
' I confess without shame that I am tired and sick of
the war. Its glory is all moonshine. It is only those
who have neither heard a shot nor heard the shrieks
and groans of the wounded, who cry aloud for more
blood, more vengeance, more desolation. War is hell.'

Caroline Stephen says truly that the foundation
of the Friends' testimony, and of the teaching of the
Gospels on which it is based, is ' a spirit of ardent
confidence in the supremacy of goodness . . . not
a suggestion that we should abandon or relax our
conflict with evil, but an assurance that we are not
at its mercy—that He who is with us is stronger than
all they who can be against us, and that in His strength
we can and must meet evil with good and overcome it.' [1]

The same writer distinguishes between the ideal
of *simplification*, as upheld by the Quakers, and the

[1] *Quaker Strongholds.*

practice of asceticism. The motive of simplicity is to prevent the frivolities of fashion from encroaching upon our time, and to be free from the guilt of *wasting* the labour of others. This is a valuable part of Quaker teaching. We have no right to employ other men on unworthy tasks, whether we pay them well or not. The luxury trades ought not to exist. But for the extravagance of the rich, all men might be employed on doing or making something useful, providing for one another's legitimate wants. Thus 'waste not' assumes the dignity of a high moral precept.

On one important branch of expenditure, female dress, I will let this lady speak to her sisters. ' The adoption of a settled costume, at any rate in mature life, is not only the most right and dignified course, but it has afforded one more proof of the truth that the lower aims of life can thrive only in proportion as they are kept in subordination to the higher. The freedom from the necessity of perpetual changes . . . has also the lower advantage of admitting a gradual bringing to perfection of the settled costume itself. We all know how exquisite, within its strictly limited range, can be the result. Its quiet beauty appeals to both the mind and the eye with a peculiar charm. I cannot think that it is unworthy of Christian women to be careful that their very dress shall speak a language of quietness, gentleness and purity—that it shall be impressed even with a touch of eternity.' What would this good woman have said if she had witnessed the short-skirted, crop-haired, flat-chested, scarlet-lipped nymphs of 1926 and 1927 ?

What is likely to be the future of this brave little band of Christian mystics, whose influence for good, both in promoting personal piety and in advancing the Kingdom of God upon earth, has been out of all proportion to their scanty numbers ? They have been warned of two dangers—one, of being assimilated to other Protestant organisations, and so losing their distinctive testimony and their peculiar strength ; the other, of being too much entangled in social politics, and so carried out of the religious atmosphere altogether. They will probably escape both ; for the mystical foundation of Quakerism is now once more increasingly recognised by Friends themselves, and they have less than other and larger bodies to gain by unworthy political alliances. The central truth of Quakerism, the indwelling presence of the Divine Spirit in the human soul, is a doctrine which appeals strongly to the present generation. The function of the Society of Friends is to bear witness to the truth of spiritual religion, to maintain the independence and self-sufficingness of this faith, and to prove, as they have done in the past, that it leads to no barren and self-centred detachment from social life and its problems, but rather to a courageous and devoted advocacy of causes in which the spirit of our religion calls for strenuous opposition to the current principles and practice of the world. This influence may be effective far beyond the limits of the Society itself, which presents religion in a form too bare and un-adorned to attract the majority. The safeguard of mysticism is the belief that we have not merely to renounce the world of ordinary experience, but to find its deeper and more spiritual meanings, and so to advance in knowledge of God, the world, and our-selves, that every aspect of our experience may be exalted and consecrated together.

HELLENISM IN CHRISTIANITY

THOSE who write about the Greeks must beware of a heresy which is very rife just now—the theory of *racialism*. Political ethnology, which is no genuine science, excused the ambition of the Germans to themselves, and helped them to wage war ; it has suggested to the Allies a method of waging peace. It will not help us to understand the Greeks. The Greeks were splendid mongrels, made up of the same elements, differently mixed, as ourselves. Their famous beauty, which had almost disappeared when Cicero visited Athens, was mainly the result of a healthy outdoor life and physical training, combined with a very becoming costume. They were probably not handsomer than Oxford rowing crews or Eton boys. Their flowering time of genius was due to the same causes which produced similar results in the Italian Renaissance. The city-state is a forcing-house of brilliant achievement, though it quickly uses up its human material. We cannot even regard the Greeks as a homogeneous mixed race. The Spartiates were almost pure Nordics ; the Athenians almost pure Mediterraneans. The early colonists, from whom sprang so many of the greatest names in the Hellenic roll of honour, are not likely to have kept their blood pure. Nor was there ever a Greek culture shared by all the Greeks. The Spartan system, that of a small fighting tribe encamped in a subject country, recalls that of Chaka's Zulus ; Arcadia was bucolic, Aetolia barbarous, Boeotia stolid, Macedonia half outside the pale. The consciousness of race among the Greeks counted practically for about as much as the consciousness of being white men, or Christians, does in modern civilisation.

Greece for our purposes means not a race, but a culture,[1] a language and literature, and still more an attitude towards life, which for us begins with Homer, and persists, with many changes but no breaks, till the closing of the Athenian lecture-rooms by Justinian. The changes no doubt were great, when politically Greece was living Greece no more, and when the bearers of the tradition were no longer the lineal descendants of those who established it. But the tradition, enshrined in literature, in monuments, and in social customs, survived. The civilisation of the Roman Empire was less Italian than Greek. After the fifth century, Hellenism—the language, the literature, and the attitude towards life—was practically lost to the West for nearly a thousand years. It was recovered at the Renaissance, and from that time to this has been a potent element in Western civilisation. The Dark Ages, and the early Middle Ages, are the period during which the West was cut off from Hellenism. Yet even then the severance was not complete. For these were the ages of the Catholic theocracy ; and if we had to choose one man as the founder of Catholicism as a theocratic system, we should have to name neither Augustine nor St. Paul, still less Jesus Christ, but Plato, who in the *Laws* sketches out with wonderful

---

[1] *Cf.* Isocrates, *Paneg.* 13, οὐ τοῦ γένους ἀλλὰ τῆς διανοίας.

prescience the conditions for such a polity, and the form which it would be compelled to take. Even in speculative thought we know that Augustine owed much to the Platonists, the Schoolmen to Aristotle, the mystics to the pupil of Proclus whom they called Dionysius. Only Greek science, and the scientific spirit, were almost completely lost, and a beginning *de novo* had to be made when the West shook off its fetters.

Hellenism then is not the mind of a particular ethnic type, nor of a particular period. It was not destroyed, though it was emasculated, by the loss of political freedom ; it was neither killed nor died a natural death. Its philosophy was continuous from Thales to Proclus, and again from Ficino and Pico to Lotze and Bradley, after a long sleep which was not death. Its religion passes into Christian theology and cultus without any real break. The early Church spoke in Greek and thought in Greek. In the days of Greek freedom to be a Greek had meant to be a citizen of a Greek canton ; after Alexander it meant to have Greek culture. None of the great Stoics were natives of Greece proper ; Zeno himself was a Semite. Of the later Greek writers, Marcus Aurelius was a Romanised Spaniard, Plotinus possibly a Copt, Porphyry and Lucian Syrians, Philo, St. Paul, and probably the Fourth Evangelist were Jews. These men all belong to the history of Greek culture. And if these were Greeks how shall we deny the name to Raphael and Michael Angelo, to Spenser and Sidney, to Keats and Shelley ? When Blake wrote :

> The sun's light when he unfolds it,
> Depends on the organ that beholds it,

he was summing up not only the philosophy of the
Lake Poets but the fundamental dogma of the maturest
Greek thought.   Would not Plato have rejoiced in
Michael Angelo's confession of faith, which Wordsworth
has translated for us ?

> Heaven-born, the soul a heavenward course must hold ;
> Beyond the visible world she soars to seek
> (For what delights the sense is false and weak)
> Ideal Form, the universal mould.
> The wise man, I affirm, can find no rest
> In that which perishes ; nor will he lend
> His heart to aught that doth on time depend.

Has the highest aspect of Greek religion ever been
better expressed than by Wordsworth himself, to whom,
as to Blake, it came by inspiration and not from books ?

> While yet a child, and long before his time,
> Had he perceived the presence and the power
> Of greatness ; and deep feelings had impressed
> So vividly great objects that *they lay*
> *Upon his mind like substances,* whose presence
> Perplexed the bodily sense.

The spirit of man does not live only on tradition ; it
can draw direct from the fountain-head.   We are dealing with a permanent type of human culture, which is
rightly named after the Greeks, since it attained its
chief glory in the literature and art of the Hellenic
cities, but which cannot be separated from Western
civilisation as an alien importation.   Without what we
call our debt to Greece we should have neither our
religion nor our philosophy nor our science nor our
literature nor our education nor our politics.   We
should be mere barbarians.   We need not speculate
how much we might ultimately have discovered for
ourselves.   Our civilisation is a tree which has its roots

in Greece, or, to borrow a more appropriate metaphor from Clement of Alexandria, it is a river which has received affluents from every side ; but its head waters are Greek. The continuity of Greek thought and practice in religion and religious philosophy is especially important, and it is necessary to emphasise it because the accident of our educational curriculum leaves in the minds of most students a broad chasm between the Stoics and the Christians, ignores the later Greek philosophy of religion altogether, and traces Christian dogma back to Palestine, with which it has very little connexion.

Our sense of continuity is dulled in another way. There is a tendency to isolate certain aspects of Hellenic life and thought as characteristic, and to stamp others, which are equally found among the ancient Greeks, as untypical and exceptional. In the sphere of religion, with which we are concerned in this essay, we are bidden to regard Plato and Euripides as rebels against the national tradition, and not as normal products of their age and country. I do not feel at liberty to pick and choose in this fashion. A national character may be best exemplified in its rebels. a religion in its heretics. If Nietzsche was right in calling Plato a Christian before Christ, I do not therefore regard him as an unhellenic Greek. Rather, I trace back to him, and so to Greece, most of the theology and philosophy of the Catholic Church, and the Christian type of mysticism. If Euripides anticipated to an extraordinary degree the devout agnosticism, the vague pantheism, the humanitarian sentiment of the nineteenth (rather than of the twentieth) century, I do not consider that he was a freak in fifth-century Athens, but that Greece showed

us the way even in paths where we have not been used
to look to her for guidance.   I am equally reluctant to
assume, without evidence, that the later Platonism,
whether we call it religion or philosophy, is unhellenic.
It is quite unnecessary to look for Asiatic influences in
a school which clung close to the Attic tradition.   It is
more to the purpose to show how a religious philosophy
of mystical revelation and introspection grew naturally
out of the older nature-philosophies, just as in our own
day metaphysics and science have both been driven
back upon the theory of knowledge and psychology.
It should not be necessary to remind Hellenists that
' Know thyself ' passed for the supreme word of wisdom
in the classical period, or that Heracleitus revealed his
method in the words ' I searched myself.'

We shall come presently to certain parts of our
modern heritage which are not Greek either by origin
or by affinity.   These will not be found in Euripides
or Plato any more than in Herodotus or Sophocles.
But some developments of religion which our Hellenists
particularly dislike, and are therefore anxious to disclaim as alien to Greek thought and practice, such
as squalid and coarse asceticism, sacramental magic,
and timid reliance on authority, are maladies of the
Greek spirit, and came into the Church from Hellenistic
and not from Jewish sources.   It was Cleanthes who
wished to treat Aristarchus as the Church treated
Galileo, for anticipating Galileo's discovery.   It was
Plutarch, or rather his revered father, who said ' You
seem to me to be handling a very great and dangerous
subject, or rather to be raising questions which ought
not to be raised at all, when you question the opinion
we hold about the gods, and ask reasons and proofs for

everything.   The ancient and ancestral faith is enough ;
and if on one point its fixed and traditional character
be disturbed, it will be undermined and no one will
trust it.'   It is true that Celsus accused the Christians
of saying ' Do not inquire ; only believe.'   But this
was not the attitude of Clement and Origen, still less
of that most courageous pioneer St. Paul ; it was rather
the attitude of the average devout pagan.   At this time
the defence of popular superstition was no longer a
matter of mere policy but of heartfelt need.   Marcus
Aurelius was a great immolator of white cows.   The
Christians were disliked, not as superstitious, but as
impious.   Alexander of Abunoteichos expelled ' Christians and Epicureans ' by name from his *séances*.
Lucian is the Voltaire of a credulous age.   As for
sacerdotal magic, Ovid explicitly ascribed the *ex opere
operato* doctrine to the Greeks.

> Graecia principium moris fuit ; illa nocentes
>   impia lustratos ponere facta putat.
> a nimium faciles, qui tristia crimina caedis
>   fluminea tolli posse putatis aqua.

The Christian Church was the last great creative
achievement of the classical culture.   It is neither
Asiatic nor medieval in its essential character.   It is
not Asiatic ; Christianity is the least Oriental of all the
great religions.   The Semites either shook it off and
reverted to a Judaism purged of its Hellenic elements,
or enrolled themselves with fervour under the banner of
Islam, which Westcott called ' a petrified Judaism.'
Christian missions have had no success in any Asiatic
country.   Nor is there anything specifically medieval
about Catholicism.   It preserved the idea of Roman
imperialism, after the secular empire of the West had

disappeared, and even kept the tradition of the secular empire alive. It modelled all its machinery on the Roman Empire, and consecrated the Roman claim to universal dominion, with the Roman law of *maiestas* against all who disputed its authority. Even its favourite penalty of the ' avenging flames ' is borrowed from the later Roman codes. It maintained the official language of antiquity, and the imperial title of the autocrat who reigned on the Seven Hills. Nor were the early Christians so anxious as is often supposed to disclaim this continuity. At first, it is true, their apologetic was directed to proving their continuity with Judaism ; but Judaism ceased to count for much after the destruction of the Holy City in A.D. 70, and the second-century apologists appeal for toleration on the ground that the best Greek philosophers taught very much the same as what Christians believe. ' We teach the same as the Greeks,' says Justin Martyr, ' though we alone are hated for what we teach.' ' Some among us,' says Tertullian, ' who are versed in ancient literature, have written books to prove that we have embraced no tenets for which we have not the support of common and public literature.' ' The teachings of Plato,' says Justin again, ' are not alien to those of Christ ; and the same is true of the Stoics.' ' Heracleitus and Socrates lived in accordance with the divine Logos,' and should be reckoned as Christians. Clement says that Plato wrote ' by inspiration of God.' Augustine, much later, finds that ' only a few words and phrases ' need be changed to bring Platonism into complete accord with Christianity. The ethics of contemporary paganism, as Harnack shows, with special reference to Porphyry, are almost identical with

those of the Christians of his day.   They differ in many
points from the standards of 500 years earlier and from
those of 1500 years later, but the divergences are neither
racial nor credal.   Catholic Christianity is historically
continuous with the old civilisation, which indeed continued to live in this region after its other traditions
and customs had been shattered.   There are few other
examples in history of so great a difference between
appearance and reality.   Outwardly, the continuity
with Judaism seems to be unbroken, that with paganism to be broken.   In reality, the opposite is the fact.

This most important truth has been obscured from
many causes.   The gap in history made by our educational tradition has been already mentioned.   And our
histories of the early Church are too often warped by
an unfortunate bias.   Christianity has been judged at
its best, paganism at its worst.   The rhetorical de-
nunciations of writers like Seneca, Juvenal, and Tacitus
are taken at their face value, and few have remembered
the convention which obliged a satirist to be scathing,
or the political prejudice of the Stoics against the
monarchy, or the non-representative character of
fashionable life in the capital.   The modern Church
historian, as Mr. Benn says, has gathered his experience
in a college quadrangle or a cathedral close, and knows
little enough about his own country, next to nothing
about what morality was in the Middle Ages, and
nothing at all about what it still is in many parts of
Europe.   In the most recent books, however, there is
a real desire to hold the scales fairly, and Christianity
has nothing to fear from an impartial judgment.

There is also an assumption, which we find even in
such learned writers as Harnack and Hatch, that the

Hellenic element in Christianity is an accretion which transformed the new religion from its original purity and half paganised the Church again. They would like to prove that underneath Catholicism was a primitive Protestantism, which owed nothing to Greece. The truth is that the Church was half Greek from the first, though, as I shall say presently, the original Gospel was not. St. Paul was a Jew of the Dispersion, not of Palestine, and the Christianity to which he was converted was the Christianity of Stephen, not of James the Lord's brother. His later epistles are steeped in the phraseology of the Greek mysteries. The Epistle to the Hebrews and the Fourth Gospel are unintelligible without some knowledge of Philo, whose theology is more Greek than Jewish. In the conflict about the nature of the future life, it was the Greek eschatology which prevailed over the Jewish. St. Paul's famous declaration, ' We look not at the things which are seen, but at the things which are not seen ; for the things which are seen are temporal, but the things which are not seen are eternal,' is pure Platonism, and quite alien to Jewish thought. Judaic Christianity was a local affair, and had a very short life.

Further, too much is made of the conflict between the official cults of paganism and Christian public worship. It is forgotten how completely, in Hellenistic times, religion and philosophy were fused. Without under-estimating the simple piety which, especially in country districts, still attached itself to the temples and their ritual, we may say confidently that the vital religion of the empire was associated with the mystery-cults and with the discipline of the ' philosophic life.' It is in this region that the continuity of Catholicism with Hellenism is mainly to be found. The philosophers at this time were preachers, confessors, chaplains, and missionaries. The clerical profession, in nearly all its activities, is directly descended from the Hellenistic philosophers.

This claim of continuity may seem paradoxical when we remember the savage persecutions of the Christians by the imperial government. Of these persecutions there were several causes. The empire, like all empires of the same type, rested partly on religious support. Augustus encouraged his court poets to advocate a revival of piety and sound morals. A government cannot inquire into religious conviction, but it can enforce conformity and outward respect for the forms of worship as ' by law established.' The Christians and Epicureans were held guilty of the same political offence—' atheism.' The State had no quarrel with the mystery-religions, which were a private matter, but open disrespect to the national deities was flat disloyalty. The pagans could not understand why the Church would make no terms with the fusion of religions (θεοκρασία) which seemed to them the natural result of the fusion of nationalities. Apuleius makes Isis say, when she reveals herself to Lucius, ' cuius numen unicum multiformi specie, ritu vario, nomine multiiugo totus veneratur orbis '; and she then recounts her various names. This more than tolerant hospitality of the spirit seemed to the mixed population of the empire the logical recognition of the actual political situation, and those who deliberately stood outside it were at least potentially enemies of society. This was the real quarrel between the Church and the empire. It is the old State religion which Augustine attacks, ridiculing

the innumerable Roman godlings whose names he
perhaps found in Varro. It is true that Plato, Euripides,
and Xenophanes had attacked the official mythology
with hardly less asperity ; but they did not escape censure, and the Christian alienation from the Olympians
was far more fundamental.

The pagan revival under the empire was rather like
Neo-Catholicism in France. It was patriotic, national-
istic, and conservative, rather than strictly religious.
Celsus, in his lost book against the Christians, seems
to have appealed to their patriotism, urging them to
support their country and its government in dangerous
times. As the Church grew in numbers and power,
and the old traditions crumbled away, largely from the
fall in the birth-rate among the upper and middle
classes, the conservatives became more anxiously
attached to their own culture, and saw in Christianity
a ' shapeless darkness ' which threatened to extinguish
' all the beautiful things in the world.' We can partly
sympathise with this alarm, though not with the foolish
policy which it inspired. The early persecutions were
like Russian ' pogroms,' instigated or connived at by
the government as a safety-valve for popular discontent. For at this time the common people hated the
Christians, and half believed the monstrous stories
about them. The attacks were not continuous, and
were half-hearted, very unlike the systematic extermination of Jews and Protestants in Spain. At
Alexandria Hadrian found a money-loving population
worshipping Christ and Sarapis almost indifferently.
A wrong impression is formed if we picture to ourselves
two sections of society engaged in constant war. The
first real war was the last, under Diocletian ; it was to

decide whether paganism or Christianity was to be the state religion. However, there is no doubt that the persecutions helped to seal the fate of the old culture.

Harnack traces three stages in the Hellenisation of Christianity. ' In the earliest Christian writings, apart from Paul, Luke, and John,' he cannot find any considerable traces of Greek influence. ' The real influx of Greek thought and life' began about 130. The exception is so important as to make this statement of little or no value. After 130, he says, ' the philosophy of Greece went straight to the core of the new religion.' A century or so later, ' Greek mysteries and Greek civilisation in the whole range of its development exercise their influence on the Church, but as yet not its mythology and polytheism ; these were still to come.' ' Another century had to elapse before Hellenism as a whole and in every phase of its development was established in the Church.' The process which he describes began, in fact, as soon as Christian preachers used the Greek language, and was never so complete as he says. The Logos-Christology, to which he justly attributes the greatest importance, is already present in St. Paul's epistles ; the name only is wanting ; and the sharp contradiction which he finds between the Christian idea of a revelation made through a person at a certain date, and the Greek idea of an apprehension of timeless and changeless truth, always open to individuals after the appropriate discipline, was faced and in part overcome by the Greek Fathers. Harnack also regards Gnosticism as an embodiment of the genuinely Greek view of revelation, forgetting that orthodox Platonism was as hostile to Gnosticism as the Church itself. In rejecting Gnosticism, the Church

in fact decided for genuine Hellenism against a corrupted and barbarised development of it.   On the other
hand, there is no period at which we can speak of a
complete conquest of Christianity by Greek ideas.
There was a large part of the old tradition which
perished with its defenders, who, obeying the melancholy law which directs human survival, died out to
make way for immigrants and for the formerly submerged classes, the people with few wants, who were
indifferent to a culture which they had never been
allowed to share.

One more cause of misunderstanding may be illus-
trated from the writings of Matthew Arnold.   He
divides the human race into Hebraisers and Hellenisers,
and classifies the modern English and Americans as
Hebraisers.   The fundamental maxim of Hebrew ethics,
according to him, is ' Walk by the light you have ' ;
of Greek ethics, ' Take heed that the light which is in
thee is not darkness.'   The Hebraiser is conscientious
but unenlightened ; the Helleniser is clear-headed but
unscrupulous.   Professor Santayana has lately noted
the same difference between the type of character
developed by the Latin nations and by the Anglo-
Saxons.   The Mediterranean civilisation, older and
more sophisticated, is careful to get its values right ;
the northern man is bent on doing something big, no
matter what, and follows Clough's advice :

Go ! say not in thine heart, And what then, were it accomplished,
    Were the wild impulse allayed, what is the use and the good ?

But Santayana does not make the mistake of regarding
the Reformation as a return to Palestinian Christianity.
This was, indeed, the opinion of the Reformers them-

selves ; but all religious innovation seeks to base itself on some old tradition. Christianity at first sought for its credentials in Judaism, though the Jews saw very quickly that it ' destroyed the Law.' The belief of the Reformers was plausible ; for they rejected just those parts of Catholicism which had nothing to do with Palestine, but were taken over from the old Hellenic or Hellenistic culture. But the residuum was less Jewish than Teutonic. On one side, indeed, the Reformation was a return to Hellenism from Romanism. Early Christian philosophy was mainly Platonic ; early Christian ethics (as exemplified especially in writers like Ambrose) were mainly Stoical. There had been a considerable fusion of Plato and the Stoa among the Neoplatonists, so that it was easy for the two to flourish together. Augustine banished Stoical ethics from the Church, and they were revived only at the Reformation. Calvinism is simply baptised Stoicism ; it is logically pantheistic, since it acknowledges only one effective will in the universe. The creed of nineteenth-century science is very similar. Puritanism was not at all like Judaism, in spite of its fondness for the Old Testament ; it was very like Stoicism. The Reformation was a revolt against Latin theocracy and the hereditary paganism of the Mediterranean peoples ; it was not really a return to pre-Hellenic Christianity. It sheltered the humanism of Shakespeare and the late-flowering English Renaissance, and Christian Platonism has nowhere had a more flourishing record than in Protestant Britain.

At the present time a more drastic revolt is in progress among the *plebs urbana*, which does in truth threaten with destruction ' what we owe to Greece.'

The industrial revolution has generated a new type of barbarism, with no roots in the past. For the second time in the history of Western Europe, continuity is in danger of being lost. A generation is growing up, not uneducated, but educated in a system which has little connexion with European culture in its historical development. The Classics are not taught ; the Bible is not taught ; history is not taught to any effect. What is even more serious, there are no social traditions. The modern townsman is *déraciné* : he has forgotten the habits and sentiments of the village from which his forefathers came. An unnatural and unhealthy mode of life, cut off from the sweet and humanising influences of nature, has produced an unnatural and unhealthy mentality, to which we shall find no parallels in the past. Its chief characteristic is profound secularity or materialism. The typical town artisan has no religion and no superstitions ; he has no ideals beyond the visible and tangible world of the senses. This, of course, opens an impassable gulf between him and Greek religion, and a still wider gulf between him and Christianity. The attempts which are occasionally made, especially in this country, to dress up the Labour movement as a return to the Palestinian Gospel, are little short of grotesque. The contrast is well summed up by Belfort Bax, in a passage quoted by Professor Gardner. ' According to Christianity, regeneration must come from within. The ethics and religion of modern socialism on the contrary look for regeneration from without, from material conditions and a higher social life.' Here the gauntlet is thrown down to Christ and Plato alike.

Quite logically the new spirit is in revolt against

what it calls intellectualism, which means the application of the dry light of reason to the problems of human life. It wishes to substitute for reason what some of its philosophers call instinct, but which should rather be called sentiment and emotion. There is no reconciliation between this view of life and Hellenism. For science is the eldest and dearest child of the Greek spirit. One of the great battles of the future will be between science and its enemies. The misologists have numbers on their side ; but ' Nature,' whom all the Greeks honoured and trusted, will be justified in her children.

The new spirit is especially bitter against the Stoical ethics, which as we have seen were revived, in all their stern strength, by Calvinism. Stoicism teaches men to venerate and obey natural law ; to accept with proud equanimity the misfortunes of life ; to be beneficent, but to inhibit the emotion of pity ; to be self-reliant and self-contained ; to practise self-denial for the sake of self-conquest ; and to regard this life as a stern school of moral discipline. All this is simply detestable to the new spirit, which is sentimental, undisciplined, and hedonistic. It remembers the hardness of Puritanism, and has no admiration for its virtues.

It is often said that the modern man has entirely lost the Greek love of beauty. This is, I think, untrue, and unjust to our present civilisation, unlovely as it undoubtedly is in many ways. It is curious that modern critics of the Greeks have not called attention to the *aesthetic* obtuseness which showed itself in the defective reaction of the ancients against cruelty. It was not that they excluded beautiful actions from the sphere of aesthetics ; they never thought of separating the beautiful from the good in this way. But they were not disgusted at the torture of slaves, the exposure of new-born children, or the massacre of the population of a revolted city. The same callousness appears in the Italian cities . at the Renaissance ; Ezzelino was a contemporary of great architects, poets and painters. I cannot avoid the conclusion that it is connected in some obscure way with the artistic creativeness of these two closely similar epochs. The extreme sensibility to physical suffering which characterises modern civilisation arose together with industrialism, and is most marked in the most highly industrialised countries. It has synchronised with the complete eclipse of spontaneous and unconscious artistic production, which we deplore in our time. Evelyn, in the seventeenth century, was still able to visit a prison in Paris to gratify his curiosity by seeing a prisoner tortured, and though he did not stay to the end of the exhibition he shows that his stomach was not easily turned. It is certain that our repugnance to such sights is aesthetic rather than moral, and probable that it is strongest in the lower social strata. Several years ago I went to the first night of a rather foolish play about ancient Rome, in which an early Christian is brought in to be very mildly tortured on the stage. At the first crack of the whip my neighbours sprang from their seats, crying ' Shame ! Stop that ! ' ; and the scene had to be removed in subsequent performances. The operatives in a certain factory stopped the engines for an hour because they heard a cat mewing among the machinery. Having with difficulty rescued the animal from being crushed they strangled it. The explanation of this extreme susceptibility must be left to psychologists ; but I am convinced that we have here a case of transferred aesthetic sensibility. We can walk unmoved down the streets of Plaistow, but we cannot bear to see a horse beaten. The Athenians set up no Albert Memorials, but they tortured slave-girls in their law-courts and sent their prisoners to work in the horrible galleries of the Laureion silver-mines.

This emergence of a new spirit, which seems to be almost independent of all traditions, makes it difficult to estimate our present indebtedness to Greece in matters of religion. It would be difficult even if the industrial revolution had not taken place. The northern Europeans have hardly yet attained to self-expression. Their religion is a mixture of Greek, Latin, and Hebrew elements which refuse to be harmonised, and which in this country sometimes clash with the ideal of a gentleman, that lay religion of the English-speaking peoples, which has no longer any connexion with hereditary status. The English gentleman is not a Greek any more than he is a Jew. His code makes Odysseus an amusing rascal ; Achilles a violent and sulky savage ; and Aristotle's $\mu\epsilon\gamma\alpha\lambda\acute{o}\psi\upsilon\chi o\varsigma$ (as has been said) is rather like a nobleman in a novel by Disraeli, but not like any other sort of gentleman. The Englishman is by nature religious ; but Christianity in its developed fôrm is a Mediterranean religion ; in all external features it might have been very different if it had been first planted north of the Alps. There is, therefore, a chronic confusion in Protestantism which makes its conflicts with the Latin Church like the battles of undisciplined barbarians against well-drilled troops.

Nevertheless, though it is so difficult to separate
the various threads which make up the tangled skein
of our modern religion, it may be worth while to make
the attempt to distinguish, first, those parts of current
Christianity which are not Greek, in the wide sense
which I have chosen for the word, and then those which,
in the same sense, are Greek by origin or affinity.

Among those elements which are not Greek, the
first place must be given to the original Gospel, of which
I have said nothing yet. Our records of the Galilean
ministry, contained in the three Synoptic Gospels, were
not compiled till long after the events which they
describe, and must not be used uncritically. But in
my opinion, at any rate, the substance of the teaching
of Christ comes out very clearly in these books. No
Hellenic influence can be traced in it ; there is not even
any sign of the Hellenised Judaism which for us is
represented by His contemporary Philo. But neither
is it possible to call the Gospel Jewish, except with
many qualifications. Christ came before his countrymen as a prophet ; He deliberately placed himself in
the line of the prophetic tradition. Like other prophets
of His nation, He did not altogether eschew the framework of apocalyptic which was at that time the natural
mould for prophecy. But He preached neither the
popular nationalism, nor the popular ecclesiasticism,
nor the popular ethics. His countrymen rejected Him
as soon as they understood Him. The Gospel was, as
St. Paul said, a new creation. It is most significant
that it at once introduced a new ethical terminology.
The Greek words which we translate love (or charity),
joy, peace, hope, humility, are no part of the stock-in-
trade of Greek moralists before Christ. Men do not
coin new words for old ideas. Taken as a whole the

Gospel is profoundly original ; and a Christian can find strong evidence for his belief that in Christ a revelation was made to humanity at large, in which the religion of the Spirit, in its purest and most universal form, was for the first time presented to mankind. This revelation has to a considerable extent passed into the common consciousness of the civilised world ; but its implications in matters of conduct, individual, social, and international, are still imperfectly understood and have never been acted upon, except feebly and sporadically. The teaching of Christ must be regarded as only one of many elements which make up what we call Christianity. The Quakers, as a body, seem to me to come nearest to what a genuinely Christian society would be.

Secondly, the Greeks escaped the evils of priestly government. The Oriental type of theocracy, with which they were familiar in the Egypt of the Pharaohs, was alien to their civilisation. Their sacrifices were for the most part of the genial type, a communion-meal with the god. But even in Greece we must remember the gloomy Chthonian rites, and the degradations of Orphism mentioned by Plato in the *Republic*. ' They persuade not only individuals but whole cities that expiations and atonements for sin may be made by sacrifices and amusements which fill a vacant hour, and are equally at the service of the living and of the dead ; the latter sort they call mysteries, and they redeem us from the pains of hell, but if we neglect them no one knows what awaits us.' This exploitation of sacramentalism was common enough in Greece ; but the Church-supported absolutism of Byzantium and modern Caesaro-papism was foreign to genuine Hellenism. It was introduced by Constantine as part of the Orientalising of the empire begun by Diocletian. As Seeley says: 'Constantine purchased an indefeasible title by a charter. He gave certain liberties and received in return passive obedience. He gained a sanction for the Oriental theory of government; in return he accepted the law of the Church. He became irresponsible to his subjects on condition of becoming responsible to Christ.'

The Greeks never had a book-religion, in the sense in which Judaism became, and Islam always was, a book-religion. But they were in some danger of treating Homer and Hesiod as inspired Scriptures. To us it is plain that a long religious history lies behind Homer, and that the treatment of the gods in Epic poetry proves that they had almost ceased to be the objects of religious feeling. Some of them are even comic characters, like the devil in Scottish folklore. To turn these poems into sacred literature was to court the ridicule of the Christians. But Homer was never supposed to contain ' the faith once delivered to the saints '; no religion of authority could be built upon him, and Greek speculation remained far more unfettered than the thought of Christendom has been until our own day.

Those who have observed the actual state of Christianity in Mediterranean countries cannot lay much stress on the difference between Christian monotheism and pagan polytheism. The early Church fought against the tendency to interpose objects of worship between God and man; but Mariolatry came in through a loophole, and the worship of the masses in Roman Catholic countries is far more pagan than the service-books. In the imagination of many simple

Catholics, Jesus, Mary, and Joseph are the chief potentates in their Olympus.

The doctrine of the creation of the world in time, which was denied by most pagan thinkers and affirmed by most Christian divines, belongs to philosophy rather than to religion. The disbelief in the pre-existence of the soul, a doctrine which for Greek thought stands or falls with the belief in survival after death, is more important, and may be partly attributable to Jewish influence. But pre-existence does not seem to have been believed by the majority of Greeks, and in fact almost disappears from Greek thought between Plato and the Neoplatonists. It is possible that this Pythagorean and Platonic doctrine may still have a future.

There are some who will insist that these differences are insignificant by the side of the fact that Christianity was the idealistic side of a revolt of the proletariat against the whole social order of the time. This notion, which made Christ ' le bon sans-culotte,' has again become popular lately ; some have even compared the early Christians with Bolsheviks. It is a fair question to ask at what period this was even approximately true. Christ and His apostles belonged to the prosperous peasantry of Galilee, a well-educated and comfortable lower middle class. The domestic slaves of wealthy Romans, who embraced the new faith in large numbers, were legally defenceless, but by no means miserable or degraded. After the second century the comparison of the Christians to modern revolutionists becomes too absurd for discussion. There is a good deal of rhetorical declamation about riches and poverty in the Christian Fathers ; but beyond this the Church seems to have done very little to protest against the economic

injustices of the fourth and fifth centuries. From first
to last there was nothing of the ' Spartacus ' movement
about the Catholic Church. As soon as the persecutions ceased, the bishops took their place naturally
among the nobility.

When we turn to the obligations of modern religion
to Greece, it is difficult to know where to begin.

The conception of philosophy as an *ars vivendi* is
characteristically Greek. Nothing can be further from
the truth than to call the Greeks ' intellectualists ' in
the disparaging sense in which the word is now often
used. The object of philosophy was to teach a man to
live well, and with that object to think rightly about
God, the world, and himself. This close union between
metaphysics, morals, and religion has remained as
a permanent possession of the modern world. Every
philosopher is now expected to show the bearing of his
system on morality and religion, and the criticism is
often justified that however bold the speculations of the
thinker, he is careful, when he comes to conduct, to be
conventional enough. The Hellenistic combination of
Platonic metaphysics with Stoic ethics is still the
dominant type of Christian religious philosophy. It is
curious to observe how competing tendencies in these
systems—the praise of isolated detachment and of
active social sympathy—have continued to struggle
against each other within the Christian Church.

The place of asceticism in religion is so important,
and so much has been written rather unintelligently
about the contrast between Hellenism and Christianity
in this matter, that I propose to deal with it, briefly
indeed, but with a little more detail than a strict
attention to proportion would justify. It has often

been assumed that a nation of athletes, who made heroes of Heracles and Theseus, Achilles and Hector, could have had nothing but contempt for the ascetic ideal. But in truth asceticism has a continuous history within Hellenism. Even Homer knows of the priests of chilly Dodona, the Selli, whose bare feet are unwashed, and who sleep on the ground. This is probably not, as Wilamowitz-Möllendorf thinks, a description of savage life, but of an ascetic school of prophets. For the fast-days which introduced the Thesmophoria were observed by the Athenian matrons in the same way ; they went unshod and sat on the bare earth ; and we may compare the Nudipedalia, ordered by the Romans in time of dearth and mentioned by Petronius and Tertullian. Prophets and prophetesses fasted at Miletus, Colophon, and other places. National fasts were ordered in times of calamity or danger, and Tarentum kept a yearly fast of thankfulness for deliverance from a siege. The flagellation of boys at Sparta hardly comes into account, being probably a substitute for human sacrifice ; but the continuance of the cruel rite till nearly the end of antiquity causes surprise. The worship of Dionysus Zagreus in Thrace was accompanied by ascetic practices before Pythagoras. Vegetarianism, which has always played an important part in the ascetic life, was obligatory on all Pythagoreans ; but in this school there was another motive besides the desire to mortify the flesh. Those who believe in the transmigration of souls into the bodies of animals must regard flesh-eating as little better than cannibalism. The Pythagorean and the Orphic rules of life were well known throughout antiquity, and were probably obeyed by large numbers. The rule of continence was far less strict than in the Catholic 'religious' life; but Empedocles, according to Hippolytus, advised abstinence from marriage and procreation, and the tendency to regard celibacy as part of the 'philosophic life' increased steadily. The Cynic Antisthenes is quoted by Clement of Alexandria as having expressed a wish to 'shoot Aphrodite, who has ruined so many virtuous women.' But the asceticism of the early Cynics and of some Stoics was based not on self-devotion and spirituality but on the desire for independence, and often took repulsive forms. Of some among them it may be said that they did not object to sensual pleasure, they only objected to having to pay for it. Desire for self-sufficiency is always part of asceticism, but in the Christian saints it has been a small part. The Greeks who practised it were from first to last too anxious to be invulnerable ; this was the main attraction of the philosophic life from the time of Antisthenes, and it remained the main attraction to the end. But Cynicism and Stoicism (which tend to run together) became gentler, more humane, and more spiritual under the Roman Empire. Seneca, Epictetus, and Marcus Aurelius often seem to be half Christian. Direct influence of Christian ethics at this early period is perhaps unlikely ; it is enough to suppose that the spirit of the age affected in a similar way all creeds and denominations. Self-mortification tended to assume more and more violent forms, till it culminated in the strange aberrations of Egyptian eremitism. It is impossible to regard these as either Greek or Christian ; they indicate a pathological state of society, which can be partly but not entirely accounted for by the conditions of the time. After a few centuries a far more wholesome type of monachism supplanted the hermits ; the anchorites of the Middle Ages retained the solitary life, but were very unlike the crazy savages of the Thebaid. In modern times, those who have been most under the Greek spirit have generally lived with austere simplicity, but without any of the violent self-discipline which is said to be still practised by some devout Catholics.   The assiduous practice of self-mastery and the most sparing indulgence in the pleasures of sense are the ' philosophic life ' which the Greek spirit recommends as the highest.   The best Greeks would blame the life of an English clergyman, professor, or philosopher as too self-indulgent ; we often forget how frugally and hardily the Greeks lived at all times.   But here we have to consider the differences of climate, and the apparent necessity of a rather generous diet for the northern peoples.

The influence of the Greek mysteries upon Christianity is a keenly debated question, in which passion and prejudice play too large a part.   The information necessary for forming a judgment has been much enlarged by recent discoveries in Egypt and elsewhere, and, as usually happens, the importance of the new facts has been sometimes exaggerated.   Protestant theology has on the whole minimised the influence of the mysteries, and has postdated it, from an unwillingness to allow that there was already a strong Catholic element in the Christianity of the first century. Orthodox Catholicism has ignored it from different but equally obvious motives.   Modernist Catholicism has in my opinion antedated the irruption of crude sacramentalism into the Church, and has greatly overstated its importance in the religion of the first-century

Christians. This school practically denies anything more than a half-accidental continuity between the preaching of the historical Christ, whom they strangely suppose to have been a mere apocalyptist, one of the many Messiahs or Mahdis who arose at this period in Palestine, and the Catholic Church, which according to them belonged to the same type of religion as the worship of Isis and Mithra. Another bone of contention is the value of the mystery-religions of Greece. The very able German scholars who have written on the subject, such as Reitzenstein and still more Rohde, seem to me much too unsympathetic in their treatment of the mystery-cults. Lastly, some competent critics have lately urged that this side of Christianity owed more to Judaism—Hellenised Judaism, of course— than has been hitherto supposed.

Plato in the *Phaedo* says that ' those who established our mysteries declare that all who come to Hades uninitiated will lie in the mud ; while he who has been purified and initiated will dwell with the gods. For, as they say in the mysteries, Many are the thyrsus-bearers, but few are the inspired.' This sacramentalism was not unchallenged, as we have already seen from Plato himself. Diogenes is said to have asked whether the robber Pataecion was better off in the other world than the hero Epaminondas, because the former had been initiated, and the latter had not. But Orphism, though liable to degradation, purified and elevated the old Bacchic rites. As Miss Harrison says, the Bacchanals hoped to attain unity with God by intoxication, the Orphics by abstinence. The way to salvation was now through ' holiness ' (ὁσιότης). To the initiated the assurance was given, ' Happy and

blessed one !   Thou shalt be a god instead of a mortal.'
To be a god meant for a Greek simply to be immortal ;
the Orphic saint was delivered from the painful cycle
of recurring births and deaths.   And Orphic purity
was mainly, though not entirely, the result of moral
discipline.   Cumont says that the mystery-cults brought
with them two new things—mysterious means of puri-
fication by which they proposed to cleanse away the
defilements of the soul, and the assurance that an
immortality of bliss would be the reward of piety.
The truth, says Mr. H. A. A. Kennedy, was presented
to them in the guise of divine revelations, esoteric doctrines to be carefully concealed from the gaze of the
profane, doctrines which placed in their hands a powerful apparatus for gaining deliverance from the assaults
of malicious demonic influences, and above all for
overcoming the relentless tyranny of fate.   This
demonology was believed everywhere under the Roman
Empire, the period of which Mr. Kennedy is thinking
in this sentence, and it has unfortunately left more
traces in St. Paul's epistles than we like to allow.
The formation of brotherhoods for mystic worship was
also an important step in the development of Greek
religion.   These brotherhoods were cosmopolitan, and
seem to have flourished especially at great seaports.
They were thoroughly popular, drawing most of their
support from the lower classes, and within them
national and social distinctions were ignored.   Their
ultimate aim cannot be summed up better than in
Mr. Kennedy's words—' to raise the soul above the
transiency of perishable matter through actual union
with the Divine.'   It has been usual to distinguish
between the dignified and officially recognised mysteries,

like those of Eleusis, and the independent voluntary
associations, some of which became important. But
there was probably no essential difference between
them. In neither case was there much definite teaching ; the aim, as Aristotle says, was to produce a
certain emotional state (οὐ μαθεῖν τι δεῖν ἀλλὰ παθεῖν).
A Passion-play was enacted amid the most impressive
surroundings, and we need not doubt that the moral
effect was beneficial and sometimes profound. When
the Egyptian mysteries of Isis and Osiris were fused
with the Hellenic, a type of worship was evolved which
was startlingly like Christianity. A famous Egyptian
text contains the promise : ' As truly as Osiris lives,
shall he [the worshipper] live ; as truly as Osiris is not
dead, shall he not die.' The thanksgiving to Isis at
the end of the *Metamorphoses* of Apuleius is very
beautiful in itself, though it is an odd termination of
a licentious novel. The Hermetic literature also contains doctrine of a markedly Johannine type, as notably
in a prayer to Isis : ' Glorify me, as I have glorified
the name of thy son Horus.' I agree with those critics
(Cumont, Zielinski, and others) who attach the ' higher '
Hermetic teaching to genuinely Hellenistic sources.
But it is not necessary to ascribe all the higher teaching
to Greece and the lower to Egypt.

Much of St. Paul's theology belongs to the same
circle of ideas as these mysteries. Especially important
is the psychology which divides human nature into
spirit, soul, and body, spirit being the divine element
into which those who are saved are transformed by
the ' knowledge of God.' This knowledge is a supernatural gift, which (in the *Poimandres*) confers
' deification.' St. Paul usually prefers ' Pneuma ' as

the name of this highest part of human nature ; in the
Hermetic literature it is not easy to distinguish between
Pneuma and Nous, which holds exactly the same place
in Neoplatonism. The notion of salvation as consisting in the knowledge of God is not infrequent in St.
Paul ; compare, for example, 1 Cor. xiii. 12 and a still
more important passage, Phil. ii. 8–10. This knowledge was partly communicated by visions and revelations, to which St. Paul attributed some importance ;
but on the whole he is consistent in treating knowledge
as the crown and consummation of faith. The spiritual
transformation of the personality is the centre of
St. Paul's eschatology. ' Though our outward man
perish, our inward man is renewed day by day.' The
' spiritual body ' is the vehicle of the transformed
personality ; for ' flesh and blood cannot inherit the
kingdom of God.' The expression ' to be born again '
is common in the mystery literature.

It would be easy to find many other parallels in
St. Paul's epistles, in the Johannine books which are
the best commentary upon them, and in the theology
of the Greek Fathers, which prove the close connexion
of early Christianity with the mystery-religions of the
empire. Twenty years ago it might have been worth
while to draw out these resemblances in greater detail,
even in so summary a survey as this. But at present
the tendency is, if not to overestimate the debt of the
Christian religion to Hellenistic thought and worship,
at any rate to ignore the great difference between the
higher elements in the mystery-religions, which the new
faith could gladly and readily assimilate, and the lower
type, the theosophy, magic, and theurgy, which was
not in the line of Hellenic development, and is not to be

found in the New Testament. Wendland, always a judicious critic, has said very truly that St. Paul stands to the mystery-religions as Plato to Orphism ; they are not the centre of his religious life, but they gave him effective forms of expression for his religious experience. Or, as Weinel says, ' St. Paul's doctrine of the Spirit and of Christ is not an imitation of mystery-doctrine, but inmost personal experience metaphysically interpreted after the manner of his time.' Writers like Loisy, who say that for St. Paul Jesus was ' a Saviour God, after the manner of Osiris, Attis, or Mithra,' and who proceed to draw out obvious parallels between the sufferings, death, and resurrection of these mythological personages and the Gospels of the Christian Church, surely forget that St. Paul was a Jew, and that there are some transformations of which the religious mind is incapable. He never speaks of Christ as a ' Saviour God.'   Even more perverse are the arguments which are used to prove that the centre of St. Paul's religion was a gross and materialistic sacramental magic. The apostle, whose antipathy to ritual in every shape is stamped upon all his writings, who thanks God that he baptised very few of the Corinthians, who declares that ' Christ sent him not to baptise, but to preach the Gospel,' is accused of regarding baptism as ' an *opus operatum* which secures a man's admission into the kingdom apart from the character of his future conduct.'   And yet in the Epistle to the Romans, as Weinel says, ' baptism only once enters his mind, and the Lord's Supper not even once.' Baptism for him is no *opus operatum*, but a ceremony of social significance, a symbol conditioning a deeper experience of divine grace, already embraced by faith. These same critics proceed to illustrate St. Paul's doctrine of the Lord's Supper by references to the religion of the Aztecs and other barbarians. But it is hardly worth while to argue with those who suppose that a man with St. Paul's upbringing and culture could have dallied with the notion of ' eating a god.' The ' table of the Lord ' is the table at which the Lord is the spiritual host, not the table on which his flesh is placed. Does any one suppose that ' the table of demons ' which is contrasted with the ' table of the Lord ' is the table at which demons are eaten? Demons had no bodies, as we learn from the οὐκ εἰμι δαιμόνιον ἀσώματον of a well-known passage in a New Testament manuscript.

Crude sacramentalism certainly came in later. Its parentage may be traced, if we will, to those mystery-mongers whom Plato mentions with disapproval. If Hellenism is the name of a way of thinking, this form of religion is not healthy Hellenism ; that it was held by many Hellenes cannot be denied.

The biblical doctrine of the Fall of Man, which the Hebrews would never have evolved for themselves, remained an otiose dogma in Jewish religion. It was revivified in Christianity under Greek influence. Man, as Empedocles and others had taught, was ' an exile and vagabond from God ' ; his body was his tomb ; he is clothed in ' an alien garment of flesh.' He is in a fallen state and needs redemption. Hellenism had become a religion of redemption ; the empire was quite ready to accept this part of Christian doctrine. The sin of Adam became the first scene in the great drama of humanity, which led up to the Atonement. At the same time the whole process was never mere history ;

its deepest meaning was enacted in the life-story of each individual. Greek thought gave this turn to dogmas which for a Jew would have been a flat historical recital. In modern times the earlier scenes in the story, at any rate, are looked upon as little more than the dramatisation of the normal experience of a human soul. But Greek thought, while it remained true to type, never took sin so tragically as Christianity has done. The struggle against evil has become sterner than it ever was for the Greeks. It must, however, be remembered that the large majority of professing Christians do not trouble themselves much about their sins, and that the best of the Greeks were thoroughly in earnest in seeking to amend their lives.

Redemption was brought to earth by a Redeemer who was both God and Man. This again was in accordance with Greek ideas. The Mediator between God and Man must be fully divine, since an intermediate Being would be in touch with neither side. The victory of Athanasius was in no sense a defeat for Hellenism. The only difficulty for a Greek thinker was that an Incarnate God ought to be impassible. This was a puzzle only for philosophers ; popular religion saw no difficulty in a *Christus patiens.* The doctrine of the Logos brought Christianity into direct affinity with both Platonism and Stoicism, and the Second Person of the Trinity was invested with the same attributes as the Nous of the Neoplatonists. But the attempt to equate the Trinity with the three divine hypostases of Plotinus was no more successful than the later attempt of Hegel to set the Trinity in the framework of his philosophy.

The subject of eschatology is so vast that it is hopeless to deal with it, even in the most summary fashion, in one paragraph. It is usually said that the resurrection of the body is a Jewish doctrine, the immortality of the soul a Greek doctrine. But the Jews were very slow to bring the idea of a future life into their living faith ; to this day it does not seem to be of much importance in Judaism. Some form of Millenarianism —a reign of the saints on earth—would seem to be the natural form for Jewish hopes to take. This belief, which was the earliest mould into which the treasure of the new revelation was poured, has never quite disappeared from the Church, and in times of excitement and upheaval it tends to reassert itself. The maturest Greek philosophy regards eternity as the divine mode of existence, while mortals are born, live, and die in time. Man is a microcosm, in touch with every rung of the ladder of existence ; and he is potentially a ' participator ' in the divine mode of existence, which he can make his own by living, so far as may be, in detachment from the vain shadows and perishable goods of earth. That this conception of immortality has had a great influence upon Christian thought and practice needs no demonstration. It is and always has been the religion of the mystic. But the Orphic tradition, with its pictures of purgatory and of eternal bliss and torment, has on the whole dominated the other two in popular Christian belief. It has been stripped of its accessories—the belief in reincarnation and the transmigration of souls, doctrines which maintain a somewhat uneasy existence within the scheme of the Neoplatonists. The picture of future retribution is even more terrifying without them. Both the philo-

sophical and the popular beliefs about the other world
are far more Greek than Jewish ; but the attempt to
hold these very discrepant beliefs together has reduced
Christian eschatology to extreme confusion, and many
Christians have given up the attempt to formulate any
theories about what are called the Four Last Things.
On such a mysterious subject, definiteness is neither
to be expected nor desired. The original Gospel does
not encourage the natural curiosity of man to know
his future fate ; and the three types of eschatology
which we have described have all their value as representing different aspects of religious faith and hope.
We must after all confess the truth of St. Paul's words,
that ' eye hath not seen, nor ear heard, neither hath it
entered into the heart of man to conceive, the things
that God hath prepared for them that love him.' The
same apostle reminds us that ' now we see through a
mirror, in riddles, and know only in part ' ; the face-to-
face vision, and the knowledge which unites the knower
and the known, may be ours when we have finished our
course. In these words, which recall Plato's famous
myth of the Cave, St. Paul is fundamentally at one
with the Platonists ; and it may well be that it is by
this path that our contemporaries may recover that
belief in eternal life which is at present burning very
dimly among us.

In conclusion, what has the religion of the Greeks to
teach us that we are most in danger of forgetting ?   In
a word, it is the faith that Truth is our friend, and that
the knowledge of Truth is not beyond our reach.   Faith
in honest seeking ($\zeta\acute{\eta}\tau\eta\sigma\iota\varsigma$) is at the heart of the Greek
view of life.   ' Those who would rightly judge of truth,'
says Aristotle, ' must be arbitrators, not litigants.'

' Happy is he who has learnt the value of research '
(ἱστορία), says Euripides in a fragment. Curiosity, as
the Greeks knew and the Middle Ages knew not, is
a virtue, not a vice. Nature, for Plato, is God's vice-
gerent and revealer, the Soul of the universe. Human
nature can participate in the divine; no one has
proclaimed this more strongly. Nature is for us;
chaos and ' necessity ' are the enemy. The divorce
between religion and humanism began, it must be
admitted, under Plato's successors, who unhappily were
indifferent to natural science, and did not even follow
the best light that was to be had in physical knowledge. In the Dark Ages, when the link with Greece
was broken, the separation became absolute. The
luxuriant mythology of the early Greeks was not unscientific. In the absence of knowledge gaps were
filled up by the imagination, and the ' method of trial
and error.' The dramatic fancy which creates myths
is the raw material of both poetry and science. Of
course, religious myths may come to be a bar to progress in science; they do so when, in a rationalising
age, the question comes to be one of fact or fiction.
It is a mistake to suppose that the faith of a ' post-
rational ' age, to use a phrase of Santayana, can be the
same as that of an unscientific age, even when it uses
the same formulas. The Greek spirit itself is now
calling us away from some of the vestments of Greek
tradition. The choice before us is between a ' post-
rational ' traditionalism, fundamentally sceptical, prag-
matistic, and intellectually dishonest, and a trust in
reason which rests really on faith in the divine Logos,
the self-revealing soul of the universe. It is the belief
of the present writer that the unflinching eye and the

open mind will bring us again to the feet of Christ, to whom Greece, with her long tradition of free and fearless inquiry, became a speedy and willing captive, bringing her manifold treasures to Him, in the well-grounded confidence that He was not come to destroy but to fulfil.

SCIENCE AND THEOLOGY

It has been my privilege to read all the essays in this volume.[1] I hope the critics and the public will endorse my opinion that they reach a high standard of excellence, and deal in a masterly manner with questions of the greatest interest and importance. The instructions of the editor were that the essays should be solid, but not too technical for the general reader. These conditions have, I think, been observed admirably.

It was also stipulated that the essays should not be directly apologetic in tendency. The book is neither a defence of Christianity nor a criticism of it. Its object is to make clear what the present state of the relations between religion and science actually is. This restriction also has been observed, but the writers have quite rightly not contented themselves with a colourless presentation. The book, after all, has a practical object, that of indicating possible terms of peace, or a *modus vivendi*, between religion and science. The writers are not all agreed as to how this is to be brought about ; but the differences between them are, in my opinion, less remarkable than their general harmony. After reading the whole volume, one is inclined to feel confident that a reconciliation is much nearer than it seemed to be fifty years ago.

[1] *Science, Religion and Reality*, Sheldon Press, 1925.

My task in summing up the work of the essayists—
it is not a debate, for the contributors have not seen
each other's work—is very difficult. There are some
subjects dealt with in the book with which I have
only a superficial acquaintance ; and there are others
which I should myself have treated somewhat differently. I have thought myself bound not to depart
from the rules laid down for the essayists, and in
particular not to turn all their arguments into an
apology for the Christian faith. A certain degree of
neutrality is, I think, imposed upon me by the task
which I have accepted, of attempting to sum up and
bring together the contributions of the different
writers. And yet I have felt that a mere *résumé* is
not what is desired from me. There may be one or
two gaps which I should try to fill. The position of
one writer may satisfy me better than that of another.
If, on reading the whole book, a clear notion of acceptable terms of peace has suggested itself to my mind,
it will be desirable that I should say so, and that I
should not shrink from ruling out suggestions which
seem to me impossible.

For instance, I have rejected with decision that
kind of agreement which rests on a delimitation of
territory. Some recent writers have said that there
can be no conflict between religion and science, because
they never meet. They move on different planes.
To this way of thinking belong all such bisections of
the field of experience as those which oppose sharply
to each other fact and value, reality and appearance,
the knowable and the unknowable, the visible and the
invisible, prose and poetry. To acknowledge such distinctions, and rest an agreement upon them, assigning

all on one side of the line to science and all on the other side to religion, is at best a proposal for an armistice; it can lead to no permanent peace. A religion which does not touch science, and a science which does not touch religion, are mutilated and barren. Not that religion can ever be a science, or science a religion; but we may hope for a time when the science of a religious man will be scientific, and the religion of a scientific man religious.

I have not concealed the fact that I write as a Christian. It would, I hope, be absurd for me to do so. But I have treated the religion of Christ as one of the permanent achievements or acquisitions of humanity like Hellenism and the Roman science of law and government. There are few scientific men, in this country at least, who would not allow so much as this, though the question remains how much of traditional Christianity is essential, and how much an accretion or an accommodation to transient conditions. This question will not be dealt with directly in this essay, though I shall not hide my conviction that some parts of the tradition are not integrally connected with the kernel of Christ's religion.

Following the usual practice now, the editor has divided the subject into two parts. The first part of the book is historical; in other words, it treats religion as a branch of anthropology. By usage, anthropology has come to mean chiefly the study of the backward races, though there is nothing in the name to exclude the social history of civilised man. In this section the relations between religion and science are brought down to recent times, and thus a transition is made to the second part, which may be called, in the broadest

sense of the word, philosophical. The importance
thus given to history will be generally approved,
though it has its dangers. It is right that we should
remember that we stand in the middle—or perhaps
nearer the beginning than the end—of a long evolutionary process, and that our thoughts and beliefs
are determined by the period at which we live. Our
civilisation has its distinguishing characteristics, like
the civilisation of classical antiquity, or of the Middle
Ages. We are what the past has made us ; and if
we can trace certain changes slowly at work in the
period preceding our own we may be able to predict
with some probability that these changes will continue,
for some time at least, to operate in the same direction.
The study of early history is certainly far more instructive in religion than in science. The rudimentary
science which may be discovered even among savages
is not interesting or important to modern research,
which discards obsolete hypotheses without scruple
or sentiment. The case is very different with religion,
if we allow the word to include myth, ritual, and
magic, through which religion has maintained its
position as a social force. Religion is a powerful
antiseptic, which preserves mummified customs that
have long outlasted their usefulness, and otiose dogmas
that have long lost their vitality. The history of
customs and beliefs which have been put under the
protection of religion is very instructive. It explains,
as nothing else can, the vast quantity of mere survivals which encumber modern life. Even outside
religious sanctions the race has contracted habits
which seem to be hard to eradicate in proportion to
the length of time during which they have existed.

These habits have become, as the proverb says, second nature. Rapid changes are impossible; even slow changes are exceedingly difficult. Nature, or habit, reasserts itself, though it has been expelled with a pitchfork. Religions, in the same way, tend strongly to revert to type. Stolid resistance to innovations is a policy which often justifies itself.

These are only some of the lessons which we may learn from history. But historicism, as we may call it, has been responsible for many errors and fallacies, especially in the most recent times. The tendency to judge movements of the human spirit by their roots instead of by their fruits is widespread, and in all the higher activities of mankind it is far less illuminating than the Aristotelian canon that the ' nature ' of a thing must be sought in its completed development, its final form. There have been writers who have treated all existing forms of religion as survivals of barbarous beliefs and customs. The error is no doubt associated with a very recent tendency to regard myth, ritual, and magic as the kernel instead of the husk of religion. If the essence of a religion were sought in the devotional life of its followers and in its influence upon the thought and action of the peoples among whom it flourishes, there would be less disposition to seek for explanations of it among the primitives of the past and the savages of the present.

Anthropologists of this type may learn something from the analogy of biology. The fact that gill-slits and a tail exist in the human embryo tells us something about the remote past of humanity, but nothing about its present or its future. It tells us nothing about Newton to know that he once had a tail. Religion in the higher sense, which alone seriously concerns us, is a phenomenon of civilised humanity. We do not care much how it began ; we want to understand it as it is or may be.

An even more serious objection is suggested by the extreme uncertainty of historical and anthropological records. In this field, if in any other, ' nothing worthy proving can be proven, nor yet disproven.' Laborious compilers may collect instances given by travellers of this or that quaint tribal custom, found in different parts of the world ; they may make ingenious theories as to the inner meaning of sacrifices and sacraments ; but can they really enter into the mind of the savage, and interpret his thoughts to civilised Europeans ? The savage, we may guess, could not explain himself if he would, and would not if he could ; for he is a shy person, imbued with the notion that certain things are not to be talked of to strangers. Some learned anthropologists have never seen a savage, and would be much alarmed if they met one ; others have travelled in barbarous countries, but have failed to master the very complicated native languages, which are not the same in any two tribes. There have been instances when the natives have wilfully made game of the investigator, whose motives for inquiring they cannot be expected to understand.

Consciously or unconsciously the champions of the historical method are often the victims of the great superstition of the last century, the belief in a natural law of progress. This delusion has been lately revived in a curiously crude form by the Italians who claim to represent the *dernier cri* in philosophy. When we find savagery called ' primitive,' and a sort of assump-

tion that the later in time is always the better, we may
suspect a survival of this superstition. Nobody treats
the history of art and poetry in this way, but the
delusion has not been completely abandoned in the
case of religion. We have discussions on what is
supposed to be a serious difficulty in the way of
accepting Christianity—that on the Christian hypothesis the highest revelation came to mankind nearly
two thousand years ago.

The truth is that all the great religions—Buddhism,
Christianity, and Islam—date from the millennium
which ends with the career of Mohammed ; and all of
them were at their best when they were fresh from
the mint. It is quite possible that religious genius
culminated at that stage in human history. Our
species has been in existence for half a million, perhaps
for a million years. The changes in bodily structure
which differentiate man from the other Primates
belong to a vast period of which there are few records.
Mental evolution has perhaps retarded the progress
of physical changes, and the use of tools seems to have
brought to an end the growth of the human brain.
Intrinsic progress there has been none, or very little,
for twenty thousand years. The vast accumulation
of knowledge, and of mechanical appliances, which we
call civilisation, may not be very favourable to religious
insight. Industrialism has been very injurious to art ;
may it not have injured religion also ? There are
reasons for thinking that civilisation has been bio-
logically a retrograde movement, which by no means
implies that it was not inevitable, or that a return from
it is possible. Man the tool-maker has made ' inanimate instruments ' (as Aristotle says) do his manual

work for him ; he is now trying to make them do his mental work for him. Nature has no objection—at a price. The price may be the progressive deterioration of our faculties. Our brains may follow our teeth, claws, and fur.

The temptation to confound accumulated knowledge and experience with intrinsic progress is almost irresistible ; but it must be resisted. It is quite unnecessary to go to Australia or Central Africa to find the savage ; he is our next-door neighbour. The mentality of the Stone Age exists on our platforms and in our pulpits. There is no superstition too absurd to find credence in modern England ; fetishes and taboos dominate London drawing-rooms. Dr. Malinowski's sojourn in Melanesia has convinced him that the mental processes of the South Sea islanders are very like those of Europeans. It is probably only politeness that prevented him from adding that a return to civilisation has convinced him that the mental processes of Europeans are very like those of Melanesians.

The belief in a law of progress, which is the soul of historicism, is a form of Millenarianism which constituted the secular religion of the nineteenth century. It was, of course, taken over by Christian progressives, who tried to find some warrant for it in the New Testament, where its only analogue is the apocalyptic Messianism which we find St. Paul and the author of the Fourth Gospel cautiously discarding. It is, however, very undesirable that Christianity should make friends with science by annexing a superstition which has nothing scientific about it. What we call progress is a biological episode which other species, such as the bees and ants, traversed long ago. The age of turmoil and experiment ended for them in the establishment of a stable civilisation, after which any further innovations have been severely and successfully discouraged. It is more likely than not that our species will come to rest in the same way, unless our present habits end in mutual extermination.

Dr. Malinowski's article shows the extreme importance of a distinction which is not always drawn, and the neglect of which has led to great confusion. Science is one thing, philosophies built upon science are another. The statement sometimes made, that mythology is primitive science, is an example of this error. Mythology is an attempt to account for facts in the natural order; it is more like primitive philosophy than primitive science. It is not true that the savage knows nothing of natural laws, or of the sequence of cause and effect. He has his own traditional lore which teaches him when to plough and sow, how to make weapons, boats, and tools, and whatever else belongs to the stage of culture in which he lives. In these essential matters the savage reasons and behaves very much like a civilised man.

And yet it is true that magic plays a large part in his life. It is resorted to in difficulties, and in connexion with mysterious and awe-inspiring events in the life of nature and of human beings. Magical rites gather round puberty, marriage, birth, death, and the corresponding processes in the vegetable world. Magic is an attempt to set in motion laws which the savage does not understand.

On the much-discussed distinction between magic and religion Dr. Malinowski seems to me to be right in rejecting the theory that magic is a private affair, while religion belongs to the community. There is much corporate magic, and much individual religion. The distinction is rather that magic always aims at producing some definite result, while primitive religion gives expression to mental states, such as sorrow, hope, and despair, without pursuing any practical aim. The separation cannot be made precise, for the cult of spirits, demons, and mythological personages has undoubtedly a practical object—namely, to placate these unseen but powerful beings, to avert their wrath and win their favour. Prayer has a practical object, though prayer is not a magical act. But the distinction is none the less valuable.

Dr. Malinowski emphasises the pragmatic and unspeculative character of religion among backward peoples. The savage (like the civilised man !) appeals to his gods and his priests when he finds himself in a quandary. The practical advantage of organised cult and sanctified custom is to stabilise valuable results already won. Innovation is made artificially difficult ; but most innovations, like most mutations in a species, are deleterious. Tribal law also keeps a social aggregate together, and gives it a great advantage in lawless societies, where raids and wars are even more frequent than under civilisation. But though the survival value of cohesion may be the real explanation of tribal ritual and custom, that is not the conscious motive of the discipline. It is honestly believed that the transgression of custom, the mishandling of ritual, and the commission of acts which shock the conscience of the community, will call down upon the tribe collectively the vengeance of the higher powers. It is a great mistake to suppose that beliefs which have, or which once had, a survival value, are adhered to because they are known to have a survival value. They are maintained with equal zeal when they are manifestly disadvantageous, when, for example, they prescribe painful and even dangerous operations as part of the ceremony of initiation into full membership of the tribe. The answer, ' It is the custom,' is final for the savage, as for the lady of fashion. There is no other reason why they behave in a certain way, so it is useless to push further inquiries.

The statement that myth is not a speculation, nor the result of contemplation of nature or of the desire to explain natural phenomena, but rather a historical record of an important event, out of which a ritual act has been born, is manifestly true only of one class of myths. The savage is not without curiosity ; he is a natural ' animist,' and he enjoys poetical and picturesque descriptions. His cosmological myths may be described as poetical nature-philosophy ; they have no close connexion with his tribal customs and disciplines.

Before leaving this subject it is worth while to notice that belief in the supernatural presupposes a belief in natural law. Where there is no law, there is no miracle. The savage dislikes the idea of a lawless universe ; and when he sees countless things happening of which he can give no rational explanation, he assumes that there is another causative principle, besides the natural order on the regularity of which he counts in sowing his fields. Having once restored his belief in law and order by this hypothesis, he is content to ascribe wind and rain and everything else

that seems irregular to supernatural agency, and then
to speculate whether this power is in any way amenable
to control. Rain-making is an almost universal
industry among savages, and we are told that twenty
years ago there were still old women in the Shetlands
who made a livelihood by selling winds to seamen.
It is a slow process to find out the limits of the possible ;
the principle of causation is fully realised, but its
operation is unknown. Lubbock gives an example of
a Kaffir who broke a piece of a stranded anchor and
died soon afterwards, upon which all the Kaffirs
looked upon the anchor as alive, and saluted it respect-
fully whenever they passed near it. We behave in
the same way when our science is at fault. A house
in which there have been two deaths from cancer is
not easily let. The savage eats a tiger, or a slain
enemy, to make him fierce ; the British parent stuffs
his boys with roast beef to make them strong. There
are to this day, I believe, remedies in the *Materia
Medica* which have no origin except sympathetic
magic.

Dr. Malinowski sums up magic as ' pseudo-science,'
and yet feels bound to find a justification for it and
a value in it. It represents, he thinks, ' the sublime
folly of hope,' which has encouraged men to face life
with courage, and therefore with some chance of
success. Without disputing this, we must remember
that the false science has been the deadliest enemy of
the true. Religion is the guardian of all the higher
values ; but magic is a will-o'-the-wisp which tempts
men to their destruction. We have only to think of
the resort to magic in modern times, to stop an
epidemic, to cure diseases, to protect soldiers against

bullets, to wash away sin, and to predict the future, to realise that we are dealing with an evil thing, a genuine survival of savagery. True religion and science have here a bond of sympathy—they have a common enemy to destroy.

The next essay, by Dr. Charles Singer, takes us into the heart of the subject, the relations between religion and science, treated historically. It should be supplemented by the two brilliant contributions of Dr. Singer to ' The Legacy of Greece,' in which justice is done, almost for the first time, to the achievements of Greek science in the classical period. The subject is an immense one, too great, as the writer would admit, to be summarised adequately in one essay, while a summary of a summary, in this concluding paper, would obviously be worthless. Accordingly, I shall not attempt to make any comments on the relations of religion and science in antiquity, nor shall I discuss the causes why science decayed and died under the Roman Empire. The Dark Ages, and even the Middle Ages which followed them, are to the scientist a melancholy chapter in human history. I shall confine my remarks to the modern period, beginning with the revival of learning in Italy. It should be said that Dr. Singer treats the period between Newton and our own day very slightly, leaving it to be dealt with, from a rather different point of view, by Professor Aliotta.

Dr. Singer ' omits any discussion of the revival of learning as irrelevant ' to his subject. His reason is that the scholars of the Renaissance were antiquarians rather than researchers, and confined themselves chiefly to unearthing the remains of the science of antiquity.

It is not easy to see what else they could have done. Greek science had done wonderful things, and had then perished and been forgotten. To disinter what could be found of these treasures was an indispensable preliminary to a new advance. And the great name of Leonardo da Vinci shows that the Italians were ready enough to turn their new knowledge to practical discoveries.

The truth is, I think, that the Reformation not only checked but obscured the scientific progress which had begun in the century which preceded it. The Reformation and Counter-Reformation were, from the point of view of secular culture, a retrogression. The Humanism of the fifteenth century was more literary and artistic than scientific, but it was ready to welcome scientific research, and would in a short time have freed itself from the ecclesiastical shackles which hampered its development. But the outbreak of fierce religious war in the sixteenth century destroyed the hopes of the humanists. It is useless to ask whether the Catholics or the Protestants were the most guilty of this set-back to civilisation. It was not Catholicism or Protestantism, but the state of war between them, which had this evil consequence. Christianity, when unmenaced, is no enemy to culture ; but as soon as war is declared, every nation or institution must subordinate all other considerations to the necessity of victory. It must curtail liberty of action, speech, and thought. It must devise and publish a fighting propaganda, in which the claims of truth and fairness are cynically disregarded. It must rest its claims on very clear and simple issues, which all can understand. When two religions are at war, there is no call for deep philosophers or subtle theologians. Both sides will rest their case on some external authority ; their dogmas will be coarsened and materialised ; they will both, while the struggle lasts, become religions of a narrow and brutal type.

It was, I believe, the terrible Wars of Religion that made the fatal rift between religion and science which we are now trying to close. It was a really disastrous accident that the greatest problem which the Christian Church has ever had to face was thrust upon it when it was distracted by an internecine conflict. That problem was the destruction of the geocentric view of the universe by the discoveries of Copernicus and Galileo. The momentous consequences of these discoveries were not at first apparent. Copernicus had no wish to provoke a battle with the Church, and his writings were not published till after his death ; Galileo was intimidated and persecuted. This was only to be expected ; but the Church of the Roman Renaissance would probably have withdrawn from an untenable position. Not so the Churches of the Spanish Inquisition, of Luther and Calvin. Catholic and Protestant vied with each other in denouncing the new theories. Nor has this disaster ever been retrieved. By degrees the Copernican astronomy has passed into the region of common knowledge ; and though Rome put it under the ban, the devout Romanist is no longer expected to assert that the earth is the centre of the universe. But the retreat of Church authority has been gradual and, as usual, unavowed ; there has never come a time when it seemed urgently necessary to consider the new situation created by the revolution in astronomy. The task has been put off from generation to generation, and to this day little has been done to relieve the strain upon the intellect and conscience of the Christian world.   Those Churchmen who airily declare that there is no longer any conflict between Christianity and science are either very thoughtless or are wilfully shutting their eyes. There is a very serious conflict, and the challenge was presented not in the age of Darwin, but in the age of Copernicus and Galileo.

The discovery that the earth, instead of being the centre of a finite universe, like a dish with a dish-cover above it, is a planet revolving round the sun, which itself is only one of millions of stars, tore into shreds the Christian map of the universe.   Until that time the ordinary man, whether educated or uneducated, had pictured the sum of things as a three-storeyed building, consisting of heaven, the abode of God, the angels, and beatified spirits ; our earth ; and the infernal regions, where the devil, his angels, and lost souls are imprisoned and tormented.   The mystics had been allowed to hold and expound a more spiritual philosophy ; there was never, I believe, a time when the saying that God has His centre everywhere and His circumference nowhere was condemned as unorthodox. But most certainly heaven and hell were geographical expressions.   The articles in the Creeds on the descent of Christ into Hades, and His ascent into heaven, affirm no less ; and it is obvious that the bodily resurrection of Christ is intimately connected with the bodily ascension.   The new cosmography thus touched the faith of the Creeds very closely.   That the Church interpreted these doctrines literally is shown by the Anglican Articles of Religion, which declare that Christ ascended into heaven ' with flesh, bones, and all things appertaining to the perfection of man's nature ; and there sitteth.' Transubstantiation was denied on the ground that the body of Christ is in heaven, and that it is contrary to the properties of a natural body to be in more than one place at the same time.

The Copernican astronomy, and all the knowledge about the heavens which has been built upon this foundation, leave no room for a geographical heaven. Space seems to be infinite, or as some prefer to say, boundless—a distinction not very intelligible except to the mathematicians; and among all the stars, planets, satellites, and nebulae which are sparsely scattered over its vast empty distances we can hardly imagine that one has been chosen as the abode of the Creator and the site of the heavenly Jerusalem. The belief in a subterranean place of punishment, which has not been disproved by astronomy, seems to have faded away without making any commotion, though I am told (I speak under correction) that the law of the land is still committed to it. If I buy a square mile of ground, I become the proprietor not only of 640 acres of the earth's surface, but of a cube with its base reaching ' from heaven to hell.'

There are also difficulties about time, but these are less serious, because though the Church rejected the belief, held by most of the Greek philosophers, that the universe had no temporal beginning, there is no reason why creation in time should be erected into a dogma. Few would say that this a vital question. Nor does the doctrine of evolution cause any serious difficulty to Christians who have rejected verbal inspiration. It was a shock to many to hear that the human race has developed out of non-human ancestors; but the question is only about the methods of creation;

Darwinism has inflicted no injury upon the Christian faith.

There are at least three positions between which the Church may make its choice.   It may condemn modern astronomy as impious and heretical, as the Inquisitors and the Reformers agreed in doing.   Luther denounced Copernicus as a fool who dared to contradict the Bible, ' an upstart astrologer who dared to set his own   authority   above   that   of   Holy   Scripture.' Melanchthon thought that those who set forth such theories must have no sense of decency ; and Calvin asked, ' Who will venture to place the authority of Copernicus above that of Holy Scripture ? '   The Roman Church has lately condemned the doctrine of evolution in terms not less stringent than these.   This is one possible policy.   It declares that there can be no truce between science and religion till science has renounced its errors and accepted the authority of the Church.

A second policy, equally open to the Church, is to admit that these traditional doctrines do not belong to the natural order with which science deals, but to claim that they possess a higher truth, to which science cannot reach.   This may be done by regarding these and other dogmas as symbolic of eternal truths, aids to the imagination in forming clear conceptions of revealed truth in a region beyond the compass of our senses. The apologist for tradition who takes this line will not be content to justify the use of symbols.   He will argue that science itself is an imaginative construction ; that the supposed laws of nature are not derived directly from our observation of the behaviour of atoms and molecules ; that what are called the assured results of science are the work of the mind upon an abstract view of reality, which neglects the values and qualitative properties of things, and attempts to construct a universe out of mathematics and chemistry. This disparagement of science as incapable of forming any adequate synthesis may be pushed so far as to reach what is called acosmism, the theory which denies the objective existence of the world or universe. The conclusion will then be, that though the dogmas in question are symbolic, they are much nearer to truth than the scientific laws which pronounce them to be impossible.

The third policy is to recognise that all theological doctrines which rest upon the geocentric theory must be recast, inasmuch as the results of astronomical science are, in their main conclusions, unassailable. I do not think I underestimate the seriousness of this step, nor the great difficulties in taking it. But anything, I believe, is better than trying to conceal an open sore which destroys our joy and peace in believing. If we adopt this third policy, we shall be driven to think of God less anthropomorphically, and of heaven as a state rather than a place—a state, too, which is eternal in a deeper sense than that of unending time-succession. But I cannot pursue this subject without transgressing the limits set for writers in this volume.

If I had any doubts that the religion of Christ can and will weather the storm, if I had any doubts that it is entirely independent of any false opinions about the nature of the universe, my readers may be certain that I should not have spoken as I have done. If I believed that Christianity stands or falls with a Ptolemaic universe, either I should be obliged to take the painful

course of confessing that I have believed and taught all
my life a creed which is as outworn as Paganism, or I
should do like thousands of others—I should hold my
tongue. But I am quite confident that this crisis will
be surmounted if the Church has the faith and courage,
and, above all, the common honesty, to face it candidly.
Only let us hear no more of clergymen thanking God
that theology and science are now reconciled, for
unhappily it is not true.

The next essay, that of Professor Aliotta, leads us on
to a new field. In the last paragraphs we have considered science as a steadily advancing army of
ascertained facts, with which religious tradition is often
at variance, and with which it must come to some sort
of agreement. Professor Aliotta shows us science on
the defensive, science divided against itself. In his
famous book, translated into English under the title
of ' The Idealistic Reaction against Science,' he has
brought together the very various hostile forces which
are assailing the fortress of Naturalism from different
sides. He finds that the dominant tendency in modern
philosophy is a reaction from ' intellectualism.' ' The
ruined shrines of the goddess of reason are invaded by
the rebel forces of feeling, will, imagination, and every
obscure and primitive instinct.' The blind power of
impulse has been exalted, and the guidance of the
intellect abandoned. Theosophy, occultism, magic,
and spiritualism have returned to the places from which
they seemed to have been finally banished. The
Professor traces for us the causes and progress of this
astonishing revolt against the view of the world which
not long ago seemed to be triumphant.

Even Kant, while discerning beyond the realm of

mathematics and physics that of ethics and aesthetics, considered these as outside the pale of true knowledge, which belongs to mathematics and physics alone. Hence arose the agnosticism of writers like Du Bois-Reymond, Huxley, and Spencer. But Spencer in his language about the Unknowable was approaching the mystics without knowing it. Since his time reflection has shown clearly that mechanism and evolution are two concepts which do not agree together. Mechanism asserts quantitative permanence and determination by mathematical law ; evolution asserts qualitative transformation which cannot be calculated mathematically. The doctrine of evolution rehabilitates history, and destroys the rigidity of the mechanical method. In practice it is associated with a valuation for which mathematics can find no place. A still harder blow was dealt when science itself began to be treated historically as a mental habit in process of evolution, the direction of this evolution being determined not by correspondence to external truth, but by practical human needs. This is the genesis of pragmatism, which disintegrates the whole structure of science, and incidentally bids every superstition which seems to work, to take heart of grace.

The varieties of Voluntarism, which starts with Kant's primacy of the practical reason, but carries this doctrine much further, cannot here be discussed. On the other hand, the general tendency of Hegelianism is to regard the world, both as given by experience and as constructed by science in its concepts, as an illusory appearance of a deeper reality, to the understanding of which we are led by speculative philosophy. The Hegelians, however, though their audacious claims for dialectic as the revealer of reality may make them impatient of laborious research, are not such enemies of science as the other schools enumerated by Professor Aliotta. In this they resemble the school of Plato, which allowed science to die, but welcomed its rebirth at the Renaissance.

There is a French school which strikes at Naturalism by affirming the contingency of natural laws. This is the thesis of Boutroux; Bergson seems to reduce the universe to a stream of forces flowing in no definite direction, a shoreless river deriving the strength for its renewal from some blind and unintelligent impulse. ' With all his metaphors,' says Aliotta, ' Bergson fails to convince us that continuous creative activity can give birth to practical discontinuous activity, and this activity in its turn to the objective world with all its determinations.' A more fundamental criticism is that a philosophy which has no place for the intelligence is a contradiction in terms.

In the last part of his book Aliotta discusses the influence of new mathematical theories as shaking the foundations of a materialistic philosophy. I must leave this topic to those who are qualified to deal with it. It is the subject of Professor Eddington's essay, which follows that of Professor Aliotta. I will only say that an outsider like myself feels a strong suspicion that the new instrument with which Einstein has presented the mathematicians is being put to uses for which it was never intended. I cannot see how a purely mathematical theory can either prove or disprove materialism. In fact, I am still unconvinced that it has much importance either for the metaphysician or for the theologian.

It appears to me that Professor Aliotta might have kept further apart the philosophical revolt against intellectualism and the revolt of biology and psychology against mechanism. The former belongs to epistemology, the theory of knowledge ; the latter belongs to pure natural science. The reaction against intellectualism is, on the whole, hostile to the claims of science ; the revolt against the tyranny of mathematics and physics is justified by the fact that these sciences have not succeeded in explaining the phenomena of life ; it is suspected that they are not, as was once supposed, universally valid principles. Thus we find some of our leading biologists inclining to some form of animism or vitalism, without showing the slightest tendency to disparage the claim of natural science to interpret the truth of phenomena, or to follow the pragmatists in denying the possibility of a disinterested and successful pursuit of things as they really are. The anti-intellectualist movement seems to me to lead to sceptical subjectivism. It discredits the authority of science, but it is equally damaging to religion, or at any rate to Christianity. For Christianity aims at nothing less than absolute truth. The Christian God is not only relative to human needs ; He is not only the ideal of human efforts. To put it technically, Christian philosophy cannot dispense with ontology ; the modern division of philosophy into the theory of knowledge, psychology, and ethics cannot be a philosophy of the Christian religion. If this be granted, the metaphysics of science needs rather more consideration than it has received in the body of this volume, and I propose to offer a few additional considerations on this subject.

It is a common error to speak of the doctrine of science when what is meant is Naturalism, which is a philosophy advocated by many students of science. Much confusion would be avoided if it were realised how little of what is called Naturalism depends directly on the results of nature-study. Let us then consider what Naturalism means.

It arose as a protest against supernaturalism, and as such has existed from the atomistic theory of Democritus to modern materialism. We find it opposing all mythology and miracle, insisting that throughout nature there runs a constant association of cause and effect, so that whatever happens could be explained simply and adequately if we knew its natural antecedents. As knowledge advanced, the hope was strengthened that all things would be discovered to be bound together in an uniform and necessary system. In almost all naturalistic theories we find an aversion from the idea of purpose. Teleology is banished as well as supernatural intervention. The machine of nature must somehow run by itself.

Now we have to distinguish between two widely different developments of Naturalism. One of these tends to an apotheosis of nature, as the life of a world-soul, which may become the object of religious reverence. Instead of ending in atheism, Naturalism may end in pantheism. This has been one of the most important lines of human thought. It is well represented in Greek philosophy, and has been the creed of many great men in modern times, of whom Goethe may serve as the type. As an example of this kind of Naturalism, ' touched with emotion,' I will quote some beautiful but little-known lines by Constance Naden :

Yes, thou shalt die ; but these almighty forces,
   That meet to form thee, live for evermore ;
They hold the stars in their eternal courses,
   And shape the long sand-grasses on the shore.

Be calmly glad, thine own true kindred seeing
   In fire and storm, in flowers with dew impearled ;
Rejoice in thine imperishable being
   One with the essence of the boundless world.

It might be better not to call this pantheistic creed Naturalism, reserving the name for the belief that the whole system of nature is calculable in terms of mathematics and mechanics. This is a clearer and more exact theory than the other ; for pantheism is generally a conglomerate of animism, poetical fancy, and mysticism ; it soon leaves the domain of exact science. True Naturalism is determined to keep within this domain, and to reduce all phenomena under a few simple, easily formulated laws. All must be measurable and ponderable.

With this object Naturalism selects as the normative sciences mathematics, physics, chemistry, and mechanics. All the phenomena of life and change, all the operations of the human mind, in spite of their apparent freedom and independence, must be theoretically capable of being reduced to problems in physics and chemistry. In its desire to find a quantitative calculus for everything alike, Naturalism divests life, whether physical or spiritual, of all that separates it from the inanimate and inorganic. So far from deifying nature, like pantheism, it devitalises it. Pantheism is romanticist, Naturalism is positivistic. Clear-sighted pantheists have expressed a strong dislike to Naturalism.

But though these two developments are antagonistic,

the popular mind easily and frequently confuses them.
The same persons who speak of men as mere machines,
the cunningest of nature's clocks, will try to bring down
will and instinct into the lowest stages of existence.
They do not realise how much they are borrowing, quite
illegitimately, from idealism, poetry, and religion, and
while they profess to build upon Naturalism an edifying
and attractive philosophy of life, they disguise from
themselves and others the bare and abject poverty of
the scheme which alone can be supported by their
primary hypothesis. One might go further and say
that even materialism could not exist if there were
nothing real except matter and energy.

The method of Naturalism is simplification. Its
ideal is to find one simple law under which everything may be brought and explained. This law can
only be purely quantitative, and since qualitative differences are incommensurable, they must be neglected
altogether. This arbitrary rejection of all the ' imponderables,' which in philosophy as in politics are
the most important factors of experience and deter-
minants of action, is an even more comprehensive
error than the omission to consider the fact of consciousness, which has so often been brought home to
Naturalism. It is, however, this latter mistake which
has caused the revolt against Naturalism within the
ranks of science itself. Naturalism is driven, by its
passion for simplification, to assume that all mental
processes are the accompaniments of material changes,
and that the material changes are the causes, while the
mental processes are inert consequences, mere ' epiphe-
nomena.' Thus the broad and deep gulf which, in our
experience, divides the living from the dead, the organic

from the inorganic, is obliterated ; the inanimate is made the norm by which the animate is to be explained. The method of simplification demands an even greater sacrifice. Physics and chemistry are theoretically capable of reduction to the fundamental laws of movement in general ; the end of the simplifying process is a statement of the nature of reality in mathematical symbols, which are valid whether there is anything corresponding to them in nature or not. And so the philosophy which professes to be grounded on the solid rock of observed phenomena, severely rejecting all subjective human valuations, ends in pure mentalism, which is independent of the existence of any external world whatever.

It is thus plain that the instinctive repugnance of the religious mind to Naturalism, however clumsy the expression which it has sometimes found, is not the wilful blindness to ascertained truth which the scientific controversialists of the last century often assumed it to be. These doughty champions of nature-study, who had, we must not forget, a good case against the theologians who wished to forbid their investigations and discredit their conclusions in advance, were in the habit of saying to the defenders of religion, ' Leave us alone, and we will leave you alone. Leave us the knowable, and keep the unknowable for yourselves. Our province is realities ; yours is dreams, and you are welcome to them.' This delimitation of territory was absolutely impossible, because both sides claimed to have an interpretation of existence as a whole. Naturalism is not science, but a jejune and self-contradictory philosophy. Its outcome is not to leave religion alone, but to destroy it, along with the other interests of the human spirit which we have agreed to call the highest part of our nature. That the controversial Naturalists were themselves high-minded and cultivated men is not disputed ; but their devotion to the good, the true, and the beautiful was built not on their philosophy but on their self-denying labours and pure unselfish lives. It is perhaps fortunate that the philosopher is the reverse of audacious, except in speculation. His books generally end in a *salto mortale* which lands him in very familiar and conventional morality.

The aim of every intellectual construction of the universe—of every world-view, as the Germans call it—is to find universal law, to comprehend all experience in a closed system. An exception (in the sense of a contradiction) does not prove the rule ; it disproves it. If there are phenomena, whether biological, psychological, or religious, which cannot be made to fit into the framework of Naturalism, Naturalism as a philosophy is overthrown. Many biologists, among others, now assert that there are such phenomena. There are some religious minds which rejoice in this new proof that *Omnia exeunt in mysterium*. It pleases them to find that the closed system is not closed, and that ' contingency is brought into the heart of things.' I am not in entire sympathy with this feeling, though I agree with Plato that ' only that which is perfectly real can be perfectly known,' and that the impasse into which Naturalism falls is an indication that the perfectly real is spiritual. But those who take refuge in gaps find themselves in a tight place when the gaps begin to close ; and those biologists who join the idealists in exposing the limitations of Naturalism are themselves in search of a wider Naturalism which will find room for life, mind, and spirit within the scheme of nature.   The inexplicable is for them, as for the naturalists of the last century, a scandal, or at least a problem.   Perhaps the most fruitful line of thought, in view of the present situation, is to consider briefly the problem of teleology, the possibility of purposiveness in nature.

It has been pointed out lately (by Mr. S. A. McDowall) that organisms are not closed systems. The general tendency to the degradation or dissipation of energy is balanced, for a time, by a building-up process in the cell and in the organism.   In this building-up process we seem to see signs of purpose, and this purpose is clearly not only individual but racial.   Although many writers speak of unconscious purpose in the sub-human and even in the vegetable world, this, he thinks, is an unintelligible idea.   Purpose is the prerogative of personality, and since it exists in ourselves, we may infer the existence of a personal Creator.

Now it is certainly true that we are convinced of the existence of a self-directing purposive activity in ourselves.   The *onus probandi* rests with those who ascribe to delusion one of the primary characters of our nature, as it is known to ourselves.   A theory which denies the truth of one of our fundamental convictions about our own minds must have very strong evidence from other quarters to make it credible.   Nor do I dispute the validity of arguing by analogy that the Creator must possess *per eminentiam* the highest qualities with which humanity is endowed.   But personality is obviously a matter of degrees.   The

argument which I have recapitulated implies that there
is somewhere a line which divides the personal from
the infra-personal, and this line can nowhere be found.
The evidence seems to me to point to a purposiveness
running through all nature, sleeping in the stone,
dreaming in the flower, and partially awake and
conscious in man, a purposiveness which points to a
God who is both immanent and transcendent. This
view, as I shall presently show, is in harmony with the
doctrine of evolution, but not with the Naturalism
which is logically bound to deny evolution.

I would rather emphasise what Professor Arthur
Thomson has said of the organic world, only extending
it to the inorganic world as well, since I believe that
here also there is no rigid line of demarcation, but a
transition, in accordance with universal law, from the
inorganic to the organic, from the inanimate to the
living. This has not yet been definitely proved ; but
it is possible, as Professor Benjamin Moore has suggested, that the colloids, or giant molecules, may supply
the link which is still missing. Professor Thomson
says : ' Only a system with order and progress in the
heart of it could elaborate itself so perfectly and so
intricately. There is assuredly much to incline us to
assert eternal providence and justify the ways of God
to man.'

If the whole of nature is purposive, it is not likely
that we can discern special purposes operating in
particular cases. The laws of nature are, on this
hypothesis, purposive laws, like all other laws ; and if
they are the laws of an omnipotent and omniscient
Being, we should expect them to act regularly and
uniformly. A machine that needs tinkering is a

faulty machine, but a machine that has no intelligence behind it can hardly be called a machine at all. All that science has done to establish the uniformity and regularity of nature's operations tells heavily in favour of the existence of a single creative intelligence, and tells with equal force against the non-Christian hypothesis of a plurality of gods, against the Manichean theory of a good and an evil spirit contending on nearly equal terms in the arena, against the hypothesis of an inert and yet intractable ' matter,' and against any other theory which makes God a spirit among other spirits, struggling with only partial success to enter into His kingdom. It is against this dualism or pluralism that scientific men, and many others who cannot claim to be men of science, protest when they reject the vulgar conception of miracle as the suspension of a lower law by a higher. They find no valid evidence for such suspensions ; but they also feel that the classification of events as natural or supernatural withdraws the natural order from the immediate jurisdiction of God, and virtually hands it over to some lower principle, or to blind and unintelligent ' necessity.'

Naturalism declares that neither purposes nor ideas are to be found anywhere in nature, neither in the whole nor in the parts. They are driven to this, not by dislike of the idea of an intelligent Creator, which does not interfere with the freedom of science in any of its branches, but by the attempt to reduce everything to the quantitative formulas which are used in physics, chemistry, and mathematics. There must be nothing in the consequent which was not in the antecedent. The Naturalist is bound by his theory to deny all real change. Evolution, if he uses the word, is a mere mechanical unpacking of what was there all the time. There is nothing in this theory of mechanical unpacking which necessarily conflicts with Aristotle's theory of entelechies. Aristotle taught that the perfect ' form ' of everything was implicit in it from the beginning, and determined the course of its development. Naturalism, however, rejects this theory because it implies a kind of vitalism or panpsychism, an inner unconscious will residing in the developing organism, or, if this is not asserted, it merely describes what happens, and gives no explanation of it. This dispute does not concern religion, which needs only to assert that, however evolution, which means continuous creation, is effected, a divine purpose is being realised in it. ' Emergent evolution ' (Lloyd Morgan) implies an immanent teleology. It is no use to deny this. If the purpose is not in the evolving organism, it must be directive from outside. We cannot explain an evolutionary process from within itself. Religious teleology is belief in an eternal purpose. Every additional proof that the world is a closely interwoven system of means carries back the evidence of purpose to the mind of the Creator Himself, and so assists religious belief. The religious difficulty in welcoming this proof arises from a different source—namely, from our moral valuation of the natural order. This belongs to a later stage of our discussion.

Here, however, it is necessary to point out again that Naturalism and Darwinian evolution do not agree together. There is, of course, a vulgar Darwinism which is exactly the jumble of Naturalism with pieces of other and incompatible philosophies already

mentioned. Darwin himself no doubt accepts the
naturalist philosophy as true within the sphere of his
own studies ; he took no interest in metaphysics. He
denies purpose as a factor within nature. Natural
selection is for him a sieve through which those forms
of life which happen to be adjusted to their environment pass. In theory, all valuation is excluded.
There is no reason why the better should survive, even
if the words better and worse had any relevant meaning. But several expressions in Darwin's writings
leave us in no doubt that he shared the confidence in
progress which, arising from very unscientific sources,
dominated the minds of his generation.

The legacy of Darwin is now in dispute. Some
reject natural selection and the struggle for existence
altogether as explanations ; indefinite variation is
opposed by orthogenesis, slight variations by saltatory
mutations. There are neo-Lamarckians and neo-
Vitalists. But besides this, reflection on Darwinism
proper, when treated as a philosophy, shows that its
outcome is not Naturalism, but something more like
sceptical pragmatism. The common notion is that
Darwin teaches that all history is development towards
a goal, and that therefore the strongest must be the
best. So, I suppose, the ideas which prevail must be
true. But although Darwin may have held this comfortable opinion, it is no part of his system. All he
has a right to say is that the ideas by which humanity
has progressed so far are called true, and that while
using the same ideas there is some probability that we
shall continue to go on in the same direction. The
true idea is the idea which prevails ; truth, in this
system, can have no other meaning. As Bradley

says : ' The one criterion for Darwinism is the abstract
success or prevalence of whatever happens to prevail,
without any regard for its character. And this leaves
us in the end with no criterion at all.' Darwinism,
in fact, is a fruitful theory of the means by which nature
works. It cannot be made the basis of a philosophy,
and it has no vital connexion with religion.

I have spoken of Naturalism as a poverty-stricken
and ultimately self-contradictory philosophy, which is
now being dethroned by its own subjects. But it is
wise to be cautious in condemning views and systems
which are now out of fashion. We have to understand what made them plausible, and to remember
that the errors against which they were a protest—
for an -*ism* is always in opposition—are probably
raising their heads again now that their adversary is
in retreat. And so I will make use of a review by
Professor Wallace of Lord Balfour's ' Foundations of
Belief,' in which Wallace earnestly deprecates the
modern tendency to disparage reason. Naturalism,
he reminds us, was in its origin a protest, not against
the supernatural in itself, but against a supernatural
conceived as arbitrary, incoherent, and chaotic ; it
was a protest against the idle profanity which thinks
it has explained an event when it has said that it is
the work of God, as if anything were not the work of
God. The world which Reason claims is one where
she may go on and never die ; a world where nothing
can be called unknowable, though much may remain
for ever unknown ; a world where, as man accumulates
more and more his intellectual and spiritual capital,
we shall move about more and more freely and wisely.
The world which the genuine Naturalist desires is not

different. It is a reign of law ; but may not the reign of law become the kingdom of the spirit ? ' To assault Naturalism and Rationalism is to strike at Nature and Reason ; it is to support supernaturalism and the materialism of authority.'

Professor Wallace is attacking what I should agree with him in thinking a dangerous tendency, but what he calls Naturalism at its best is not consistent Naturalism. The passage which I have summarised shows how alarmed a Hegelian may be by an assault upon the authority of science. We have now to consider, assuming that the attempt to reduce life, mind, and spirit to the quantitative categories of physics, chemistry, and mathematics has definitely failed, what philosophy is likely to commend itself to thoughtful students of nature, in the place of what we have called Naturalism.

Of one thing we may be certain. Science will never renounce the attempt to bring everything under a single system of laws. Science must be monistic, for under any other dispensation science could not exist. The dualism of nature and supernature is intolerable to science. And therefore, since the attempt to explain mind materialistically and life mechanically appears to have failed, nothing remains but to explain nature spiritually. Even the partition of the world into the animate and the inanimate is distasteful to science, which dislikes any lines that cannot be crossed.

There are many signs that this solution will be attempted. Professor J. S. Haldane says : ' It was formerly assumed that as we trace life backwards to its simpler forms, we are tracing it towards a primitive world of physical mechanism. This is not the case. We are really tracing life into what we had wrongly assumed to be a world of physical mechanism. It may be many years before the significance of the phenomena of life for our conceptions of visible reality are generally understood ; but assuredly this general understanding will in time be reached.' How far this movement towards panpsychism has already gone may be realised by the following words from an essay by Professor Carveth Read : ' It is reasonable to suppose that every cell that goes to constitute the body has its own consciousness, of which we are never distinctly aware, though each cell may contribute something to our total subjectivity ; and even in the central nervous system, with its prepared lines of connexion, it is only in the cortex that consciousness becomes identified with ourselves, and only in the focus of attention that it becomes clear and coherent.' On this theory we are literally nations of living individuals. And if such tiny entities as the cells of the body are to be regarded as having their own life, and the germs of consciousness, it seems likely that some thinkers will go back to the speculations of Fechner, a very remarkable philosopher whose works are now receiving much attention on the Continent, though they have unfortunately not been translated into English. Like the later Platonists and many others in antiquity, Fechner regards the earth and the other spheres as animated beings of a highly spiritual kind. As the spirits of men, with all the life in the earth, are comprised as moments in one conscious earth-spirit, so the earth-spirit is included with all the other sidereal spirits in one conscious spirit of the universe, God.

I am not defending this theory, which to many will seem fantastic. There is something absurd in the idea that a vast aggregation of incandescent gas must have a soul of a dignity proportioned to its bulk. But it is surely significant that panpsychism is once more being taken seriously. And with panpsychism comes teleology, and perhaps, as some think, the admission of freedom and contingency. What we call mechanism may be the teleology of the inorganic world.

If Fechner is ever studied in this country, he will be found to have laid down with great power and insight a spiritual philosophy which may be acceptable to a speculative student of nature. To the sceptical biologist or pragmatist who undermines our faith in the objective truth of our convictions, he replies with much force : We should not need religious faith if its objects did not exist. For if man has made belief in those objects because he needs it, he did not create the circumstance that he needs belief in them for his continuance and welfare, and is therefore obliged by that necessity to make it. The production of this faith by man must therefore be based on the same real nature of things which produced man with his needs. It would be to impute an absurdity to the nature of things, and it would be contrary to experience, so far as we can speak of experience in such a matter, to say that nature has constituted man in such a way that he can only prosper while he cherishes a belief in a thing that is not. We may hope that what Fechner calls the Day-view of the world (in contrast with the Night-view which he rejects) will dissipate the mists of the scepticism which would cut us off from any real knowledge of things as they are.

I have written at some length on the philosophy of science, because science, no less than religion, aims at formulating a general view of reality, within which its more abstract investigations may be set. Neither science nor religion can claim less ; both involve a philosophy. There is, in my judgment, something of a gap between the scientific essays in this book ; the philosophy of science is not adequately dealt with. I could have wished that the filling of this gap had fallen into more competent hands ; but I thought that the book would be incomplete without some such discussion as I have tried to supply. If I am right, the materialistic monism of the last century is giving place to a spiritualistic monism which is still in a very tentative stage. The whole problem of the interplay of the psychical with the physical is very far from settled, and the difficulties seem to be extremely formidable. It is, however, obvious that any theory which finds room for mind and spirit as essentially parts of the field of inquiry must be far nearer to the religious view of reality than the Naturalism of the last century. To the religious view of the world we must now turn.

Perhaps the first caution which we shall do well to bear in mind is that religion is not always true or good. As Dr. Oman has said, we are dealing with human nature when our subject is religion, just as much as when we are discussing art or politics or social life. There is much bad and false religion, which we shall discard, just as we should discard bad and false science. We wish to take both religion and science at their best, and to consider how they stand towards each other.

We have said enough about the religion of the backward races. Let us consider religion as we know it in civilised modern Europe. We shall find it full of distortions and corruptions which explain, if they do not justify, the hostile attitude which some reformers take to religion, at least in its institutional forms.

Alienists tell us that the highest of our mental faculties are the first to yield to morbid conditions of the brain. Decadent races or individuals will have a decadent religion. The close connexion between religion and morals is loosened; the religious conscience, except in relation to some tradition of the elders which has no real ethical sanction, becomes blunter than that of the respectable man of the world. The happy and joyous temper, which characterises a fresh and confident faith, degenerates into moroseness, or into the vapid hilarity of the seminary. Religion relapses into mere cultus, which is the husk of religion; its genial symbolism petrifies, and offers a stolid opposition to the best-established secular knowledge. In order to retain the allegiance of the masses, it stoops to fraud and deception, and endeavours either to impede education or to control it. A decadent religion does far more harm than good in the national life. If we blame the pioneers of modern science for the acerbity of their language about the religion of their day, we must in justice remember that the religion of their day contained much rotten material.

Next, we must remember that religion, like some chemical substance, is never found pure, and it is not at all easy to isolate it in order to learn its properties. We have seen in the earliest part of this

book how difficult it is to separate religion from magic
in the beliefs and practices of savages. The difficulty
is not less among civilised peoples. Religious beliefs
always impinge upon natural science. They may at
first have been myth, symbol, or poetry, since primitive
man does not distinguish clearly between these and
the field of strict science ; or they may once have
seemed probable explanations of phenomena ; but it
is far more difficult for religion to correct its mistakes
than it is for science. A doctrine which has acquired
a mysterious or sacramental value is too precious to
be sacrificed ; its place cannot be taken by a new
symbol manufactured for the purpose. Pieces of
obsolete science, imprisoned like a fly in amber in the
solid mass of a religious creed, may have become the
casket in which the soul keeps her most valued
treasures. They are defended fiercely by believers,
not because as brute facts they have much value for
religion, but because they have become charged by
association with spiritual values which ' must be given
through something.' Religion clings like a climbing
plant to extraneous supports of many different
kinds ; the supports may become rickety, but the
vine has grown round them and entangled itself with
them.

   There is so much even in the highest religion that
seems archaic and obstructive, that some thinkers,
like Comte in the last century and Croce at the present
day, can make out a case for treating religion as half-
baked philosophy, and predicting its disappearance.
There are, however, no signs that this is likely to
happen ; and if we examine religion as we know it,
not only in its first beginnings but in its fullest maturity,

we shall understand why neither philosophy nor science can take its place.

Religion for most of us, I think, is born in the anti thetic consciousness of alienation from, and of communion with, the unseen power which surrounds us. The sense of alienation begins with the mere feeling of impotence in face of an indifferent or unfriendly world. Then our dissatisfaction turns inward, and becomes a sense of guilt. We realise that it is our self-centredness which puts us at enmity with our surroundings, and in the sacrifice of self-will we find our peace. The sense of communion with God is equally important as an element in all religion. It finds ritual expression in most religions, but its own language is prayer, which is the pulsation of the heart of religion. We need not trace the evolution of prayer from a half-magical incantation to the sublimation of petition in ' Thy will be done,' and the ' prayer of union ' of the saintly mystic. It is only necessary to say that the consummation of communion with God coincides with the final resolution of the sense of estrangement from Him. In both aspects of religion there is a spiritual death and resurrection to a higher life, in which the ' I yet not I ' of St. Paul is no longer a contradiction.

A similar antithesis is that between the two processes of expansion and sinking deeper into ourselves, which mark the progress of the religious life. The expansion movement throws out what Carlyle calls organic filaments into our environment, enlarging our personality by establishing new affinities and sympathies with our fellow-men, with nature, and with God. This enlargement of sympathy is so far from

dissipating our personality, that it deepens and in-
tensifies it.   It is only by going forth out of ourselves
that we can attain to a really personal life.   Here
again we see that two apparently divergent movements
meet at the top.   Those only who are willing to lose their
' soul,' their separate individuality, in larger interests
and self-forgetting activities, can hope to find it unto
life eternal.

At the present day, when psychology attracts so
much more attention than metaphysics or dogmatic
theology, the old question whether the organ of religious
faith is the intellect, or the will, or the feelings, is
much debated.   Some of the disputants are in great
danger of falling back into the discarded faculty-
psychology, which treats our undivided human nature
as if it were a bundle of separable forces or attributes.
In particular, a large school of thought cherishes a
curious animus against what it calls intellectualism,
and argues as if it were possible and desirable to banish
reason and logic from religion altogether.   I shall
follow Dr. Oman in discussing this question of the
faculties which religion uses, but I shall take my own
line in developing the argument.

But before weighing the claims of the intellect,
the will, and the feelings in the production of religious
faith, there is a preliminary truth to which I attach
the greatest importance.   We have spoken already of
the quantitative and qualitative differences between
things, and have rejected the attempt of Naturalism
to reduce everything to quantitative terms.   To do
this would be to rule out all valuation, if it were not
true to say, as I shall argue presently, that the rigid
order and uniformity at which Naturalism aims is

itself a value. The whole case for a spiritual interpretation of the world rests on the belief that the
tendency to attach values to all experience is not only
a psychological necessity which we cannot escape,
but an avenue leading to objective truth. I do not
think that any religious view of the world, or any
genuinely religious conviction, is possible if we do not
believe that value is as objective as existence, and
inseparably connected with it. I am not afraid to
say that there can be no existence without value, and
no value without existence. I know well that in
putting forward this claim for our value judgments
we are in danger of an intractable dualism, which we
must not seek to escape either by reducing the world
of becoming to a mere appearance, or the eternal
world to an unrealised ideal. We cannot solve the
problem by setting an imperfect world in the present
against a perfect world in the future. As I have said
elsewhere, we cannot levy unlimited drafts on the
future to avoid bankruptcy in the present, like the
belligerents in the late war. If the world of becoming
is unreal, the will is an illusion, and time, space, and
moral choice disappear with it. If, on the other
hand, the ultimate values have no objective existence,
but are merely regulative ideals on which we are to
model our conduct, we have no absolute standard
left, and are abandoned to subjective and fluctuating
valuations. My own conviction, if I may quote from
myself, is that ' reality is neither mental nor material,
but a realm in which thought and thing, fact and
value, are inseparable, neither having any existence
apart from its correlative. The real world is a coherent
organic unity, spaceless and timeless, but including

all happenings in space and time in their proper relations to itself—that is to say, *sub specie aeternitatis.*

The attributes of ultimate reality are values ; and
we may follow the usual classification by saying that
the ultimate values known to us are goodness, truth,
and beauty. Windelband even says : ' There can be,
as regards content, no further universal values beyond
these three, because in these the entire province of
psychic activity is exhausted.' We are nearest to
God, and to knowledge of the world in which His
attributes are reflected, when we can see and feel these
ultimate values without us and within.

Science is not, as some have erroneously supposed,
a description of fact without valuation. Such a
description would be utterly impossible, and it should
be superfluous to point out how widely the world as
known to science differs from the final analysis of
material objects into electrons and protons. The
mind of the scientist constructs its own world, in which
certain values alone are looked for—those of coherence
and uniformity and commensurability. It seems that
at present observation gives only approximate or
average regularity. This may or may not be philosophically important. But it is most important to
realise that physics and chemistry aim at only an
abstract picture of the world. All that falls under
the heads of goodness and beauty is omitted. And
yet, if we are right, these are just as real as those
aspects of existence which can be weighed and counted.

This theory of ultimate values is at the root of all
that I have to say about religion. It follows that I
am opposed to what may be called psychologism, the
theory that we cannot get beyond the study of mental

states as such. I believe, on the contrary, that our knowledge of the ultimate values, so far as it goes, brings us into touch with the truth of things, with the mind and will of the Creator. I accept Plato's well-known canon that only the perfectly real can be perfectly known ; and perfect knowledge is no mere intellectual process, but an enhancement of the whole personality till it becomes capable of ' knowing even as we are known.' The unity of knower and known, through the love which passes knowledge (but which has not passed by knowledge), is the ideal consummation of spiritual growth.

In saying this, I have in part anticipated what I have to say about the place of intellect, will, and feeling respectively in the life of faith. But my criticism of what seem to me one-sided views will be better understood if my general standpoint is known.

There have been many who have found the source and the essence of religion in pure feeling, which they have tried to isolate from thought and will. It would be a mistake to place the mystics in this class. Emotional theism is not the same as mysticism, which is an intensely active inner life, usually involving a strenuous exercise of the will, and often profound thought. The exaltation of a religion of feeling was naturally popular among the romanticists, among whom Schleiermacher was the most famous theologian. He found the origin of faith in an undifferentiated feeling of the Infinite and Eternal. Some, like Jacobi, have claimed that faith is its own evidence ; that as we can say with Descartes, ' Cogito, ergo sum,' so we can say ' I pray, therefore God is.' This kind of apologetics admits of no refutation and carries no

conviction. Immediate and infallible revelation of
this kind is not given to man. But Schleiermacher's
plea for the trustworthiness of the emotions cannot be
so summarily dismissed. The life of devotion does
carry its own evidence with it. We must only demur
to its being called pure feeling. There is nothing
intrinsically good or bad about feeling. Flowers and
weeds bloom there side by side. We cannot even
speak of truth of feeling, unless we extend feeling to
include the formation of ideas. I do not think religious
feeling is ever aroused, except by ideas of objective
truth and value; but these ideas are certainly not
generated by feeling.

It is not to be denied that the stimulation of violent
emotions may leave permanent traces on the mind.
This was doubtless discovered empirically, and orgiastic
worship was practised with this end. The undifferentiated, inchoate religious sense is thus intensified and fixed, to the great and lasting injury of
the spiritual life. The fruits of emotional revivalism,
if they are permanent, are chiefly bad.

This is, perhaps, the best place to mention the
concept of ' the Holy,' which since Otto's famous book
has been given a new importance in English books on
the psychology of religion. The idea of holiness has
its history, like other religious ideas, and the history
is not edifying. The holiness of Jehovah, as exemplified by the death of Uzzah for touching the ark, was
much more like electricity than any moral quality.
The whole history of taboo might be introduced here.
But Otto is right in emphasising the feeling of awe,
dread, and fascination as an essential part of religion.
It is generally mixed with superstitious elements,

and should never be the dominating feeling in the approach of the Christian to his Father in heaven. ' He that feareth is not made perfect in love.' The impression made by Otto's book may lead to this feature being somewhat over-emphasised.

Another school, which is well represented in our day, makes faith an affair of the will. It is pointed out that people in general are not convinced by pure reasoning, but that they believe what they wish to believe. Hobbes declared that even the axioms of Euclid would be disputed if men's passions were concerned in them. But the question is not whether men do actually form their opinions in this way, but whether they ought to do so ; and the answer to this question depends on whether we have any confidence in human reason or not. The primacy of the will over the intellect goes with sceptical empiricism. It is the root of the philosophy called pragmatism and of the revolutionary movement in the Catholic Church called modernism. It is not possible to discuss either of these in this essay.

The word intellectualism, used in a disparaging sense, is in common use among the opponents of speculative idealism, especially when the Hegelians are being attacked, and also among modernists in attacking the Catholic system of dogma, based on the ' Summa ' of St. Thomas Aquinas. It is a matter of faith with Catholics that ' the one true God can be known with certainty by the natural light of reason.' This, it will be observed, is quite different from the ' ontologism ' of Jacobi, mentioned above. The knowledge of God's existence, for the Catholic, is of the nature of a valid inference. The rationalistic proof

of religion may take several forms. Paley's argument
is well known : ' The marks of design are too strong
to be gotten over. Design must have a designer.
That designer must be a Person. That Person is
God.' To this section would belong, if there were
room to discuss them, the famous four proofs of God's
existence—the ontological, cosmological, and teleological arguments, with which Kant dealt very
roughly. The ontological argument has no doubt
been often formulated faultily ; but it seems to me a
fair argument to say that the conception of God can
hardly be a purely subjective notion. A mystic might
go further. The intellect is trying to formulate and
explain an actual experience, the essence of which is
that it is known or felt not to be purely subjective.
The cosmological argument, as restated by Lotze,
is not concerned with a Prime Mover but with an
immanent ground of the World. There must be an
ever-present energy, which is the source of all cosmical
movement. The teleological argument, which Kant
treats with respect, has since his time been repudiated
by the majority of scientists. But though the simple
teleology of Paley is out of date, we must protest
against the assumption that uniform law and order
are incompatible with the idea of purpose. I am inclined to think that the very conception of law implies
purpose. These arguments are sometimes called
proofs, though they are not demonstrations ; they
are, however, closely inwoven with the texture of
rational experience.

Intellectualism, in the disparaging sense, may take
the form either of pantheistic naturalism or of speculative idealism. The rationalism of the deists lost

sight of the meaning of faith ; it ended in a ' common sense ' attitude, from which the religious valuation of the world has quite disappeared. Its practical outcome was utilitarianism, which, though philosophically weak, provided many excellent men with a calculus of personal conduct and of social reform. I shall not attempt any description or criticism of speculative idealism, as expounded in the numerous disciples of Hegel. The tide is running strongly against this type of philosophy. But I agree with Sir Henry Jones, that ' the intellectual ardour of the world cannot be damped, far less extinguished, by any theory, blindly advanced in the interests of religion, of the radical insecurity of knowledge, or of the incompetence and untrustworthiness of human reason.'

The special quarrel of the modern schools with the idealists is connected with the repudiation by the former of ' absolutism.' Here I must take leave to paraphrase from what I have already written (' Faith and its Psychology,' 1909). To give up the conception of reality as a single system would be to give up both philosophy and science. If the world is ' wild,' as William James thinks, only wild men, whom we do not permit to be at large, would be at home in it. ' And yet so great is the fear engendered by the conception of a cosmos which shuts man up in an iron framework, that we find Lotze reducing natural laws to mere conceptual generalisations ; we find Ritschlians warning the intelligence away from the domain of religion ; we find Professor James and his followers constructing the universe of enigmatical atoms dignified by the name of persons, and rushing into polytheism.'

We cannot regard particular facts as real, and the

laws which connect and regulate them as only subjective. 'Mere ideas' cannot bind together 'real
objects.' Or if the objects also are said to be subjective, everything disappears at once into dreamland,
including the reasons for doubt. The sceptic cannot
throw his opponent if his own feet are in the air.

We pursue the Absolute, not because we are
intellectualists, but because we must. The opponent
of absolutism generally sets up an Absolute of his own
without knowing it. Even the principle of relativity
has become, with some of its defenders, a kind of
absolute.

The objection to intellectualism loses its force if
we use intelligence in the Platonic sense, not of the
logic-chopping faculty, but of the whole personality
become self-conscious and self-directing, under the
guidance of its highest part. In my other books I
have attempted to show in detail how the spiritual
life is or should be a harmonious development of the
whole man, passing, as Clement of Alexandria says,
from faith to knowledge, and from knowledge to that
love which 'unifies the knower and the known.' In
this state of enlightenment there is no more discord
between the will, the intellect, and the feelings, and
the objects of our reverence—the True, the Beautiful,
and the Right—are more and more blended, like a
triple star.

It seems strange that a warning should be necessary
to take our religion seriously. But we cannot look
about us without noticing the extraordinary frivolity
of much which passes for religious interest. In
Southern Europe, especially, religion is largely a social
diversion, a spectacular performance, an artistic enjoy-

ment.   The attitude of our own public towards popular superstitions, half belief and half make-belief, is too common among church-goers.   The scientific man cannot understand this playfulness where matters of the highest moment are at stake.   Nothing repels him more from the worship of the churches.   It is difficult for a student of science to realise how weak the love of truth is in the majority, and how widespread the mistrust of reason.   The real sceptic does not write books on agnosticism ; he never thinks at all, which is the only way to be perfectly orthodox.

It is, I think, a valuable reflection of Otto that much injury is done to the cause of religion by separating the question of human immortality from the truth or falsehood of the religious view of the world generally. It is of the essence of religion, in its higher forms, to distinguish between the transient, unsatisfying flux of things, and the permanent, satisfying reality which lies behind it.   This distinction has been embodied in countless mythologies and eschatologies, but the conviction which creates them is fundamental.   So long as we discuss immortality merely as the question whether the individual continues to exist as a con-scious being after his death, we have taken it out of its religious context.   For religion this question is significant only as a part of the much larger conviction that the true nature of things lies behind their visible appearances, and beyond time and space.   The mere question of survival in time, and for a time, is almost frivolous to the religious mind.   What is essential is the conviction that, in the words of Plotinus, ' nothing that really is can ever perish,' or, as Goethe puts it, ' all that is transitory is only a symbol.'   I honestly

believe, as Otto does, that the destruction of the
supramundane physics of the Middle Ages by the discoveries of astronomy will be found to have done a
good service to religion, by forbidding it to seek its
treasure and its everlasting home in space and in time.
I have not room to follow Otto in his penetrating
analysis of our conceptions of time and space.   As
he says, the arguments of which Kant was the pioneer,
though they do not remove the curtain which separates
being from appearance, at any rate force it to reveal
itself as a curtain.

The religious conception is made up essentially
of a belief in the pre-eminence of the spiritual world
over the natural, and rejects the common scientific
view that ' mind is but a kind of *lusus* or *luxus naturae*,
which accompanies it at some few places, like a
peculiarly coloured aura or shadow, but which must,
as far as reality is concerned, yield precedence to
"Nature" in every respect.' And although it is certain
that when religion is in any way complete, it includes a belief in the everlastingness of our spiritual
nature, and its independence of fleeting phenomena,
it is a mistake so to isolate the question of survival
that opponents may dictate both the questions and
their answers. If this pre-eminence and autonomy
of the spiritual be not granted, it is misleading to use
the word God at all, and those who do so are open to
F. H. Bradley's gibe that ' they call the Unknowable
God only because they don't know what the devil
else to call it.'

The naturalist arguments against a spiritualistic
interpretation of nature are certainly formidable.
Briefly, the best answer to them is to remind opponents

that without the free and creative activities of the mind there could be no Naturalism. Further, it is legitimate to point out that if the spiritual faculty is given fair play, and suffered to develop normally, suspicion and distrust of it must disappear. We do not disparage the results of science, or throw doubt upon them, when we affirm that they are the creation of the free spirit which finds in nature those laws which their and our Creator has planted alike in the conscious and in the unconscious world. ' The world we know, the world of sound, light and colour, of all properties whatsoever, of the ugly or the beautiful, of pain and pleasure, is in the most real sense the product of consciousness itself.' The spirit is never dumb, and it speaks a different language from that of mathematics or physics.

I pass to the psychology of religious belief as it has been studied from another side. The literature is abundant ; a satisfactory survey of the subject is Professor Pratt's ' Religious Consciousness.' This writer makes a useful fourfold classification, which we may call either four aspects of religion, or four temperamental kinds of religion. These are : the traditional, based on the authority of the past ; the rational ; the mystical ; and the practical or moral. These four aspects are to be found in every genuinely religious person ; but in varying degrees according to circumstances, temperament, and, not least, according to age.

Wordsworth's well-known line, ' Heaven lies about us in our infancy,' can hardly be accepted without qualification. The child's mind is a garden where flowers and weeds grow together. The perverted

o

ingenuity of the psycho-analysts has laid bare the roots of unpleasant vices even in the apparent innocence of the nursery. The child believes in God because he has been told that He exists, and probably imagines Him as resembling in character one or both of his parents. He readily assimilates the supernatural stories of the Old Testament, and it is a serious problem how to teach him without making him believe many things which he will afterwards learn to be untrue. It is not easy for his elders to know what really goes on in the mind of the child. Much of the religiosity which unwise parents delight to observe in their children is pure imitation or innocent hypocrisy. And on the other side, the child's inner life is often a turmoil of terrors and anxieties of which his parents know almost nothing. And yet we must always remember that young children not infrequently have an exquisitely beautiful saintliness of character, ' walking with God ' in a simple directness of realisation which is rare in adult life, except among the highest saints. Sometimes when a child is called early from this world, the experience of sickness seems to accomplish in a few months all that a lifetime of devotion and sustained moral effort could have produced.

The period of adolescence has engaged the attention of many researchers, especially in America. It is said to be a time of storm and stress, of repressed cravings, morbid brooding, and alternations of communion with and alienation from God. The ages between eighteen and twenty-five are the usual time for what is called conversion. The subject has been investigated in America by means of the questionnaire, a method which, in my opinion, is unsafe if much reliance is placed upon it. It selects those who are willing to answer such questions and omits the large number of those who refuse to answer them. It assumes a power to analyse one's own heart and motives which is by no means common. It does not allow for the great influence of suggestion, especially in such matters as instantaneous conversion. There are some Christian bodies in which the young are taught to expect a sudden turning to God, and in these bodies it is reported as a common experience. Roman Catholics and Anglo-Catholics do not expect it, and for them it is an unusual event. John Wesley believed that it is almost universal, and reported that ' in London alone I found 652 members of our society who were exceeding clear in their experience, and whose testimony I could see no reason to doubt. Every one of these, without a single exception, has declared that his deliverance from sin was instantaneous, that the change was wrought in a moment. As I have not found, in so long a space of time, a single person speaking [of a gradual change], I cannot but believe that sanctification is commonly, if not always, an instantaneous work.' A living Wesleyan minister of large experience has told me that among modern Methodists instantaneous conversion is very far from being felt by all.

There is also a danger of overestimating the ' storm and stress ' of adolescence. Very many persons develop healthily and happily without it. The special psychical disturbances caused by sex are no doubt very common, but they have been greatly exaggerated by Continental writers, unless we may flatter ourselves (and I am not sure that we may not do so) that a much

larger proportion of young people in England preserve
their innocence than in other great countries.

In middle life we have come to take ourselves for
better and for worse. We have learned that there are
some things which we are good for and others that we
are bad for, and we no longer kick against the pricks.
We live in our work and in our affections and ideals ;
we are what we are interested in. We have given up
our claim to ' unchartered freedom,' and are beginning
to understand that our perfect freedom consists in
service and submission to God. As I have said elsewhere, ' Lucan speaks of

> Libertas, cuius servaveris umbram
> Si quidquid iubeare velis.

But in religion it is the substance, and not the shadow
of liberty, which is gained in this way.' In middle
life, petition forms a smaller and smaller proportion
of our prayers. Our creed is simplified, and intensified.
God becomes for us less an object than an atmosphere.

Dr. Brown, like all modern psychologists, attaches
the greatest importance to the mystical experience, the
essence of which is that the soul believes itself to have
come into immediate communication with a spiritual
power or presence above itself. It may be hoped
that we shall have no more attempts, like that of
Murisier, to prove that all mysticism is pathological.
If the student chooses to take for his examples only
the extreme types of ecstasy, it is no doubt easy to show
that the subjects of these trances were often in a morbid
state of the brain or nerves. Even among visionaries,
however, there have been many men and women of
robust health and keen intelligence. But if we realise,

as is certainly the truth, that what is called mysticism is only a further development of an universal religious practice, that of prayer, we shall put aside these attempts to discredit religion at its base.   It is the conviction of all religious people that in prayer we are speaking to One who hears us, and this is the strongest argument that the religious quest is not vain.   Dr. Brown mentions that many persons fail to achieve anything like the mystical experience, and regards this as an argument against the value of the mystic's testimony, except to the psychologist.   But, so far as we can judge, very many persons are religiously ungifted, just as many are indifferent to music.   They may be excellent people, but they are, so to speak, deaf on this side.   There are many also who have never given long and concentrated attention to the unseen world ; they do not ' practise the presence of God.'   Such persons do not receive the mystical experience, because they have not earned it.   They have not even attempted to climb a mountain which, as all who have climbed it testify, is long, steep, and difficult.   There are specialists in the spiritual life, as in other things.   Their testimony is of supreme value in their own sphere ; and it is an error to say that what they have seen and felt is valid only for themselves, because others cannot share it.   It is not thus that we treat the authority of genius in other subjects.

But there is a question of special interest in the study of mysticism, to which Dr. Brown calls attention.   The mystic nearly always describes his initiation into the higher mysteries as a progressive simplification, in the course of which he closes one avenue after another through which ideas might reach him from the world of sense, and at last reaches a point where time and space and individuality drop away from him, leaving him ' alone with the Alone.' The interesting question is whether in this experience of simplification and nakedness the soul really has an intuitive perception of the Unity which lies behind all multiplicity, of an eternal mode of existence which transcends time and space, or whether this is an illusion and not in reality a deeper experience than the definite and brightly coloured images of the normal consciousness.

The question is very difficult, especially when we remember that we have not ourselves enjoyed this ineffable experience, and that those who have had it agree that it has been the culminating point of their life of devotion.

It is well known that the Vision of the One forms the apex of those systems of philosophical mysticism of which the scheme of Plotinus is the type. He was led to his doctrine of the superessential One by three distinct paths. His dialectic led him to acknowledge in the real or intelligible world a unity in duality, a complete correspondence between thought and its object, which nevertheless remain two in one, not simple unity. The same method of rising from multiplicity towards unity which he had used in all his philosophy, compelled him to take the last step, and postulate a final and complete unification in the Absolute ' beyond existence.' It is part of his greatness to realise that without some duality of thought and its object there can be no existence ; and yet that this duality cannot be absolutely final. Secondly, he feels that the soul cannot be in bliss unless it has something above itself to worship and aspire to, ' always attaining, and always striving on.' 'All things pray, except the First Principle,' as Proclus says. Thus belief in the Absolute gives him an object which the beatified spirit can adore. And thirdly, he has experienced the blank trance, and he thinks that in those moments he has risen even above the spiritual world, and been merged in the immediate presence of the Absolute, the First Principle.

Many who have followed the mystics so far will shrink back at this last claim. How can any finite spirit so transcend the conditions of its existence as to share, even for a moment, the life or consciousness of the Absolute ? And if this belief is illusory, are we not thrown back upon the full and rich life of the spirit among other spirits as the highest state which man can attain ? Some who have been repelled by the bleak isolation of the mystic's final climb might welcome this conclusion. Dr. Brown emphasises transcendence of space and time in ecstasy as perhaps an important experience. But in fact much of our higher life is timeless and spaceless ; it is not only in ecstasy that we rise beyond these forms of thought.

The last essay in the book deals not with religion in general but with Christianity in particular. What is its position among other religions ? Is it, in any real sense, unique ? Can we expect that it will ultimately conquer the world ?

These questions cannot be answered without a clearer definition of what we mean by Christianity than Professor Webb's essay contains. The future of Christianity as an institution—the fate of the Churches —is, from the point of view of these essays, not a matter of supreme importance. As a great historical

institution, Christianity can be characterised only as
the religion of the white race. Although it arose on
Semitic soil, it had made its choice between Europe and
Asia long before the end of the first century. The
Jews would have none of it, thus transformed; the
Asiatic Christians made a poor fight against a genuinely
Oriental religion, that of Islam. From the second
century till the present day, Christianity has been the
most European and the least Asiatic of religions. Its
great expansion in modern times has been due to the
unparalleled expansion of the white race. It has
made no triumphs worth boasting of among the
brown, black, or yellow peoples. The gospel itself, no
doubt, may exercise a wide influence upon Buddhism,
Hinduism, and Mohammedanism. There is a cult of
Amida in Eastern Asia which is said to be not unlike the Logos-Christology of the early Church. But
the European nations, arrogant, domineering, and
rapacious, have done little to recommend the name of
Christianity in Asia and Africa; and it is hardly
probable that the European Churches, which have
formed their customs and forms of government to suit
Western conditions, will impose their organisations
upon the immemorial religious traditions of the East.
That the Gospel of Christ will one day ' convert the
world '—that is to say, the religiously minded in all
nations—is not beyond the possibility of hope; but
an universal institutional Church is as chimerical an
idea as an universal Empire.

It is not scientific to pick out all the superiorities
of Western civilisation and put them down to the
credit of Christianity. European civilisation has been,
like Hellenism, a permanent enrichment of humanity,

and the religion of Europe has borne many exquisite flowers. But unless, like the Roman Catholic
Modernists, we assume that every transformation which
helped the Church to survive and prosper was a legitimate development of the original design, we shall not
find it easy to affiliate Hildebrand, Oliver Cromwell,
and Cardinal Manning to the Gospel as it was preached
to the fishermen of Galilee.   Organised religion is not,
in modern times, one of the strongest forces in human
affairs. As compared with patriotism and revolutionary aims, it has shown itself lamentably weak.
The strength of Christianity is in transforming the lives
of individuals—of a small minority, certainly, as Christ
clearly predicted, but a large number in the aggregate.
To rescue a little flock, here and there, from materialism,
selfishness, and hatred, is the task of the Church of
Christ in all ages alike, and there is no likelihood that
it will ever be otherwise.   To many the most pressing
question is whether the Churches will ever make it
easier for students of science to profess themselves
church-members without doing violence to their scientific conscience. What the institutions will decide is
quite uncertain.   But there are already large numbers
of Christians who find it possible to follow Christ while
accepting the conclusions of science and the scientific
attitude of mind.   These are far more important than
their isolation from ecclesiastical life might lead us to
suppose. It is to individuals that we must look for
encouraging signs, not to institutions. Science has
learned this lesson in its own sphere ; it must look at
religion in the same way. The right note was already
struck at the Renaissance. Leonardo da Vinci ex-
claims : ' Let bigots talk at leisure and heed them not.

The study of Nature is well-pleasing to ·God, and is akin to prayer. Learning the laws of Nature, we magnify the first Inventor, the Designer of the world ; and we learn to love him, for the great love of God results from great knowledge. Who knows little, loves little. If you love the Creator for the favour you expect of Him, and not for His most high goodness and strength, wherein do you excel the dog, who licks his master's hand in the hope of dainties ? But reflect how that worthy beast, the dog, would adore his master if he could comprehend his reason and his soul.' Whether our dogs would respect us more if they knew us better may be seriously doubted ; but I think we may say of natural science what Bacon said of philosophy, that while a little knowledge often estranges men from religion, a deeper knowledge brings them back to it ; though we ought to add that the religion to which deeper knowledge brings us is not the same as that from which superficial knowledge estranges us.

SCIENCE AND ULTIMATE TRUTH

I NEED not say how greatly I appreciate the honour of having been invited to lecture here,[1] in this renowned centre of medical science. The distinction is all the greater when I remember that this lectureship was founded in memory of a brilliant member of your brotherhood, whose premature death was felt as a severe personal loss by his colleagues and pupils, and also that I have been appointed to lecture in succession to one of the most celebrated men of our time. It is a wholly undeserved honour, for I have no claim to be counted a man of science. My duties have called me to the studies of classical scholarship, theology, and philosophy. But I hope I may claim not only to have an intelligent interest in scientific subjects, and not least in those which concern bodily health and social hygiene, but to have what I may call a scientific conscience, which leads me to look at questions as men of science look at them, and to sympathise with the point of view which they usually take. I have also been led by my personal experience to feel a very great moral respect and admiration for the medical profession, and for other scientific men, among whom, not to name the living, I may mention especially Sir Francis Galton, one of the best and greatest men whom I have known. The disinterested search for truth is

[1] See Introduction.

certainly one of the highest and noblest careers that
a man can choose.

There have been three periods of history when
knowledge has advanced by leaps and bounds. These
are, the time of the ancient Greeks, the Renaissance,
and our own age. The achievement of the ancient
Greeks is perhaps the most wonderful when we consider the poverty of their apparatus ; but they suffered
for their preference of speculation to applied science.
The greatest accession of positive knowledge has come
in our own time.

And what a brilliant pageant it is ! How shall we
compare the cramped and limited vision of the universe
which spread itself to the imagination of mankind in
old time with the tremendous vistas opened out to
us by modern science ? We are told that one hundred
millions is an underestimate of the number of stars
already photographed, though not more than ten
thousand are visible with the naked eye. There may
be, and probably are, other universes, dimly visible
as nebulae, besides the Galactic universe in which
we live. The diameter of our own system has been
guessed as 3000 to 4000 light-years, the velocity of
light being 186,000 miles per second. The total
number of stars is supposed, even by those who reject
the idea of infinite extension, to run into thousands of
millions. Of these, some are growing hotter, others
colder, and the transmutation of elements, which
has only lately come within actual observation, seems
to cover the whole series from hydrogen and helium
to the heaviest atoms. Among the very distant stars
there are two, Canopus and Rigel, which by comparison reduce our sun to a very tiny dwarf. The

much smaller diameter of Betelguese is stated as 215 million miles. So much for unimaginable magnitudes. When we turn from the infinitely great to the infinitely small, the wonder is not less. The word atom means by derivation that which is too small to be further divided. But every atom, it has been revealed, is a miniature solar system, with electrons, in numbers which determine the nature of the element, whirling round a central nucleus.

In your own science, what a romance seems to be coming into view in the occult properties of the ductless glands, which indicate the strangest possibilities in the future, not only of curing disease, but of altering character and, perhaps, arresting the progress of old age. Every year some new and fascinating discovery is made.

The Psalmist, long before the age of science, was struck with the smallness of human life in the great spaces of nature. ' I will consider thy heavens, even the work of thy fingers, the moon and the stars which thou hast ordained. What is man that thou art mindful of him ? ' What is man but a species which, during a brief period, has been dominant over other species on a dwarf planet, revolving round a dwarf sun, which is an average undistinguished specimen of a large class of elderly stars which have seen better days ? What is man, that God should be mindful of him, or that he should take himself seriously ? Well, man is a being that knows all the things that we have mentioned and much besides. This wonderful and glorious vision of a boundless universe, all, as far as can be ascertained, compounded of the same elements and obeying the same laws, is either reflected in his mind or created by his mind. We must not regard the world of science as an objectively existing fact, wholly independent of us who observe it.

So we are thrown back on the troublesome and perhaps insoluble problem of knowledge, which has exercised all the philosophers, especially since Kant stirred up these fundamental questions a hundred and fifty years ago. The history of philosophy since Kant is strewn with the wrecks of systems. The only question is whether any ship is left afloat.

Hume, after investigating the problem with great acuteness, came to the despairing conclusion that though ' the cause or causes of order in the universe probably bear some remote analogy to human intelligence,' this proposition ' affords no inference that affects human life, or can be the source of any action.' This is to deny the rationality of science. Kant, unwilling to accept such a negation of all that religion means by belief in God, thinks that he has found a way out by building up, from man's moral instincts, the assurance of a moral Creator, who has ordained that life on earth shall be the discipline of our spiritual growth. Thus he introduces the idea of *Value* as a constituent of reality, and this idea of Value is now one of the fundamental elements in all living philosophy. Reality, for him, is a moral system, the *raison d'être* of which is the working out of ultimate good in a world of conscious spirits. Most of us now feel that Kant's outlook is too individualistic, and that in rejecting the idea of divine immanence he is condemned to a purely deistic theory of God. But it is from him that was developed, or rather revived, for the Platonists taught it, the belief in eternal,

intrinsic values, as not less real and significant than
the world of facts with which science deals. Our
judgments of value are as objective as our judgments
of fact ; we pronounce the verdicts of good and bad,
better and worse, beautiful and ugly, with as much
confidence and impartiality as we declare the results
of quantitative measurement. We feel with Lotze
that if we put these considerations of value out of
our minds, and in the interests of what we call truth
confine ourselves to a view of reality which excludes
them, we are ' glorying in renouncing what no man
has a right to renounce.'   There are some conclusions
which without being demonstrably false are rejected
as intolerable. Such are the theories that the universe
is a chaos, that it is intrinsically unknowable, that it
is a dream of our own (solipsism), and that the world
of values has no relation to the world of facts. And
it is not true to say that our refusal to accept this last
theory is based upon any private hopes and fears,
any more than the scientist's refusal to believe in a
chaotic universe, or in a world-order which is in con-
spiracy to deceive him, is based on any personal
predilections.

The conception of Value enters far more deeply
into purely scientific research than is commonly recognised. True reality as opposed to mere appearance
is itself a value. That which ' only appears ' is not
non-existent ; it differs in value from what we call real
existence, and what we call really existent depends
largely on what we are interested in. Physicists tell
us that the real nature of things is in the atoms, and
that a table or chair is only a phenomenon. From
this point of view, I suppose, a microbe is nearer

reality than a man. That is because they choose
to study nature from the point of view of the microbe.
They are radical pluralists. Some philosophers, beginning from the other end, have argued that ' the One
remains, the many change and pass.' The distinction
is psychological ; it is a matter of interest or valuation.
The historian, who also aspires to be scientific, studies
the sequence of events with other values in his mind.
Natural science confines itself to the logical value of
generalisation ; history studies those moral and social
values which, though they transcend human lives,
are actualised in human experience. Every kind of
valuation rests on selection and abstraction. The
faith in Order which makes natural science possible
is only one example of a wider faith.

The philosopher has the ambitious aim of unifying,
or harmonising, these points of view. His three
ultimate values are generally said to be the Good, the
True, and the Beautiful, but he tries to relate them
all to one suprasensuous reality. He is impelled to
appeal, even from the collective social mind, to a
supreme court beyond experience. The religious mind
is also convinced that the ultimate values are rooted
in the nature of reality, and by them, but especially
by the Idea of the Good, as it is revealed to conscience,
it tests all objects of experience. Here, again, we get
a standard of valuation which is unquestionably valid,
though it differs from the standards which are used
by natural science. Because physics, history, and
religion have their different valuations of experience,
we are obliged to concede a large measure of autonomy
to the different studies. A complete philosophy
would find room for all, and would show how they

supplement each other. But this is an ideal consummation. We need not wait for this final reconciliation to allow on the one hand that science, in endeavouring to discover and establish universally valid laws, is working in the service of one of the ultimate values, unified truth, and on the other that religion, judging all things by the standard of moral worth, is assuming no fiction, but a certain fact, namely, that the Idea of the Good is real, and that the human mind is in relation with it.

I do not think that what Otto has called ' the Holy,' and defined as the special province of religion, can be marked off as separate from the ultimate values already mentioned, the Good, the True, and the Beautiful, and added to them as a fourth. To do so would be to deprive these ultimate values of their consummation in religion, and to leave religion empty and bloodless. I should rather say that in religion these supreme values are recognised as the attributes of a supramundane Power, which is revealed in them, and the recognition of ' the Holy ' in them follows from this conviction, which is given in what is known as the mystical experience.

But this belongs rather to the final stage in my argument. Let me attempt, in the short time at my disposal, to summarise the chief solutions, other than the theistic, which have been advocated in the last century, in the attempt to determine the relations of the mental and the material, of value and fact.

The Kantian theory of knowledge had the very unfortunate result of opposing *knowledge*, which for him is attainable only in the study of nature, to *faith*, which is the basis of our moral life. This was

P

obviously to put the defenders of every kind of idealism in a highly disadvantageous position. This unlucky separation is the ground of all the naturalistic philosophies of the nineteenth century. Our Victorian naturalists did not call themselves materialists ; but they followed Kant in opposing faith to knowledge of reality, and they did all their thinking in material-istic terms. The three marks of real naturalism are : (1) the ideal of simplification, (2) the rejection of purpose or design, (3) the denial of reality to the realm of spiritual values. All idealistic and spiritual beliefs were for it a kind of luminous haze, floating inertly and idly over the field in which real work is done. The idealists on their side took up the challenge, but their reply was to disparage the significance, and even to impugn the reality, of the world as known to science. Lotze agrees with Kant that ' a chasm that cannot be filled divides the world of facts from the world of values.' ' With the firmest conviction of the undivided unity of the two we combine the most distinctly conscious belief in the impossibility of this unity being known.' He perhaps hardly realises how this belief in an irremediable cleft within our intelli-gence must destroy our confidence that either our facts or our values are anywhere near the truth. This fundamental scepticism has infected a great deal of modern philosophy. It inflicts the most serious injury on both science and religion : on science, because it suggests that we reach the reality of nature by eliminating from it mind and consciousness ; and on religion because it favours the notion that faith is fundamentally irrational, and its dogmas exempt from being brought to the bar of ordinary evidence. With materialism entrenched on one side, and superstition on the other, it is no wonder that the imaginary ' chasm ' really begins to yawn between the two.   On one side of the gap we have the materialistic physicians of France and Germany teaching that thought is a secretion of the brain, comparable to bile and other animal juices, and on the other we have Victorian bishops anathematising Darwin and Huxley.   Truly, as Professor Whitehead has lately said, the intolerant use of abstractions is the major vice of the intellect.

The theory of the chasm clearly will not work. What is to become of the sciences which deal with both facts and values, of biology, for example, and still more of psychology, if there is no way of crossing from one world to the other ?   Mechanical theories tried to extend their domain over the field of the borderland sciences, till those sciences themselves rebelled.   Not only psychology, but biology, as represented by some (by no means all) of its leaders, is searching for some principle which will liberate it from bondage to the laws of the inanimate and inorganic.   The critics of this new movement in biology condemn it as a revival of the old discredited vitalism, which called in a hypothetical ' vital principle ' to account for the seemingly rational and purposive agencies in living beings, which, as was argued, are far beyond the scope of merely physical and chemical reactions.   That this hypothesis was merely an *asylum ignorantiae* is evident, and it went the way of ' phlogiston ' and other imaginary entities.   On the other side, the opponents of the mechanical philosophy asked whether a self-feeding, self-stoking, self-repairing, self-reproducing machine can with any appropriateness be called a machine at all. The attempt to fit the phenomena of life and consciousness within the framework of mere mechanism seems to be hopeless. But the question remains, whether the new vitalists have really escaped the errors of the old. It seems to me that without intending it they frequently lapse into speaking of their entelechies, psychoids, or whatever name they prefer, as agents acting from outside upon the physical organism ; and this resembles the method of the old vitalism. I shall try to indicate, before the close of this lecture, in what direction I think we must look for a solution of the problem. I do not think that psychical energy can be added to other forms of energy as an efficient cause, as if mind were a special form of energy. The fundamental question is whether the physical is a closed system, uninfluenced by the psychical world. Whether the closed system is to be called a mechanism or not is not of primary importance. The great difficulty is that the principle of the conservation of energy seems to leave no room for any other principle, and that this principle seems to reduce consciousness to a continuous mirror of a system which works independently of it—a supposition which is really intolerable.

The word evolution is loosely used in two incompatible senses. Sometimes it is a mechanical unpacking of that which was there all the time ; there is no gain in the process, but equivalence. This is, I suppose, what is meant by the evolution of a star, which passes through great changes of temperature and bulk, contracting, heating, and cooling, but without any change, addition, or subtraction (except loss of mass by radiation) in the ultimate units of which it is composed. I suggest that in the interest of clearness this should be called *genesis*, not evolution. But in biology, growth and real change are the facts to be understood ; and if we look for the explanation of these facts in the primordial elements, as the sciences of physics and chemistry necessarily do, we are leaving out the very facts which have to be accounted for ; we are really denying the fact of change which is the crux of the problem. There are few things in the world so difficult to explain as real change ; it appears to me that most scientists are far from realising the complexity of this metaphysical puzzle. James Ward, who is a champion of free will and of pluralism, postulates what he calls creative synthesis, and this is the foundation of Bergson's philosophy ; but the idea of new creation contradicts what the physicist means by causation, and the popular formula ' emergent evolution ' does not, I think, remove the difficulty, but only softens and disguises the breach of continuity.

The words cause and causation are used with the same carelessness ; the two problems are to a large extent the same. The real meaning of causality, as used by mechanicists, is that there is nothing new in the world ; the cause is merely the form which the effect had previously. But this is a misuse of the word causality, which, in the interests of clearness of thought, ought to be banished from physics altogether. To turn *post hoc* into *propter hoc* is illegitimate, and we might even question whether, on strictly mechanistic principles, the time-series is not theoretically reversible. We might also ask why we are never tempted to say that summer is the cause of winter, or night of day. Is it that we do not speak of causation

unless we imagine that there is some contingency—
that the sequence might not occur ? Efficient causation cannot be discovered within physical phenomena,
and no logical necessity binds together the successive
stages of a sequence. That the particular depends on
the general is, I think, the principle which must take
the place of the untenable notion of inter-phenomenal
causality ; and we may be driven back upon the idea
of a single creative First Cause as the only real cause
in the universe.

I have said that Kant's dualism of knowledge and
faith, in which knowledge is confined to the world of
phenomena, had an unfortunate influence on much of
the thinking of the nineteenth century. The system
of Comte is a salient example of this dualism. He
held that we can never transcend the subjectivity
which belongs to the human mind generally. We are
rigidly confined to a subjective view of reality, which
we must accept as true. Accordingly, philosophy and
theology are merely transitional forms through which
the human spirit arrives at what he calls Positivism,
which is a worship of the idea of humanity. Practically,
he denies that there is anything behind appearances,
and so condemns religion and philosophy alike.
Science he would only allow to exist on condition of
confining itself to purely utilitarian ends. Astronomy,
for example, he regards as waste of time.

Positivism is more dogmatic than Agnosticism.
But the inconsistencies of Herbert Spencer's Agnosticism are by this time notorious. What are we to say
of a thinker who first lays down that we are absolutely
precluded from knowing anything except phenomena,
all that lies behind it being not only unknown but

inherently unknowable, and then invests his Unknowable with some at least of the attributes of a personal deity, speaking of it as ' an Infinite and Eternal Energy by which all things are created and sustained,' and ascribes to this Infinite and Eternal Energy ' manifested alike within us and without us,' ' not only the manifestations themselves but the law of their order ' ? Some have argued, not unreasonably, that Spencer was being led, unconsciously or in spite of himself, to the position of the philosophical mystics —that the Godhead in himself is unknowable, dwelling in the light that no man can approach unto, the light that to the dazzled vision of finite beings appears as darkness, but that God, as the author of nature and the self-revealing Spirit in our consciousness, is neither unknowable nor unknown. Instead of ridiculing a contradiction so patent and so seemingly perverse, we should see in Herbert Spencer a good example of the strength of the theistic position, and especially of the theology of the Platonising mystics, which has made captive a thinker so little disposed to treat the names of these religious philosophers with respect.

But there is another aspect of Herbert Spencer's system which must be briefly criticised. It has been a fundamental assumption, or act of faith, with many philosophers that the logical sequence of ascending values is either closely connected with, or accurately reflected in, the course of evolution in the phenomenal world. The older form of this optimism was somewhat different. Plotinus, for example, found the scale of spiritual values reflected in the world of events, not as a sequence of ascending values in time, but as degrees of truth and reality, the most valuable

being the most real, the less valuable the less real,
till at the bottom of the scale we find the inert and
valueless substratum which he calls ὕλη, trembling on
the verge of absolute non-existence.

The assumption that the order of the world is
found, on full examination, to justify the demands
of intellectual, moral, and aesthetic optimism is
common to Plotinus and to Spencer; but the form
which Spencer gives to it is hardly tenable. All that
can be justifiably deduced from Darwin's theory of the
survival of the fittest is that the tendency of nature,
or at least of organic nature, is towards stability. If
we must find some philosophy in it, it points rather
towards sceptical pragmatism than to any other view.
That which survives is thereby proved to be the fittest,
the best, if we will. But Darwinism gives us no
criterion at all whereby we may pronounce one order
of beings higher than another. This however was
hidden from the scientists of the last century, who
were, to a strange degree, under the sway of a naturalistic optimism which regarded an actual event as, by
the fact of its occurrence, of superior value to an
event which did not occur. Moreover, they regarded
evolutionary change as a progressive increase in values.
To appraise this supposed increase in values, they
took two standards. One was that the complex is
of higher worth than the simple, and the other was
that as humanity is the roof and crown of things, all
nature may be represented as groaning and travailing
to produce at last her consummate masterpiece, our
noble selves. There is a certain provincialism about
this last assumption, characteristic of a self-complacent
age. It was not peculiar to the naturalists, for Hegel

also suggests that the Absolute had at last attained self-consciousness and self-expression in the kingdom of Prussia a hundred years ago. As for the superiority of the complex over the simple, you doctors know that in this conflict the severely simple microbe, multiplying by fission, does not always get the worst of it. Moreover, there is no reason to connect the simple with the past, and the complex with the future. To do so is to generalise from one swing of the pendulum.

It is, I think, very interesting to find that the evolutionary optimism of Hegel, which had so much influence on the protagonists of biological evolution, synchronised with the philosophical pessimism of Schopenhauer. If it is merely the will to live, to live anyhow, which makes the world go round, where, he asked, in this universal striving shall we find any value ? Is mere living, whether for oneself or in one's descendants, living without reference to any intrinsic values, a thing of any worth ? Would it not be better to refuse this irrational prompting and make an end of it ? Were not the Indian sages right in finding salvation in Nirvana ?

After all, evolutionary optimism is broken on the certain knowledge that the entire world of forms, including man and all his achievements, is destined to pass into the unconscious and inorganic mass out of which it arose. Involution is as much a law of nature as evolution. There is no escape from this doom, though some of the leading naturalists in the nineteenth century often wrote as if they had forgotten it. Let us hope, by all means, for some amelioration in the human lot in the near future ; but let us not

forget two indubitable facts—first, that there is no
law of progress ; we must work out our own salvation ;
and second, that life is given to our race, as Lucretius
says, not in fee simple, but in usufruct. The time
will come and must come, whether suddenly or
gradually, when this planet will no longer be inhabit-
able, and when, as far as the consciousness of finite
beings in this world goes, the human race will be as
if it had never been. All that is in the world, the lust
of the flesh, the lust of the eyes, and the pride of life,
passeth away. ' *Horum naturam . . . Una dies dabit
exitio, multosque per annos Sustentata ruet moles et
machina mundi.*'

There is only one way in which we may have
confidence that we may escape this doom. We may
find in our earthly experience the sure traces of eternal
values which, independently of time, independently of
the sequence of events, have a being in themselves,
or in the mind of the Supreme Being in whom all
things consist, and which, accordingly, are not only
the ever-receding goal of a historical process.

This brings me to the constructive part of my
lecture. Hitherto I have been trying to show why
certain solutions, proposed and advocated since the
illustrious Kant, fail to satisfy me. I have not even
mentioned them all. I have not discussed the theory
of Mentalism, which turns the tables on Materialism
by teaching that nothing exists except as an object
of thought. Nor have I spoken of the pluralistic
theories now so popular, according to which reality
consists of a society of conscious spirits, with or without a supreme Spirit, who is sometimes added as a
constitutional President of the Republic. I do not

myself think that these theories are of much value. They owe much of their attractiveness to the relatively dignified position which they concede to the individual, and to their promise to deliver mankind from the paralysing grip of determinism. The societies of spirits are to be free and independent, citizens of a democracy. I will leave these theories alone ; I have not time to discuss them, and they would lead me away from the conclusion towards which I wish to bring you.

I mentioned Hegel just now. He is usually supposed to have taught that the Absolute realises himself only in conscious spirits. The world, according to him, it has often been said, is as necessary to God as God is to the world. There is, I believe, no doubt that this last sentence fairly represents his teaching. But he is a very difficult writer ; and his critics are not agreed whether he really means to subordinate the Deity to the time-process, or whether the self-explication and self-realisation of which he speaks is a logical rather than a temporal process. In considering this question, which is vital to the position which I wish to put before you, I am obliged to part company with a thinker for whom I have the greatest respect, and to whom I am indebted in some of my writings, and not least in this lecture—Professor Pringle-Pattison, the author of that fine book, ' The Idea of God.'

This writer says : ' The metaphorical language in which Lotze, not to mention Hegel and others, speaks of nature as striving towards self-expression and rising as it were stage by stage towards its self-completion in mind, is clearly not intended as the record of a historical progress. Such expressions are an analysis of ideal stages, or "moments," as idealistic writers are fond of calling them, aspects of one total fact which can only be known truly as a whole or system. Hence I was at pains to insist that questions of the apparent historical genesis of the higher or more complex from the lower or simpler have no philosophical importance, seeing that philosophically considered the lower or simpler phases are not independent facts existing as a *prius*, but abstract aspects of a single fact, which is fully expressible only in terms of self-conscious experience.'

I am not convinced that Hegel's historical process of reality is meant to be taken metaphorically; he builds so much upon it. And I think I could prove that the Hegelian school, or most of them, really believe that without self-conscious finite spirits God would be only potentially existent. He realises Himself in them. Either, then, when the human race disappears, some other vehicle must be found in which the Absolute may realise himself, or God will literally die. I do not call this Theism at all, and if we have to abandon the nineteenth-century dream of unending progress, I do not see that it has any attractiveness to the religious mind. Let me illustrate the Professor's standpoint by a few quotations.

I agree, of course, entirely with the fine words : ' The presence of the Ideal is the reality of God within us '; and ' from the same fontal reality must be derived those ideals which are the master light of all our seeing, the elements, in particular, of our moral and religious life.' But I am not satisfied with the following : ' Apart from our actual experience, God or the Absolute is a subject waiting for predicates,

an empty form waiting to be filled.' (Why should it
be *our* experience which forms the predicates of the
Divine Being ?) ' If knowledge has the same meaning
in the two cases, the existence of a thing can no more
depend on God's knowing it than on my knowing it.'
The Professor has just rejected the philosophy of
mentalism or subjective idealism, as I too should
reject it. Without surrendering to this theory, which
would deprive the external world of all extra-mental
existence, we may fairly hold that the real world
consists neither of mind apart from matter, nor of
matter apart from mind, but in the unity in duality
of subject and object, of mind and the world perceived
by mind. If there is no Supreme Being behind the
immanent Spirit which lives and moves within the
world, we must take God and the world as correlatives,
neither of which has any existence without the other.
But if the creative Ideas are the thoughts of a Supreme
Being who ' spake and it was done,' who ' made the
heavens by his word, and all the hosts of them by the
breath of his mouth,' then we can hardly say that the
existence of the world does not depend on God's
knowing it. The relation of God to the creatures is
not the same as the relation of the human mind to its
objects. Again we read : ' As soon as we begin to
treat God and man as two independent facts, we lose
our hold upon the experienced fact, which is the
existence of the one in the other and through the
other. . . . God has no meaning to us out of relation
to our own lives or to spirits resembling ourselves in
their finite grasp and infinite reach ; and in the nature
of the case we have absolutely no grounds for positing
his existence out of that reference.' This seems to

deny the transcendence of God, who is regarded as
merely immanent in the minds of conscious beings.
But without forsaking the standpoint of human
experience we may surely say that the highest flights
of religious intuition, the contemplations of the great
mystics, as well as the more ordinary experiences of
communion with the Unseen in prayer, affirm constantly that God is not merely the inner side of the
cosmic process ; the Being with whom devotion brings
us into contact is emphatically not one of whom it
might be said that ' without the creature God would
not be God.' Besides this witness from experience,
the quest of absolute unity, which attracts the philosopher as much as the ideal of unbroken continuity
attracts the scientist, leads us to postulate an unknown
and ineffable Godhead above the attributes, harmonious on the whole but not to be fully unified, under
which the nature of the Creator is known to us. It
seems to me an error to say that we have no grounds
for positing the existence of God outside His relation
to ourselves. The religious mind thrills rather to the
words of Emily Brontë, in the wonderful poem which
she wrote when she was dying :

> With wide-embracing love
> Thy Spirit animates eternal years,
> Pervades and broods above,
> Changes, sustains, dissolves, creates, and rears.
>
> Though earth and man were gone,
> And suns and universes ceased to be,
> And Thou were left alone,
> Every existence would exist in Thee.

Again we read : ' God is known to us as creator of
the world ; we have no datum, no justification what-

ever, for supposing his existence out of that relation.'
' God exists as creatively realising himself in the world.'
I cannot see how these Hegelian utterances can escape
the charge that God is being placed inside the time-
process, subordinated to the category of time, and
incomplete so long as the world is incomplete. The
' far-off divine event ' to which Tennyson looks forward
is, on this showing, an event in God no less than in
the creation. To make his position quite clear, the
Professor says that we must ' abandon the conception
of God as a changeless and self-sufficient unit.'

I am particularly anxious in this lecture not to
assume the rôle of a Christian apologist. This lecture
is a humble attempt to sketch out a metaphysics of
natural science, which may be less open to objection
than the materialism, epiphenomenalism, positivism,
agnosticism, and pluralism, which have, for various
reasons, been found unsatisfactory. I have insisted
that although the sciences, for their own limited purposes, may disregard almost all qualitative estimates
of reality, those qualitative estimates, or valuations,
have quite as good a right to be regarded as true
interpretations of the real as the facts and laws with
which science is concerned. This claim rules out all
the one-sided philosophies of naturalism. Purely
scientific considerations have rendered also untenable
those theories which levy unlimited drafts on the
future. The future, says Anatole France, is a con-
venient place in which to store our dreams. To throw
our ideals into the future, says Bosanquet, is the death
of all sane idealism. If the consequences of this
admission are fully faced, I do not think we shall be
able to get much comfort from the contemplation of

the Hegelian God, who is likely, it seems, to end in ignominious stagnation, perhaps even in a return to unconsciousness, long before he can fully realise himself. I plead frankly for the theistic hypothesis as involving fewer difficulties than any other. I am quite unable to understand why our idealist philosophers, in spite of their earnest religious interests, seem to treat the theistic hypothesis as almost beneath their notice. I think they object to the one-sided relation of a First Cause to the universe. But I cannot see why there should not be such a one-sided relation.

Let us then suppose that there is a Supreme Being, who is independent of the universe in much the same sense in which Shakespeare was independent of his plays. Being Shakespeare, it was certain that he would write plays, and just the plays which he did write ; but his plays are the necessary expression of his mind and character, not the necessary conditions of his existence. Of the motives of the creation, and of the manner of creation, we know nothing whatever. We cannot penetrate the mind of the Absolute ; and I think we must frankly confess that while the return journey to God, the path of salvation, is known to us, the downward journey, the path of creation, is unknown to us. This has often been made a reproach against the school of philosophy to which I belong. We fail, we are told, to account for the world. Well, the world is a solid fact, which we have to accept, not to account for ; I see no reason why we should be admitted behind the scenes while our business is on the stage.

If I had to picture to myself how the world may be related to its Creator, I should say that though the

innermost nature of the Supreme Being is unknown
to us, He has revealed Himself under the three
attributes of Goodness, Truth, and Beauty. These
eternal and ultimate Values are not inactive thoughts ;
they necessarily produce an eternal world—a sphere
of spaceless and timeless existence—in which they
live. This is the heaven of the Christian, the intelligible (or spiritual) world of the Platonist. This
is the ultimately real world ; of the Absolute, the
fountain of all values, we cannot use any of the
categories of human thought, not even that of existence. But the divine thoughts which in heaven are
fully accomplished are also Energies. By the will of
the Creator they are to pass into outward expression
as acts. This, we may suppose, is the purpose for
which space and time, and the world in space and time,
exist. They are the field in which the thoughts of
God, transmuted into vital laws and acts of will,
express themselves. Will can only be exercised in
the presence of something which retards or resists it ;
this involves the existence of duration ; the notion of
vital law seems to require a connected system arranged
in a temporal sequence. Such a world as we know
would seem to be demanded if the thoughts of the
Creator are to appear as operative energies. This,
of course, is speculation ; it may be worthless ; but
it is the only way in which I can think of the relation
of the world of becoming to the world of being, of the
temporal to the eternal.

I should go on to say that in the apprehension of
these eternal Values, and in earnest striving to co-
operate with the divine will in actualising them, lies
the whole duty of man and the path by which he can

Q

claim his status in the eternal world. The Platonists held that the Soul is on the confines of the eternal and of the perishing. It has an insecure footing in the upper world, which it may fully attain or lose. Above the soul is the Intelligence, *Nous*, which St. Paul and later Christian thinkers called *Pneuma*, Spirit. This is in a sense super-personal, belonging entirely to the eternal world. The highest human life is that of Soul raised to Spirit.

You will remember that, following almost all the best authorities, I have named three eternal and ultimate Values : the Good, which is the goal of all moral endeavour ; the True, which is the goal of all scientific and all philosophical inquiry ; and the Beautiful, which all pure Art strives to realise. It follows that there are three paths up the hill of the Lord, which, we may suppose, meet and unite near the top, and that the path of science is one of them. It also follows, I think, that as a saint may be a very holy man without knowing much of science or art, and a poet or artist may be satisfied with his own inspiration, so the man of science may specialise, without fearing that he is losing the pearl of great price while pursuing lesser ends. Any worthy object of study, pursued disinterestedly, has a universal value, and does not permit its votary to be very seriously narrowed by his zeal—though of course the saint, the poet, and the man of science may all cut a poor figure in keeping their households in order and managing their investments. But the scientist should not try to build a philosophical system on his abstract field of knowledge. He should recognise that there are other avenues to truth, not less important than

his own, and that in those fields he must be content
to learn from those who are specialists in them, as
they should be content to learn from him on his own
subjects.

I know that religion, science, and art are all jealous
of each other, because each of them claims, in a sense,
to cover the whole field, that is, to interpret all experience from its own point of view. Philosophy tries
to mediate between them, and the task has so far been
beyond its powers. Some of the new philosophies
undermine the authority of science, as some of the
older systems undermined the authority of religion.
Complete reconciliation is not in sight ; but there is
no reason for hostility, which reacts unfavourably upon
our whole view of life. For the eternal Values are not
entirely separate from each other ; they are, if my
view be correct, a triple star, the attributes under
which the one Supreme Being has revealed to us His
nature and His will ; and we shall be harmoniously
developed men in proportion as we can make our own
something of what the saint, the scientist, and the
artist respectively find in their experience of life.

There are some, I know, who picture to themselves
Religion as retreating from one position to another
before the victorious advance of science, and now
preparing to die in its last ditch. That is not at
all my opinion. Organised Religion is certainly in
retreat, but why ? I do not think that scientific discoveries have so much to do with it as is often supposed. I should say rather that Religion has in the
past tried to coerce the irreligious, by garish promises
and terrifying threats—both promises and threats
being offered in grossly materialistic language. When

these promises and threats lost their cogency it
secularised itself further and announced that its object
was to promote a comfortable organisation of society.
These irreligious appeals have failed ; the irreligious
no longer care for the menaces or promises of the
Church, and they have no respect for the priest in
politics.   But the religious appeal is in no way
weakened.   Now, as always, the soul of man lives by
admiration, hope, and love ; and when these are fused
in homage to the unseen but ever-present Being, the
' Value of Values,' as a medieval thinker called him,
who exists unchanged behind the flux of phenomena,
the appropriate reaction, *worship*, is set up, and the
human spirit sets forth again ' on its adventure brave
and new,' less hampered than formerly by the frag-
ments of obsolete science and philosophy which the
new knowledge has helped us to discard.

FAITH AND REASON

THIS is, I believe, the twelfth of the annual Conferences held under the auspices of the Churchmen's Union. Whether this year's meeting is to complete the series, or whether these Conferences, which have attracted so much interest and been productive of so much good, are to be continued, I am glad that this year we are assembled not to controvert the opinions of others, nor even to defend ourselves, except indirectly against misunderstandings and misrepresentations, but to testify to the faith that is in us. We are here, primarily, to help each other, though we hope that in formulating our own beliefs we may perhaps help others too.

The general title of the papers which are to be read this week is ' The Faith of a Modern Churchman.' The indefinite article was not chosen without a purpose. We want the readers of the papers to speak for themselves, not for the Society. We are not a well-drilled army, all marching in step. We have no party programme, no official syllabus of opinions, which we all have to defend. We agree only in our confidence that the Spirit of Truth, and of Truthfulness, guides and blesses honest enquiry, and that ' the Bible of the race ' is still being written. We reverence tradition, but we will not be fettered by it. God is still revealing Himself ; and if it is true that ' the invisible things of Him from the foundation of the world are clearly seen, being understood by the things that are made, even His eternal power and Godhead,' then we must expect that the mass of new knowledge about the things that are made, which science has revealed to us, will prove to have important bearings even on our beliefs about invisible things, and especially about the manner in which the power of the Godhead is exercised. And when we speak of science, we include not only the study of natural law, but the scientific study of history, and Biblical criticism.

There are of course many who accept the principles of free enquiry, but are not Christians or Churchmen. We are Christians and Churchmen, and we hope that we can give a reason for the faith that is in us without being false to the strictest obligations of intellectual honesty.

We have discarded the two infallibilities, the infallible Church and the infallible Book. Neither of them is primitive. The former grew in the struggle, first with Paganism, and then with heresy, in the course of which Christianity was changed from a religion of the Spirit to a religion of authority. The latter was the basis of another religion of authority, at war with the first. It seems to all Liberal Churchmen that belief in the Holy Spirit holds a far less central position in traditional Christianity, whether Catholic or Protestant, than it does in the New Testament. I am thinking not only of St. Paul and the Fourth Gospel, but of the Acts of the Apostles, in which the appeal to the guidance of the Spirit, or (in one place) the Spirit of Jesus, is the leitmotiv of the whole book.

We have been called by others, and we sometimes

call ourselves, Modernists. I have always disliked the
name, which seems to me even less suitable than the
long word Latitudinarians, which was hurled at the
Christian rationalists and Platonising theologians of
the seventeenth century, and which, as one of the
victims complained, ' they have taught themselves
to pronounce as glibly as if it were shorter by four or
five syllables.' We are not Modernists, except in the
sense in which Irenaeus claims that all Christians
are Modernists ' *Omnem novitatem attulit semetipsum
afferens.*' We are not Modernists, because our Christianity is no new thing, but older, we may venture
to say, than either Catholicism or Protestantism. We
find it in St. Paul and St. John, and we reverently hold
that we find it in the teaching of Christ Himself. For
though our Lord shows no obligation to Greek thought,
which from the time of St. Paul onwards has had a
marked influence upon Christian theology and worship,
it is surely no accident that as soon as the Church
began to speak and write in Greek, it began to think in
Greek, and that the original Gospel, with all its essential
features unaltered, came to Europe, and conquered
there, in a Greek dress. Most of us, I think, are
glad to find that what was best in the old civilisation,
its spirit of unfettered enquiry, its long tradition of
deep thought, its reverence for knowledge, its robust
faith that divine truth is accessible to man, was carried
over into the new religion, and preserved a real continuity with the glories of the ancient culture, so soon
to be eclipsed in the welter of barbarism. In any
case, whether we value the heritage of Greece or not, it
is certain that the tradition which we wish to follow,
whether we call it Greek, or Platonic, or mystical, or

Liberal, or Renaissance, has a history within the Christian Church. It was weak only during the Dark Ages ; it took fresh life at the Renaissance, and has maintained itself in the Church, by the side of Catholicism and Protestantism, ever since. No one, I think, can justly dispute our right to be in the Church, and to carry on, to the best of our ability, a tradition which has been, on the whole, a singularly honourable one. We wish to deal with the new knowledge which has come to us, whether scientific or historical, in the same spirit in which the Greek theologians dealt with Greek philosophy, the Schoolmen with the partially rediscovered Aristotle, and the Renaissance scholars with the newly recovered Greek Testament. We try to be up to date with our science and our scholarship ; but there is nothing ' modern ' in our desire to add to our faith knowledge, or in our hope that the Spirit of Christ is still with us, to guide us into all truth.

I have been asked, by way of introduction to the other papers which will be read at this Conference, to say something about the relations of Faith and Reason. Both words need careful consideration, for they are not always used in the same sense, and we have to remember that Christians do not all speak the same language. I do not want to inflict upon you a learned discussion of technical terms, but I think we must try to define what we mean by Faith and by Reason.

When we use the word Faith, without special reference to religion, we mean either the holding for true of something which is neither verified by experience nor demonstrated by logic, or else confidence in the wisdom and integrity of a person. We have two verbs, ' believe ' and ' trust,' which correspond to these two meanings of Faith.

Pistis, in Plato, means unverified conviction, or incomplete science ; it is a stepping-stone to real knowledge, but belongs itself to the region of opinion. But in later Greek philosophy the word rises somewhat in dignity. Plutarch, for example, says, or quotes his father as saying: ' The ancient ancestral Faith is sufficient, than which it is impossible to mention or discover anything clearer. If the common foundation for the pious life is shaken at any point, the whole becomes insecure.' Philo, and, I believe, some of the magical papyri, use the word in an exalted sense. Proclus, in agreement with the magical papyri, though not with Plotinus, actually puts Faith above Reason. ' Those beings which are not enlightened by Reason are necessarily deprived of Faith, which is above Reason.' The following passages from Proclus are extremely interesting : ' There are three constitutive factors of divine things, which are present in all the higher modes of being, Goodness, Wisdom, and Beauty. And there are three contributory factors, which are secondary to those just named, but which pervade all divine dispensations—Faith, Truth, and Love.' Faith is ' that which establishes everything and settles it in the Good.' This, as we shall see, is not quite the Christian doctrine.

Faith in the Synoptic Gospels is a spirit of receptiveness towards Christ and His teaching, loyalty to His person.

In St. Paul's epistles, I would call special attention to Gal. iii. 23 : ' before the coming of the Faith,' words which show that the first Christians felt their

Faith to be as new a thing as their Hope and their
Love ; and to ' the household of Faith ' for the Church.
I do not think that *Pistis* in St. Paul is ever equivalent
to mere *fiducia,* the subjective assurance of Lutheran-
ism ; we must remember that at that time belief involved a changed life and membership of a persecuted
society. ' The new and significant peculiarity of
Paul's conception of Faith,' says Pfleiderer truly, ' is
the mystical union with Christ, the self-identification
with Christ in a fellowship of life and death . . .
Life in the Faith means the same as " Christ liveth in
me." ' The words in Romans xiv, 23, ' whatever is not
of Faith is sin,' do not mean ' all works done before
justification are sinful ' ; they merely mean, in this
context, that whether we observe dietary rules or not,
we are to have a clear conscience. While we are here
' we walk by Faith, not by sight ' : the form of the risen
Christ is hidden from us ; but some day we shall see
face to face. Then Faith will not be abolished, but
will become eternal (1 Cor. xiii). Lastly, the Christian
' stands fast in the Faith ' (1 Cor. xvi 13), but also
grows in Faith, and attains the status of the full-grown
man by coming unto ' the unity of the Faith, and of the
knowledge of the Son of God.' In these passages we
have a deep conception of Faith, which has determined
the Christian use of the word.

In the Epistle to the Hebrews we have the famous
but obscure definition : ' Faith is the assurance of [or,
giving substance to] things hoped for, the proving [or,
test] of objects not seen.' I have not space to discuss
the meaning of the disputed words, on which Chry-
sostom's comment is noteworthy : ' Whereas things
that are matters of hope seem to be unsubstantial,

Faith gives them substance, or rather does not give it, but is itself their being.' This, in modern language, seems to make Faith rather too subjective. There are two other important sentences about Faith in this Epistle. 'Without Faith it is impossible to please Him, for He that cometh to God must believe that He is, and that He is a rewarder of them that diligently seek Him.' Again, 'Faith is the seeing of the invisible One,' God, during our earthly pilgrimage. Augustine's comment is, ' *Errabant adhuc et patriam quaerebant ; sed duce Christo errare non poterant. Via illis fuit visio Dei.*'

The word *Pistis* does not occur in the Fourth Gospel ; it is, I think, avoided like the other party catchwords of the time, *Wisdom* and *Knowledge*. But the use of the verb seems to lay about equal stress on the two meanings of conviction and complete trust.

In the earlier Fathers the doctrine is quite explicit that, to quote Ignatius, ' Faith and love towards Christ Jesus are the beginning and end of life. The beginning is Faith, the end is Love.' This is further developed by Clement of Alexandria, in admirable language, which I must find space to quote. ' Faith, which the Greeks disparage as futile and barbarous, is a voluntary anticipation, the assent of piety—the substance of things hoped for, the evidence of things not seen, as the Apostle says. Others have defined Faith as a uniting assent to an unseen object. If then it be choice, the desire is in this case intellectual, since it desires something. And since choice is the beginning of action, Faith is the beginning of action, being the foundation of rational choice, when a man sets before himself, through Faith, the demonstration which he anticipates. Voluntarily to follow what is expedient is the beginning of understanding it. Unswerving choice, therefore, gives a great impetus towards knowledge.' Again : ' Fear develops into Faith, and Faith into Love. But I do not fear my Father as I fear a wild beast ; I fear and love Him at once. Blessed therefore is he who has Faith, which is compounded by love and fear.' Once more : ' Faith is a compendious knowledge of essentials, while knowledge is a sure and firm demonstration of the things received through Faith, carrying us on to unshaken conviction and scientific certainty. There is a first kind of saving change from heathenism to Faith, a second from Faith to knowledge ; and knowledge, as it passes on into love, begins at once to establish a mutual friendship between the knower and the known. Perhaps he who has reached this stage is " equal to the angels." ' I do not think we shall find sounder teaching about the nature of Faith anywhere than in Clement. Faith begins as an experiment, and ends as an experience. It begins as a resolution to stand or fall by the noblest hypothesis, as Frederic Myers says; but it is verified progressively as we go on. It passes into knowledge, and knowledge in turn passes into love, which unites knower and known. This is the mystical ascent to God, of which Faith is the first step. There is in it, and there must be, an element of real moral venture ; but it is not irrational ; as we climb higher, we can see further.

Augustine recognises three elements in Faith—*assensus, notitia, fiducia*. ' There are,' he says, ' three classes of credible things : those which are always believed and never understood, such as historical events; those which are understood as they are believed, such as all subjects of human reasoning; and those which are first believed and afterwards understood, such as those about divine matters, which cannot be understood except by the pure in heart; and this condition comes from keeping the moral law.' It is well known that Anselm said *Credo ut intelligam*, and that Abelard altered this into *Intelligo ut credam*. The Schoolmen were not agreed as to the respective claims of primacy for Faith and knowledge.

Catholicism has always been rationalistic, up to a point. Thomas Aquinas taught that divine truth is divided, not in itself, but in its relation to our faculties. Part of it can be known by human reason, part of it only by revelation. The existence of God is demonstrable, though it requires brains and education to follow the argument. Faith involves an act of the will, but it is not an arbitrary choice; it presupposes some knowledge. I do not find the position of Aquinas very clear. He makes it plain that there is a moral and an intellectual element in Faith; but on the intellectual side it seems to rest on Church authority, which he does not permit us to scrutinise. But it is important to know that this limited rationalism is still the orthodox Catholic doctrine; the Vatican Council of 1870 anathematised those who say that the one true God cannot be certainly known by the light of natural reason.

I will not go into the Reformation controversies about Faith. The Council of Trent condemned the propositions that justifying Faith is nothing but confidence in the mercy of God, who forgives our sins for the sake of Christ, and that man is absolved and justified because he firmly believes that he is absolved and justified. This protest against identifying Faith with mere *fiducia* was made necessary by the language of Luther himself, Melanchthon, and the Confession of Augsburg.

The Anglican Homilies teach that Faith is not merely belief, but also trust and hope. Saving Faith ' is not dead, but worketh by charity, as St. Paul declareth. If thou have it, thou hast the ground of all good works.'

The pragmatist doctrine of Faith, as an act of violence exercised by the will upon the intellect to make it accept what we find it helpful to believe, has doubtless been often acted upon at all times, but it has never been crudely avowed till our own time. According to George Tyrrell : ' A certain sense of unreality is part of the trial of Faith. . . . We hold to a belief in obedience to the command of God. . . . But this will not prevent that seeming black to us which God tells us is white.' ' The great mass of our beliefs are reversible.'

This is the teaching of the real ' Modernists,' who are anything rather than Liberals.

I have argued elsewhere that Faith is belief in the objective existence of a realm of values, which religion connects with the name of God. I have also protested against the opinion, which is widely held, that while science, by a deliberate abstraction, contemplates a world of facts without values, religion contemplates values apart from facts. When we consider that both science and religion desire to know things as they are, this bisection of experience would seem to be suicidal to both alike. It is true, and very important, that science tries to express everything in terms of quantity, which shall be commensurable, while religion, and the other spiritual activities of the human mind, are interested almost entirely in quality. But the scientific view of the world is not indifferent to quality or value. It seeks to find law, harmony, uniformity in nature ; it regards disorder and inexplicable irregularity as a scandal to be removed by more patient observation. Here surely we have a Faith, that fuller knowledge will confirm that belief in the character and methods of the cosmic process which we have adopted because it seems to us to be the worthiest as well as the most probable. The reign of law is certainly a hypothesis which belongs to our judgments of value ; a strictly impartial weighing and counting of atoms would hardly have led us to it. And, on the other hand, it is surely untrue to say that the objects of religious contemplation are unrealised ideals, ends towards which action is directed. ' He that cometh to God must believe that He *is*.'

Science and religion, philosophy and politics, have all alike suffered from the nineteenth-century passion for throwing ideals into the future. We can dream that the future will realise all our hopes, though prudence might suggest that as it is not yet born, it is too early to baptise it. A great part of the quarrel between science and religion arises from divergent opinions not about the world as it is, but about what it will be. Faith, for a vast number of people, means a belief that the scheme of things will gradually, or suddenly, be remoulded nearer to our heart's desire. Thus, in forming our estimate of the world, we levy unlimited drafts on the future, like Mr. Lloyd George's Government. These drafts are not likely to be honoured. A saner idealism would look for its values in the world we know, around us and within ; and as these values are real existents, and accessible to all who seek them in the right way, they will bring the faith of the scientist and the faith of the religious mystic very much nearer together. What estranges them at present is very largely that they reciprocally doubt the solvency of each other's investments in ' futures.' This is also what exacerbates politics.

The ultimate values, which religion calls the revealed attributes of God, are the objects of Faith. The familiar classification into a triple star—three sisters that never can be sundered without tears—cannot be improved upon. As Goethe says, in Carlyle's translation :

> As all nature's myriad changes
> Still one changeless power proclaim,
> So through thought's wide kingdom ranges
> One vast meaning, e'er the same :
> This is Truth—eternal Reason—
> That in Beauty takes its dress,
> And, serene through time and season,
> Stands complete in Righteousness.

Lotze thinks that our appreciation of these ultimate values is given intuitively, and I think he is right. They are absolute, as being incapable of being resolved into each other or into anything else. They are ends, never means. ' If a man desires the good life except for itself,' says Plotinus, ' it is not the good life that he desires.' Or, as Spinoza says, ' Blessedness is not the reward of virtue, but virtue itself.' The same is true of the worship of Truth, and of Beauty. The rival claims of the three may sometimes conflict, but chiefly when our service is impure and not wholly disinterested. Complete unification is forbidden by the conditions of finite existence, but we are able to discern that they are the attributes of the same supreme Being.

There has been endless discussion whether we have a distinct faculty for the knowledge of God. The faculty-psychology is rightly discredited, and it is probable that the champions of the intellect, the will, and of a special mystical sense, transfigured and exalted feeling, are not so far apart as in controversy they seem to be. Nevertheless, mistakes are often made, and it is worth while to call attention to them.

Emotional theism is not the same thing as mysticism. The intuition in which the mystic believes, and which he hopes to attain, is the pearl of great price, to procure which all else must be surrendered. The mystics do not make things easy for themselves. But emotional theism, as we frequently encounter it, is a soft and easy creed. ' Dreaming is easy and thinking is difficult ' ; the emotionalist steeps himself or herself in luxurious feeling and pathetic imagination, which make no severe call upon either the will or the intellect. ' The heart has its reasons which the intellect knows not of.' How often have these words of Pascal been abused to justify a temper too indolent to enquire, too bigoted to doubt, a voluptuous devotionality allied perhaps to refined aestheticism, but totally alien to the austerity and penetrating sincerity of the Gospel !

It is rather deplorable that Robert Browning, in his later poems, should have seemed to countenance a Faith resting on pure feeling ·

> Wholly distrust thy knowledge, then, and trust
> As wholly love allied to ignorance.

And :

> So let us say—not, Since we know, we love,
> But rather, Since we love, we know enough.

R

This is surely not the real Browning, unless we say that it is the product of a strongly-willed optimism contending with intellectual pessimism. It may be that Faith begins in an emotion, and that in the beatific vision it ends in what we may call pure feeling ; but it has to pass through those intermediate stages which Clement describes, and which, as Proclus says, are complex, though the lowest and highest things are simple.

That Faith is purely an act of the will is equally false, and equally popular as a theory. Of course, the wish is often father to the thought ; and Hobbes may be right when he says that even the axioms of geometry would be disputed if men's passions were concerned in them. But Hobbes does not say that they could be disproved or rendered doubtful if men's interests lay in denying them. It is also true that we can in the first instance ' adhere to ' (the expression is well chosen) a creed because we choose, and then cut off our retreat by refusing to listen to arguments on the other side, and above all by making a personal wager by so acting that we should be losers if it were false. As Clough says :

> Action will furnish belief ; but will that belief be the true one ?
> That is the point, you know. However, it doesn't much matter.

This is pragmatism before William James. But how does he know that it doesn't much matter ?

Among the Schoolmen, the Englishman, William of Occam, was a champion of the will and practical reason against the moderate intellectualism of Aquinas. This philosophy is naturally allied to scepticism, and may be easily turned into the service of a blind acceptance

of authority. Kant, as is well known, distinguished
between the theoretical and practical reason, and
attempted to restore, through the latter, those fundamental beliefs which, according to him, could not be
established by the former. This was to admit a rift
within the reason. Some of his successors have gone
much further, and have sought to discredit the reason
itself. Herbert Spencer was, I think, justified in his
protest :

'Let those who can, believe that there is eternal war
between our intellectual faculties and our moral obligations. I for one can admit no such radical vice in the
constitution of things.'

This disparagement of the intellect is connected
with the separation between judgments of fact and
judgments of value, to which I have already taken
strong exception. This is the philosophy which is
connected with the name of Ritschl. There is a strong
sceptical element in Newman, though he would have
been shocked at the developments of his position by
the Roman Catholic Modernists. Many modern writers,
such as Kidd and Lord Balfour, have defended a Faith
based on sceptical anti-intellectualism. Lord Balfour
sets up ' authority ' against reason. He calls authority
the rival and opponent of reason, and makes it stand
for ' that group of non-rational causes, moral, social,
and educational, which produces its results by psychic
processes other than reasoning.' It ' coerces the operations of reason to a fore-ordained issue,' which is
fortunate, since ' reason is a force most apt to divide
and disintegrate.' I cannot see why these non-rational
processes, which coerce the operations of reason to
a fore-ordained issue, should be called ' authority.'

They seem to me a dignified phrase for what the school-boy calls fudging his sums.

But we cannot afford to despise this revolt against the intellect, for it has affected much of our recent philosophy and theology. The two most notable theological books since the war, Heiler's ' Catholicism ' and Otto's ' The Holy,' are both irrationalist in tendency, especially the latter. I am disposed to think that the mechanism and determinism of nineteenth-century science are very unwelcome to the temper of our generation, which is wilful, superstitious, and sentimental. The naturalists of Queen Victoria's reign built on their scientific studies a superstructure of badly designed philosophy, an incongruous mixture of atomism and pantheism, which the religious mind rightly refused to accept. Then a revolt against materialism broke out within the domain of science itself. Many biologists, and most psychologists, have broken loose from mechanistic determinism, as we saw in our Conference last year. Thus the authority of science is divided and shaken. The study of religious psychology seems to have diminished the importance of reason as a constitutive factor of Faith, and there are men who for various causes would be glad to be given freedom to believe—' at their own risk,' as is sometimes added—what they would like to be true.

Modern anti-intellectualism is not based on the primacy of the will over the intellect, so much as on the genuinely pragmatist contention that all our beliefs are founded on practical needs. Our whole picture of the world, it is said, is a selection from the mass of experience, an artificial construction determined by our necessities and interests. We notice

what helps or harms us ; what does not concern us we
neglect and hardly perceive at all.   Even the so-called
laws of nature are only instruments to be used ; they
are diagrams which may be approximately correct, but
they have no sacredness in themselves ; we are not
obliged to believe them.   I have collected elsewhere
some characteristic utterances by members of this
school.   'No fact,' says Le Roy, 'has any existence
and scientific value except in and by a theory ; whence
it follows that strictly speaking it is the savant who
makes the scientific facts.'   'A dogma is a truth
belonging to the vital order ; it presents its object
under the forms of the action commanded to us by it,
and the obligation to adhere to it concerns properly
its practical significance, its vital value.'   This suggests not obscurely that it does not matter to Faith
whether a historical dogma ever went through the form
of taking place or not.   But as all other events are in
the same position, there is here no special disparagement of those which are miraculous.   To take his own
example, when we say that Jesus rose from the dead,
we only mean that we should 'treat Him as if He were
our contemporary.'

George Tyrrell, in slightly more guarded language,
takes the same view :

'Beliefs that have been found to foster and promote
the spiritual life of the soul must so far be in accordance
with the nature and the laws of that will world with
which it is the aim of religion to bring us into harmony ;
their practical value results from and is founded in
their representative value.'   'Mistakings of faith-
values for fact-values are to be ascribed to the almost
ineradicable materialism of the human mind.'

I can withdraw nothing of what I wrote in 1909 on this subject :

' Such a philosophy would never have attracted Christian priests except at a time of exceptional difficulty and perplexity. The aid which it brings is illusory ; it enables a man to blow hot and cold with the same mouth and feel no qualms, but it offers no solution of the problem.' ' This almost absolute scepticism about objective truth, if followed to its logical conclusion, would lead us, as it has led Loisy, far outside Christianity. A scepticism which denies all confidence even to the instrument of thought, obliterating the difference between fact and fiction, history and fable, has hardly enough ground left on which to plant its own feet. This school has betrayed some of the *arcana imperii* of Catholicism, but, as might be expected, this has not diminished the determination of the hierarchy to repudiate it.'

The relation of Faith to authority requires a little more consideration. Authority in the religious sphere generally means absolute or infallible authority, such as Catholics ascribe to the Church, some Protestants to the Bible, and a few mystics to the Inner Light. In fact, there are no such infallible authorities. Alan of Lille in the thirteenth century wittily said ' Authority has a nose of wax ; it can be twisted either way.' But of course we can decide for ourselves that we will follow one authority only, and refuse to listen to any others. It is not a very dignified position, for it amounts to saying ' I will believe because I choose.' This kind of religion cannot be anything better than an anodyne ; but an anodyne is unfortunately just what many people want from their religion.

What authority means for a Catholic has been
clearly stated by Cardinal Newman. The authority of
the Church ' has the prerogative of an indirect jurisdiction on subject-matters which lie beyond its own
proper limits, and it most reasonably has such a jurisdiction. It could not properly defend religious truth
without claiming for that truth what may be called its
pomoeria, or, to take another illustration, without
acting as we act, as a nation, in claiming as our own
not only the land on which we live, but what are called
British waters. The Catholic Church claims not only
to judge infallibly on religious questions, but to
animadvert on opinions in secular matters which bear
upon religion, on matters of philosophy, of science, of
literature, of history, and it demands our submission
to her claim. It claims to censure books, to silence
authors, and to forbid discussions. It must of course
be obeyed without a word.' This is the terrible slavery
of soldiers on the march. ' Their's not to make reply,
Their's not to reason why, Their's but to do and die.'

The tyranny of the infallible Book is less shocking,
because it is weaker. ' The Bible,' says Chillingworth,
' is the religion of Protestants.' I do not think I need
waste time over it here, since Oxford is not in Tennessee.

Nor need I say much about the supposed infallibility
of individual inspiration, the ' testimony of the Holy
Spirit.' It is still sometimes abused, as when people
ask for a ' leading ' on some question which they have
to decide, and then omit to use their best judgments
upon it, or to ask for good advice. The early Quakers,
as the Friends of to-day admit, fell into the error of
making the inner light something wholly alien to man's
nature. ' The light of which we speak,' says Barclay,

'is not only distinct but of a different nature from the soul of man and its faculties.' This is to make the inner light itself external, and it may lead to absurdities, as when a Quaker woman exclaimed : ' Jerusalem ? It has not yet been revealed to me that there is such a place.'

Authority, like a good educator, ought to aim at making itself superfluous. We cannot do without it, but our progress in the spiritual life may be measured by the extent to which our Faith rests no longer on authority but on experience. Faith, as we found Clement saying, must pass into knowledge, the state in which God's commands are no longer arbitrary edicts, but are understood and accepted by our minds. This is the ' reasonable service ' of which St. Paul speaks. To give authority any higher place than this implies the one really bottomless scepticism, which denies that the human mind can distinguish truth from falsehood in criticising an alleged revelation.

I think I have made it plain how I understand Faith. There is, I believe, in all of us an innate attraction for things that are true and pure and noble and of good report. The act by which we resolve, God helping us, to take our stand on this side is the initial act of Faith. In proportion as we adhere to this resolution, we come to see more clearly what God means us to make of our lives. The facts and laws of the spiritual world become more familiar to us ; we begin to have the testimony of the Holy Spirit within us that our prayers are heard ; and though we may too often forget God, we do not seriously think that He forgets us, or doubt His exist- ence. Those who have advanced further in the life of grace tell us all that the saints and mystics say about

the irradiation of the whole personality by the felt
presence of the Holy Spirit. Their testimony is so
clear and so consistent that we cannot suspect it of
being unreal. It does not, of course, certify us of the
truth of any event in the past or future; but as our
best moments are, almost from the first, connected
with the figure of the human Christ, and with His
recorded words, we are surely justified in following
St. Paul's example, and calling the spiritual presence
which envelops us the Spirit of Christ. So far as we
have a living Faith, it seems to be an enhancement
of our whole personality, and though in some persons
the will is the strongest faculty, in others the intellect,
in others the affections, it does not seem that Faith
strengthens one part of our nature and starves another.
When this happens, it means that we have been badly
taught; and this happens very often, for imperfect, and
worse than imperfect, conceptions of Faith are very rife.

We have now to consider the second noun in our
title—the word Reason. The word in this connexion
means the intellectual side of our nature, treated as
something apart from the will and feelings. A religion
which rests on reason is called rationalism; and when
we have mentioned this word we feel at once that we
are in a controversial atmosphere. A rationalist, in
common speech, means one who applies to religious
matters the same tests that he uses in judging the things
of this world; and we assume, not always rightly, that
he comes to negative conclusions.

I have shown that there is a rationalistic element
in orthodox Catholicism, and we hear the charge of
'intellectualism' brought against the Greeks, against
the Schoolmen, and against philosophers of the school

of Hegel. I do not think that the criticism is justified in the case of the later Greek teachers. The word *Nous*, which they used for the highest of our faculties, is carefully distinguished from the discursive reason, which has an honourable place, but not the highest. So much misunderstanding has been caused by translating *Nous* by ' intellect ' or ' intelligence,' that I prefer to render it by ' spirit ' when dealing with the later Platonists. The Christian Platonists, in fact, used *Pneuma* where their Pagan contemporaries used *Nous*.

The Schoolmen undoubtedly used their admirable logical training on the dogmas of religion, and often forgot that the concepts of religious thought cannot be manipulated like counters. But, if I may venture to speak with very scanty knowledge of scholastic theology, I do not think that the contempt expressed for it by some Modernists is justified. I have read with profit some of the modern Jesuit manuals, which follow the methods of St. Thomas Aquinas.

The Panlogism ascribed to Hegel is perhaps open to the charge of intellectualism, though I thoroughly dislike the word. The time has probably passed when these grandiose constructions could seem to have solved the riddle of the universe. There are, however, some powerful religious thinkers still among us who acknowledge a great debt to Hegel.

Rationalism suggests to most of us a type of religion which flourished especially in the seventeenth and eighteenth centuries. It has done valuable and necessary work in driving out the intruding forces of ecclesiastical authority from secular subjects. You will not have forgotten the amazing sentences which I read a few minutes ago from Cardinal Newman. But the claim to judge spiritual truth by what is called common sense, rejecting with scorn all that can be called mysticism, soon carries us out of religion properly so called. The rationalist may become a mere moralist, or he may write a book like Paley's 'Evidences,' on which a Cambridge don pronounced a suitable epitaph when he said that Paley had the merit of reducing Christianity to a form eminently fitted for examination purposes.

The Cambridge Platonists, and especially Benjamin Whichcote, are full of the praises of Reason. From Whichcote's 'Aphorisms' we may quote:

'A man has as much right to use his own understanding in judging of truth, as he has a right to use his own eyes to see the way.' 'He that gives reason for what he saith has done what is fit to be done and the most that can be done. He that gives no reason speaks nothing, though he saith never so much.'

'When the doctrine of the Gospel becomes the reason of our mind, it will be the principle of our life.' 'Reason discovers what is natural, and receives what is supernatural.'

Nevertheless, the Cambridge group were not rationalists in the ordinary sense, but devout disciples of the Platonists, in whose writings they had steeped themselves. Their aim is to establish the autonomy of the Christian faith as a self-evidencing religion of the Spirit. If Whichcote talks rather too much about Reason, without clearly defining what Reason means in spiritual matters, his friend John Smith, whose university sermons are perhaps the best ever written, makes it abundantly clear that it is only the spiritually enlightened mind that can reason truly on divine things. He says :

' God is not better defined to us by our understandings than by our wills and affections. He is not only
the eternal Reason, that almighty mind and wisdom
which our understandings converse with ; but He is
also that unstained Beauty and Supreme Good which
our wills are perpetually catching after ; and where-
soever we find true Beauty, Love, and Goodness, we
may say, here or there is God.' ' Reason in man being
Lumen de lumine, a light flowing from the Fountain
and Father of lights, it was to enable man to work out
of himself all those notions of God which are the true
ground-work of love and obedience to God, and conformity to Him ; and in moulding the inward man into
the greatest conformity to the nature of God was the
perfection and efficacy of the religion of nature. But
since man's fall from God, the inward virtue and vigour
of Reason is much abated, the soul having suffered
a πτεροῤῥύησις, as Plato says, a *defluvium pennarum* :
those principles of divine truth which were first
engraven upon man's heart with the finger of God are
now, as the characters of some ancient monuments,
less clear and legible than at first. And therefore God
hath provided the truth of divine revelation. . . . But
besides this outward revelation, there is also an inward
impression of it, which is in a more special manner
attributed to God. We cannot see divine things but
in a divine light. . . . He that made our souls in His
own image and likeness can easily find a way into them.
. . . Thus it is God alone that acquaints the soul with
the truths of revelation ; and He also it is that does
strengthen and raise the soul to better apprehensions
even of natural truth, God being that in the intellectual
world which the sun is in the sensible, as some of the

ancient Fathers love to speak, and the ancient philosophers too, who meant God by their *Intellectus Agens*,
whose proper work they supposed to be not so much to
enlighten the object as the faculty.'

When we come to the Deists, we are sensible at
once of a sharp fall of temperature.   One of the first,
Charles Blount, who says that ' Faith is like a piece of
blank paper, on which you may write as well one
miracle as another,' protests that his own religion is
based entirely on reason.   He was modern enough to
commit suicide because he was not allowed to marry
his deceased wife's sister.   Toland's ' Christianity not
Mysterious ' made him famous.   He is more interested
in the content of Christianity than in the evidences for
it.   All that we are required to believe can be understood and proved.   ' If by knowledge be meant understanding what is believed, I stand by it that Faith is
knowledge.'   Toland ended in a kind of pantheism.   In
nearly all these writers, and in their orthodox opponent
Butler, there is a cool common sense which seems to
belong to ethics rather than to religion.   After a time
attention was concentrated on so-called evidences, and
this era of arid rationalism came gradually to an end.

It may be worth while to compare St. Paul's words
with the tones of these cultivated but unspiritual
reasoners.   ' My speech and preaching were not in
persuasive words of wisdom, but in demonstration of
the Spirit and of power ;   that your faith should not
stand in the wisdom of men but in the power of God.
Howbeit we speak wisdom among them that are
perfect ;   yet a wisdom not of this world . . . but we
speak the wisdom of God in a mystery, even the wisdom
that hath been hidden, which God fore-ordained before

the world unto our glory.' Spiritual wisdom, you see, is unchanging and eternal ; it is communicated to us in types and shadows dim—in symbols—till we grow up into the power of understanding it. This wisdom is something very different from the dry rationalism, whether orthodox or deistic, of the eighteenth century. The writers of this period, on both sides, had forgotten the meaning of Faith. They wanted to prove Faith, not experimentally, but logically. This is just what cannot be done. They wanted to find a place for God in their scheme. But God is too big to be fitted into a frame. He is not one of the factors for which science has to account.

The upshot of the whole matter is that Faith leads us to a Reason above rationalism. Spiritual things are spiritually discerned. But whereas organised religion has spread its aegis over a multitude of beliefs which do not concern spiritual things, and which can be established or rebutted only by the natural under-standing, we must be on our guard against insidious attempts to disparage the findings of Reason, or to oust it from its proper province. In spite of much recent philosophy, this is not a sceptical âge ; it is not an age when the triumphs of natural science and scholarship can be bowed out of court as irrelevant to the seeker after truth ; it is not an age when the same event can be said to be true for faith but untrue for science. We must be humble, for we are compassed by mysteries, and our spiritual faculties are poor and dull ; but we can be, and we must be, perfectly honest with ourselves and with others. As Harnack says : ' If piety should suffer in the process, there is a stronger interest than that of piety—namely, that of truth.'

THE TRAINING OF THE REASON

THE ideal object of education is that we should learn all that it concerns us to know, in order that thereby we may become all that it concerns us to be. In other words, the aim of education is the knowledge not of facts but of values. Values are facts apprehended in their relation to each other, and to ourselves. The wise man is he who knows the relative values of things. In this knowledge, and in the use made of it, is summed up the whole conduct of life. What are the things which are best worth winning for their own sakes, and what price must I pay to win them? And what are the things which, since I cannot have everything, I must be content to let go? How can I best choose among the various subjects of human interest, and the various objects of human endeavour, so that my activities may help and not hinder each other, and that my life may have a unity, or at least a centre round which my subordinate activities may be grouped? These are the chief questions which a man would ask who desired to plan his life on rational principles, and whom circumstances allowed to choose his occupation. He would desire to know himself, and to know the world, in order to give and receive the best value for his sojourn in it.

We English for the most part accept this view of

education, and we add that the experience of life, or
what we call knowledge of the world, is the best school
of practical wisdom. We do not however identify
practical wisdom with the life of reason, but with that
empirical substitute for it which we call common
sense. There is in all classes a deep distrust of ideas,
often amounting to what Plato called *misologia*,
'hatred of reason.' An Englishman, as Bishop
Creighton said, not only has no ideas ; he hates an idea
when he meets one. We discount the opinion of one
who bases his judgment on first principles. We think
that we have observed that in high politics, for
example, the only irreparable mistakes are those which
are made by logical intellectualists. We would rather
trust our fortunes to an honest opportunist, who sees
by a kind of intuition what is the next step to be taken,
and cares for no logic except the logic of facts. Reason,
as Aristotle says, ' moves nothing '; it can analyse
and synthesise given data, but only after isolating
them from the living stream of time and change. It
turns a concrete situation into lifeless abstractions,
and juggles with counters when it should be observing
realities. Our prejudices against logic as a principle
of conduct have been fortified by our national experience. We are not a quick-witted race ; and we
have succeeded where others have failed by dint of a
kind of instinct for improvising the right course of
action, a gift which is mainly the result of certain
elementary virtues which we practise without thinking
about them, justice, tolerance, and moderation. These
qualities have, we think, and think truly, been often
wanting in the Latin nations, which pride themselves
on lucidity of intellect and logical consistency in

obedience to general principles. Recent philosophy
has encouraged these advocates of common sense,
who have long been ' pragmatists ' without knowing
it, to profess their faith without shame. Intellect
has been disparaged and instinct has been exalted.
Intuition is a safer guide than reason, we are told ;
for intuition goes straight to the heart of a situation
and has already acted while reason is debating. Much
of this new philosophy is a kind of higher obscurantism ;
the man in the street applauds Bergson and William
James because he dislikes science and logic, and values
will, courage and sentiment. He used to be fond of
repeating that Waterloo was won on the playing fields
of our public schools, until it was painfully obvious that
Colenso and Spion Kop were lost in the same place.
We have muddled through so often that we have come
half to believe in a providence which watches over
unintelligent virtue. ' Be good, sweet maid, and let
who will be clever,' we have said to Britannia. So we
have acquiesced in being the worst educated people
west of the Slav frontier.

I do not wish to dwell on the disadvantages which
we have thus incurred in international competition—
our inferiority to Germany in chemistry, and to almost
every Continental nation in scientific agriculture.
This lesson we are learning, and are not likely to forget.
It is our spiritual loss which we need to realise more
fully. In the first place, the majority of Englishmen
have no thought-out purpose in life beyond the call
of ' duty,' which is an empty ideal until we know what
our duty is. Confusion of means and end is especially common in this country, though it is certainly
to be found everywhere. The passion for irrational

s

accumulation is one example of the error, which causes
the gravest social inconvenience. The largest part of
social injustice and suffering is caused by the unchecked
indulgence of the acquisitive instinct by those who have
the opportunity of indulging it, and who have formed a
blind habit of indulging it. No one, however selfish,
who had formed any reasonable estimate of the relative
values of life, would devote his whole time to the
economic exploitation of his neighbours, in order to
pile up the instruments of a fuller life, which he will
never use. To regard business as a kind of game is,
from the highest point of view, right, and our nation
gains greatly by applying the ethics of sport to all our
external activities ; but we err in living for our games,
whether they happen to be commerce or football. A
friend of mine expostulated with a Yorkshire manu-
facturer who was spending his old age in unnecessary
toil for the benefit of a spendthrift heir. The old man
answered, ' If it gives him half as much pleasure to
spend my half-million as it has given me to make it,
I don't grudge it him.' That is not the spirit of the
real miser or Mammon-worshipper. It is the spirit of
a natural idealist who from want of education has no
rational standard of good. When such a man inter-
venes in educational matters, he is sure to take the
standpoint of the so-called practical man, because he
is blind to the higher values of life. He will wish
to make knowledge and wisdom instruments for the
production of wealth, or the improvement of the
material condition of the poor. But knowledge and
wisdom refuse to be so treated. Like goodness and
beauty, wisdom is one of the absolute values, the divine
ideas. As one of the Cambridge Platonists said, we

must not make our intellectual faculties Gibeonites, hewers of wood and drawers of water to the will and affections. Wisdom must be sought for its own sake or we shall not find it. Another effect of our *misologia* is the degradation of reasonable sympathy into sentimentalism, which regards pain as the worst of evils, and endeavours always to remove the effects of folly and wrong-doing, without investigating the causes. That such sentimentalism is often kind only to be cruel, and that it frequently robs honest Peter to pay dishonest Paul, needs no demonstration. Sentimentalism does not believe that prevention is better than cure, and practical politicians know too well that a scientific treatment of social maladies is out of the question in this country. Others become fanatics, that is to say, worldlings who are too narrow and violent to understand the world. The root of the evil is that a whole range of the higher values is inaccessible to the majority, because they know nothing of intellectual wealth. And yet the real wealth of a nation consists in its imponderable possessions—in those things wherein one man's gain is not another man's loss, and which are not proved incapable of increase by any laws of thermodynamics. An inexhaustible treasure is freely open to all who have passed through a good course of mental training, a treasure which we can make our own according to our capacities, and our share of which we would not barter for any goods which the law of the land can give or take away. ' The intelligent man,' says Plato, ' will prize those studies which result in his soul getting soberness, righteousness and wisdom, and will less value the others.' The studies which have this effect are those which teach us to admire and understand the good, the true, and the beautiful. They are, may we not say, humanism and science, pursued in a spirit of 'admiration, hope, and love.' The trained reason is disinterested and fearless. It is not afraid of public opinion, because it ' counts it a small thing that it should be judged by man's judgment '; its interests are so much wider than the incidents of a private career that base self-centred indulgence and selfish ambition are impossible to it. It is saved from pettiness, from ignorance, and from bigotry. It will not fall a victim to those undisciplined and disproportioned enthusiasms which we call fads, and which are a peculiar feature of English and North American civilisation. Such reforms as are carried out in this country are usually effected not by the reason of the many, but by the fanaticism of the few. A just balance may on the whole be preserved, but there is not much balance in the judgments of individuals.

Matthew Arnold, whose exhortations to his countrymen now seem almost prophetic, drew a strong contrast between the intellectual frivolity, or rather insensibility, of his countrymen and the earnestness of the Germans. He saw that England was saved a hundred years ago by the high spirit and proud resolution of a real aristocracy, which nevertheless was, like all aristocracies, ' destitute of ideas.' Our great families, he shows, could no longer save us, even if they had retained their influence, because power is now conferred by disciplined knowledge and applied science. It is the same warning which George Meredith reiterated with increasing earnestness in his later poems. What England needs, he says, is ' brain.'

Warn her, Bard, that Power is pressing
    Hotly for his dues this hour,
Tell her that no drunken blessing
    Stops the onward march of Power.
Has she ears to take forewarnings,
    She will cleanse her of her stains,
Feed and speed for braver mornings
    Valorously the growth of brains.
Power, the hard man knit for action
    Reads each nation on the brow ;
Cripple, fool, and petrifaction
    Fall to him—are falling now.

And again :

She impious to the Lord of hosts
The valour of her offspring boasts,
Mindless that now on land and main
His heeded prayer is active brain.

These faithful prophets were not heeded, and we
have had to learn our lesson in the school of Experience.
She is a good teacher, but her fees are very high.

The author of 'Friendship's Garland' ended with
a despairing appeal to the democracy, when his jere-
miads evoked no response from the upper class, whom
he called barbarians, or from the middle class, whom
he regarded as incurably vulgar. The middle classes
are apt to receive hard measure ; they have few friends
and many critics. We must go back to Euripides to
find the bold statement that they are the best part of
the community and ' the salvation of the State ' ; but
it is, on the whole, true. And our middle class is only
superficially vulgar. Vulgarity, as Mr. Robert Bridges
has lately said, ' is blindness to values ; it is spiritual
death.' The middle class in Matthew Arnold's time
was no doubt deplorably blind to artistic values ; its
productions survive to convict it of what he called

Philistinism ; but it is no longer devoid of taste or indifferent to beauty. And it has never been a contemptible artist in life. Mr. Bridges describes the progress of vulgarity as an inverted Platonic progress. We descend, he says, from ugly forms to ugly conduct, and from ugly conduct to ugly principles, till we finally arrive at the absolute ugliness which is vulgarity. This identification of insensibility to beauty with moral baseness was something of a paradox even in Greece, and does not fit the English character at all. Our towns are ugly enough ; our public buildings rouse no enthusiasm ; and many of our monuments and stained glass windows seem to shout for a friendly Zeppelin to obliterate them. But we British have not descended to ugly conduct. Pericles and Plato would have found the bearing of this people in its supreme trial more ' beautiful ' than the Parthenon itself. The nation has shaken off its vulgarity even more easily and completely than its slackness and self-indulgence. We have borne ourselves with a courage, restraint, and dignity which, a Greek would say, could have only been expected of philosophers. And we certainly are not a nation of philosophers. We must not then be too hasty in calling all contempt for intellect vulgar. We have sinned by undervaluing the life of reason ; but we are not really a vulgar people. Our secular faith, the real religion of the average Englishman, has its centre in the idea of a gentleman, which has of course no essential connexion with heraldry or property in land. The upper classes, who live by it, are not vulgar, in spite of the absence of ideas with which Matthew Arnold twits them ; the middle classes, who also respect this ideal, are further protected by sound moral traditions ;

and the labouring classes have a cheery sense of humour which is a great antiseptic against vulgarity. But though the Poet Laureate has not, in my opinion, hit the mark in calling vulgarity our national sin, he has done well in calling attention to the danger which may beset educational reform from what we may call democratism, the tendency to level down all superiorities in the name of equality and good fellowship. It is the opposite fault to the aristocratism which beyond all else led to the decline of Greek culture— the assumption that the lower classes must remain excluded from intellectual and even from moral excellence. With us there is a tendency to condemn ideals of self-culture which can be called 'aristocratic.' But we need specialists in this as in every other field, and the populace must learn that there is such a thing as real superiority, which has the right and duty to claim a scope for its full exercise.

The fashionable disparagement of reason, and exaltation of will, feeling, or instinct would be more dangerous in a less scientific age. The Italian metaphysician Aliotta has lately brought together in one survey the numerous leaders in the great 'reaction against science,' and they are a formidable band. Pragmatists, voluntarists, activists, subjective idealists, emotional mystics, and religious conservatives have all joined in assaulting the fortress of science which half a century ago seemed impregnable. But the besieged garrison continues to use its own methods and to trust in its own hypotheses; and the results justify the confidence with which the assaults of the philosophers are ignored. We are told that the scientific method is ultimately appropriate only to the abstractions of mathematics. But Nature herself seems to have a taste for mathematical methods. A sane idealism believes that the eternal verities are adumbrated, not travestied, in the phenomenal world, and does not forget how much of what we call observation of nature is demonstrably the work of mind. The world as known to science is itself a spiritual world, from which certain valuations are, for special purposes, excluded. To deny the authority of the discursive reason, which has its proper province in this sphere, is to destroy the possibility of all knowledge. Nor can we, without loss and danger, exalt instinct or intuition above reason. Instinct is a faculty which belongs to unprogressive species. It is necessarily unadaptable and unable to deal with any new situation. Consecrated custom may keep Chinese civilisation safe in a state of torpid immobility for five thousand years ; but fifty years of Europe will achieve more, and will at last present Cathay with the alternative of moving on or moving off. Instinct might lead us on if progress were an automatic law of nature, but this belief, though widely held, is sheer superstition.

We have to convert the public mind in this country to faith in trained and disciplined reason. We have to convince our fellow-citizens not only that the duty of self-preservation requires us to be mentally as well equipped as the French, Germans, and Americans, but that a trained intelligence is in itself ' more precious than rubies.' Blake said that ' a fool shall never get to Heaven, be he never so holy.' It is at any rate true that ignorance misses the best things in this life. If Englishmen would only believe this, the whole spirit of our education would be changed, which is much more important than to change the subjects taught.   It does not matter very much what is taught ; the important question to ask is what is learnt.   This is why the controversy about religious education was mainly fatuous.   The ' religious lesson ' can hardly ever make a child religious ; religion, in point of fact, is seldom taught at all ; it is caught, by contact with someone who has it.   Other subjects can be taught and can be learnt ; but the teaching will be stiff collar-work, and the learning evanescent, if the pupil is not interested in the subject.   And how little en- couragement the average boy gets at home to train his reason and form intellectual tastes ! He may probably be exhorted to ' do well in his examination,' which means that he is to swallow carefully prepared gobbets of crude information, to be presently disgorged in the same state.   The examination system flourishes best where there is no genuine desire for mental culti- vation.   If there were any widespread enthusiasm for knowledge as an integral part of life, the revolt against this mechanical and commercialised system of testing results would be universal.   As things are, a clever boy trains for an examination as he trains for a race ; and goes out of training as fast as possible when it is over.   Meanwhile the romance of his life is centred in those more generous and less individual competi- tions in the green fields, which our schools and uni- versities have developed to such perfection.   In classes which have small opportunities for physical exercises, vicarious athletics, with not a little betting, are a disastrous substitute.   But the soul is dyed the colour of its leisure thoughts.   ' As a man thinketh in his heart, so is he.' This is why no change in the curriculum can do much for education, as long as the pupils imbibe no respect for intellectual values at home, and find none among their school-fellows. And yet the capacity for real intellectual interest is only latent in most boys. It can be kindled in a whole class by a master who really loves and believes in his subject. Some of the best public school teachers in the last century were hot-tempered men whose disciplinary performances were ludicrous. But they were enthusiastic humanists, and keen scholars passed year by year out of their class-rooms.

The importance of a good curriculum is often exaggerated. But a bad selection of subjects, and a bad method of teaching them, may condemn even the best teacher to ineffectiveness. Nothing, for example, can well be more unintelligent than the manner of teaching the classics in our public schools. The portions of Greek and Latin authors construed during a lesson are so short that the boys can get no idea of the book as a whole; long before they finish it they are moved up into another form. And over all the teaching hangs the menace of the impending examination, the riddling Sphinx which, as Seeley said in a telling quotation from Sophocles, forces us to attend to what is at our feet, neglecting all else—all the imponderables in which the true value of education consists. The tyranny of examinations has an important influence upon the choice of subjects as well as upon the manner of teaching them; for some subjects, which are remarkably stimulating to the mind of the pupil, are neglected, because they are not well adapted for examinations. Among these, unfortunately, are our own literature and language.

It is therefore necessary, even in a short essay which professes to deal only with generalities, to make some suggestions as to the main subjects which our education should include. As has been indicated already, I would divide them into two main classes— science and humanism. Every boy should be instructed in both branches up to a certain point. We must firmly resist those who wish to make education purely scientific, those who, in Bacon's words, ' call upon men to sell their books and build furnaces, quitting and forsaking Minerva and the Muses and relying upon Vulcan.' We want no young specialists of twelve years old ; and a youth without a tincture of humanism can never become

A man foursquare, withouten flaw ywrought.

Of the teaching of science I am not competent to speak. But as an instrument of mind-training, and even of liberal education, it seems to me to have a far higher value than is usually conceded to it by humanists. To direct the imagination to the infinitely great and the infinitely small, to vistas of time in which a thousand years are as one day ; to the tremendous forces imprisoned in minute particles of matter ; to the amazing complexity of the mechanism by which the organs of the human body perform their work ; to analyse the light which has travelled for centuries from some distant star; to retrace the history of the earth and the evolution of its inhabitants—such studies cannot fail to elevate the mind, and only prejudice will disparage them. They promote also a fine respect for truth and fact, for order and outline, as the Greeks said, with a wholesome dislike of sophistry and rhetoric. The air which blows about scientific studies is like the air of a mountain top—thin, but pure and bracing. And as a subject of education science has a further advantage which can hardly be over-estimated. It is in science that most of the new discoveries are being made. ' The rapture of the forward view ' belongs to science more than to any other study. We may take it as a well-established principle in education that the most advanced teachers should be researchers and discoverers as well as lecturers, and that the rank and file should be learners as well as instructors. There is no subject in which this ideal is so nearly attainable as in science.

And yet science, even for its own sake, must not claim to occupy the whole of education. The mere *Naturforscher* is apt to be a poor philosopher himself, and his pupils may turn out very poor philosophers indeed. The laws of psychical and spiritual life are not the same as the laws of chemistry or biology ; and the besetting sin of the scientist is to try to explain everything in terms of its origin instead of in terms of its full development : ' by their roots,' he says, ' and not by their fruits, ye shall know them.' This is a contradiction of Aristotle ($\dot{\eta}$ $\phi\acute{v}\sigma\iota\varsigma$ $\tau\acute{\epsilon}\lambda o\varsigma$ $\dot{\epsilon}\sigma\tau\acute{\iota}\nu$), and of a greater than Aristotle. The training of the reason must include the study of the human mind, ' the throne of the Deity,' in its most characteristic products. Besides science, we must have humanism, as the other main branch of our curriculum.

The advocates of the old classical education have been gallantly fighting a losing battle for over half a century ; they are now preparing to accept inevitable defeat. But their cause is not lost if they will face the situation fairly. It is only lost if they persist in identifying classical education with linguistic proficiency. The study of foreign languages is a fairly good mental discipline for the majority; for the minority it may be either more or less than a fair discipline. But only a small fraction of mankind is capable of enthusiasm for language, for its own sake. The art of expressing ideas in appropriate and beautiful forms is one of the noblest of human achievements, and the two classical languages contain many of the finest examples of good writing that humanity has produced. But the average boy is incapable of appreciating these values, and the waste of time which might have been profitably spent is, under our present system, most deplorable. It may also be maintained that the conscientious editor and the conscientious tutor have between them ruined the classics as a mental discipline. Fifty years ago, English commentatorship was so poor that the pupil had to use his wits in reading the classics; now if one goes into an undergraduate's room, one finds him reading the text with the help of a translation, two editions with notes, and a lecture note-book. No faculty is being used except the memory, which Bishop Creighton calls 'the most worthless of our mental powers.' The practice of prose and verse composition, often ignorantly decried, has far more educational value; but it belongs to the linguistic art which, if we are right, is not to be demanded of all students. Are we then to restrict the study of the classics to those who have a pretty taste for style? If so, the cause of classical education is indeed lost. But I can see no reason why some of the great Greek and Latin authors

should not be read, *in translations*, as part of the
normal training in history, philosophy, and literature.
I am well aware of the loss which a great author
necessarily suffers by translation; but I have no
hesitation is saying that the average boy would learn
far more of Greek literature, and would imbibe far
more of the Greek spirit, by reading the whole of
Herodotus, Thucydides, the *Republic* of Plato, and
some of the plays, in good translations, than he now
acquires by going through the classical mill at a public
school. The classics, like almost all other literature,
must be read in masses to be appreciated. Boys
think them dull mainly because of the absurd way in
which they are made to study them.

I shall not make any ambitious attempt to sketch
out a scheme of literary studies. My subject is the
training of the reason. But two principles seem to
me to be of primary importance. The first is that we
should study the psychology of the developing reason
at different ages, and adapt our method of teaching
accordingly. The memory is at its best from the age
of ten to fifteen, or thereabouts. Facts and dates,
and even long pieces of poetry, which have been
committed to memory in early boyhood, remain with
us as a possession for life. We would most of us give
a great deal in middle age to recover that astonishingly
retentive memory which we possessed as little boys.
On the other hand, ratiocination at that age is difficult
and irksome. A young boy would rather learn twenty
rules than apply one principle. Accordingly the first
years of boyhood are the time for learning by heart.
Quantities of good poetry, and useful facts of all kinds
should be entrusted to the boy's memory to keep:

it will assimilate them readily, and without any mental
overstrain.   But eight or ten years later, ' cramming '
is injurious both to the health and to the intellect.
Years have brought, if not the philosophic mind, yet
at any rate a mind which can think and argue.   The
memory is weaker and the process of loading it with
facts is more unpleasant.   At this stage the whole
system of teaching should be different.   One great
evil of examinations is that they prolong the stage
of mere memorising to an age at which it is not only
useless but hurtful.   Another valuable guide is fur-
nished by observing what authors the intelligent boy
likes and dislikes.   His taste ought certainly to be
consulted, if our main object is to interest him in the
things of the mind.   The average intelligent boy likes
Homer and does not like Virgil ; he is interested by
Tacitus and bored by Cicero ; he loves Shakespeare
and revels in Macaulay, who has a special affinity for
the eternal schoolboy.

My other principle is that since we are training
young Englishmen, whom we hope to turn into true
and loyal citizens, we shall presumably find them
most responsive to the language, literature, and history
of their own country.   This would be a commonplace,
not worth uttering, in any other country ; in England
it is, unfortunately, far from being generally accepted.
Nothing sets in a stronger light the inertia and thought-
lessness, not to say stupidity, of the British character,
in all matters outside the domain of material and
moral interests, than our neglect of the magnificent
spiritual heritage which we possess in our own history
and literature.   Wordsworth, in one of those noble
sonnets which are now, we are glad to hear, being

read by thousands in the trenches and by myriads at home, proclaims his faith in the victory of his country over Napoleon because he thinks of her glorious past.

> We must be free or die, who speak the tongue
> That Shakespeare spake; the faith and morals hold
> That Milton held.   In everything we are sprung
> Of Earth's best blood, have titles manifold.

It is a high boast, but it is true.   But what have we done to fire the imagination of our boys and girls with the vision of our great and ancient nation, now struggling for its existence ?   What have we taught them of Shakespeare and Milton, of Elizabeth and Cromwell, of Nelson and Wellington ?   Have we even tried to make them understand that they are called to be the temporary custodians of very glorious traditions, and the trustees of a spiritual wealth compared with which the gold mines of the Rand are but dross ? Do we even teach them, in any rational manner, the fine old language which has been slowly perfected for centuries, and which is now being used up and debased by the rubbishy newspapers which form almost the sole reading of the majority ?   We have marvelled at the slowness with which the masses realised that the country was in danger, and at the stubbornness with which some of the working class clung to their sectional interests and ambitions when the very life of England was at stake.   In France the whole people saw at once what was upon them ;   the single word *patrie* was enough to unite them in a common enthusiasm and stern determination.   With us it was hardly so ; many good judges think that but for the *Lusitania* outrage and the Zeppelins, part of the population would have been half-hearted about the war, and we should have failed to give adequate support to our allies. The cause is not selfishness but ignorance and want of imagination ; and what have we done to tap the sources of an intelligent patriotism ? We are being saved not by the reasoned conviction of the populace, but by its native pugnacity and bull-dog courage. This is not the place to go into details about English studies ; but can anyone doubt that they could be made the basis of a far better education than we now give in our schools ? We have especially to remember that there is a real danger of the modern Englishman being cut off from the living past. Scientific studies include the earlier phases of the earth, but not the past of the human race and the British people. Christianity has been a valuable educator in this way, especially when it includes an intelligent knowledge of the Bible. But the secular education of the masses is now so much severed from the stream of tradition and sentiment which unites us with the older civilisations, that the very language of the Churches is becoming unintelligible to them, and the influence of organised religion touches only a dwindling minority. And yet the past lives in us all ; lives inevitably in its dangers, which the accumulated experience of civilisation, valued so slightly by us on its spiritual side, can alone help us to surmount. A nation, like an individual, must ' wish his days to be bound each to each by natural piety.' It too must strive to keep its memory green, to remember the days of old and the years that are past. The Jews have always had, in their sacred books, a magnificent embodiment of the spirit of their race ; and who can say how much of their incomparable tenacity and ineradicable

hopefulness has been due to the education thus imparted to every Jewish child? We need a Bible of the
English race, which shall be hardly less sacred to each
succeeding generation of young Britons than the Old
Testament is to the Jews. England ought to be, and
may be, the spiritual home of one quarter of the
human race, for ages after our task as a World-Power
shall have been brought to a successful issue, and
after we in this little island have accepted the position
of mother to nations greater than ourselves. But
England's future is precious only to those to whom
her past is dear.

I am not suggesting that the history and literatures
of other countries should be neglected, or that foreign
languages should form no part of education. But the
main object is to turn out good Englishmen, who
may continue worthily and even develop further
a glorious national tradition. To do this, we
must appeal constantly to the imagination, which
Wordsworth has boldly called 'reason in her most
exalted mood.' We may thus bring a little poetry
and romance into the monotonous lives of our hand-
workers. It may well be that their discontent has
more to do with the starving of their spiritual nature
than we suppose. For the intellectual life, like divine
philosophy, is not dull and crabbed, as fools suppose,
but musical as is Apollo's lute.

Can we end with a definition of the happiness and
well-being, which is the goal of education, as of all
else that we try to do? Probably we cannot do better
than accept the famous definition of Aristotle, which
however we must be careful to translate rightly.
'Happiness, or well-being, is an activity of the soul

directed towards excellence, in an unhampered life.'
Happiness consists in doing rather than being; the
activity must be that of the soul—the whole man
acting as a person; it must be directed towards
excellence—not exclusively moral virtue, but the best
work that we can do, of whatever kind; and it must
be unhampered—we must be given the opportunity
of doing the best that is in us to do.   To awaken the
soul; to hold up before it the images of whatsoever
things are true, lovely, noble, pure, and of good report;
and to remove the obstacles which stunt and cripple
the mind: this is the work which we have called The
Training of the Reason.